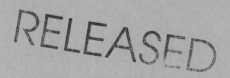

RELEASED

The 'Kept Men'?

THE 'KEPT MEN'?

The First Century of Trade Union Representation in the British House of Commons, 1874–1975

WILLIAM D. MULLER

Associate Professor of Political Science,
State University of New York, Fredonia

HARVESTER PRESS LTD
HUMANITIES PRESS INC

First published in Great Britain in 1977 by
THE HARVESTER PRESS LIMITED
Publisher: John Spiers
2 Stanford Terrace, Hassocks
Sussex
and in the USA by
Humanities Press Inc,
Atlantic Highlands, N.J. 07716

© 1977 William D. Muller

Harvester Press
British Library Cataloguing in Publication Data
Muller, William D
    The kept men: the first century of trade
    union representation in the House of Commons
    Bibl. – Index.
    ISBN 0–85527–184–1
    1. Title
    328.41'07'3   JN1129.L32
    Great Britain. Parliament. House of Commons
    Trade-unions – Great Britain – Political
    activity – History

Printed in Great Britain by
Redwood Burn Ltd., Trowbridge, Wiltshire

To the blessed memory of

John C. Muller (1900–1965)
and
Dorothea M. Muller (1901–1964)
and
for Barbara

Contents

Acknowledgements

Many people have assisted me in the preparation of this study and I can recognise only a few of them. The most important individual was Professor Arnold J. Heidenheimer of Washington University, St. Louis, Missouri. Without his constant prodding and criticism as both teacher and adviser, the project would have never been completed. Only a student can understand the difference a teacher makes.

The data for the study were collected with the assistance of many people in the British labour movement during three visits to the United Kingdom in 1964, 1967, and 1970. Three of the forty Labour MPs who gave their time and energy for interviews and correspondence deserve special recognition. They are: the Rt. Hon. Charles Loughlin; the Rt. Hon. Richard Marsh; and the Rt. Hon. Charles Pannell (now Lord Pannell). Several Labour Party officials were also very helpful. In particular, the help of Mrs. Irene Wagner, the Party Librarian, in permitting access to the party's newspaper clipping files, in arranging contacts and providing other materials, deserves my thanks and appreciation. Without her assistance the project would have been long delayed (and perhaps impossible).

I am also indebted to the officials of more than twenty unions, who gave their time for interviews, answered my correspondence, and provided me with a wealth of documentary material for the years since 1964. Their comments and insights kept me from many deadends in the course of my research. Only one union of all those contacted, the Association of Scientific, Technical and Managerial

Staffs (ASTMS), refused to cooperate in any way whatsoever.
I was also able to examine numerous union reports and journals at
the libraries of the Trades Union Congress and the London School of
Economics. Their collections of trade union materials helped greatly
to minimise my personal solicitation of these documents from individual unions, saving both me and the unions considerable time
and energy. I am particularly indebted to the library staff of the London School of Economics.

In the United States I have been assisted in securing secondary
material for the study by the library staffs of the University of
Florida, Texas Technological College (now University), and, especially, the State University of New York, Fredonia. Since I was
working away from the major metropolitan areas, the interlibrary
loan facilities of these institutions were indispensible. Other
American assistance was provided by the computer facilities of the
University of Florida and Texas Technological College, for the
statistical analysis in Chapter V.

A number of British students of politics contributed to the study.
The original idea of studying the sponsored MPs was suggested by
Professor Jean Blondel of Essex University, during a brief visit to the
University of Florida in the 1963–64 academic year. Dr. David
Butler of Nuffield College, Oxford, provided much of the background
data on the three groups of MPs used in the analysis in Chapter V.
Earlier drafts of the entire study or part of it have been read by
Professor Robert T. McKenzie of the London School of Economics,
Mr. Tom Ponsonby of the Fabian Society, and Professor Martin
Harrison of Keele University. Professor Harrison's comments and
criticism were especially helpful in revising the study, and he provid-
ed the major impetus for its eventual publication. Without his encouragement, I would have given up long ago.

Two other residents of the United Kingdom also provided help and
encouragement while I was working on the study. John Terzza,
NALGO Public Relations Officer, has proved to be both a friend to a
stranger in his country and an aid in my research. John King has also
provided insights into British politics which a resident of the colonies
is not likely to have on his own.

Financial assistance while finishing the manuscript was provided
by summer faculty fellowships from the Research Foundation of the
State University of New York in 1968 and 1969. These grants gave
me six valuable months to work on the study. The first grant was es-

pecially important in enabling me to work out some difficult organisational problems presented by the study.

Three Fredonia graduate students: Robert J. Butcher, Walter T. Thurneau, and Cynthia Rupert, helped with various parts of the study. Miss Rupert's work was especially important and is cited in the appropriate place. The critical editorial comments of Mrs. Norma M. Braude were of major assistance in turning the normal prose of an American social scientist into something more readable.

An earlier, somewhat longer, version of this study has been deposited with the Labour Party Library in London. Mrs. Barbara Griffiths's typing skills turned the pre-1974 version of the manuscript into a legible format.

Finally, none of the people mentioned above can be blamed in any way for errors of omission or commission in the study. Such errors or faults that remain are solely the responsibility of the author.

Dunkirk, New York
London, England
May Day, 1975

Tables

Figures

Abbreviations

* Union names are those used in 1970–71 and may not correspond with more recent practice. Because of continuing union mergers, it is difficult to ensure that any published work will use current names.

Introduction

I

In a 1954 House of Commons debate on the need for additional public financial assistance for Members of Parliament, a Conservative MP, Walter Elliott, referred to what he termed 'kept men' in the House, i.e. those Members who receive financial assistance from extraparliamentary bodies.[1] The largest number of these so-called 'kept men' are the Labour MPs whose candidatures have been 'sponsored' or financially supported by various unions affiliated to the Labour Party. Two such men, David Kirkwood and George Buchanan, were specifically referred to during the 1954 debate to illustrate the financial problems that force some members to accept outside support. The 'kept men' in this study are the trade-union sponsored Members of Parliament, whose status 'is a long and honoured tradition of the House of Commons'.[2]

Technically all Labour parliamentary candidates and therefore Labour MPs must have their candidatures supported by one of the organisations affiliated to the Labour Party. The major organisations sponsoring MPs under these rulers are constituency Labour parties (CLPs) and trade unions. In addition, a small group of Labour Members are backed by the Co-operative Party. Common usage, however, reserves the term 'sponsored MP' for the trade-union supported Members, and this study will do the same. Since 1950 over one-third of the Labour MPs at each election have been sponsored by unions. There were 114 union-sponsored MPs returned at the 1970 General Election, 124 at the February 1974 Election, and 127 in October 1974.

II

From the time it first met, the British House of Commons has included some form of functional, in addition to territorial or geographical, representation, and this has been accepted by almost all British theories of representation.[3] All sorts of groups – farmers, teachers, local government officials, businessmen, doctors, and trade unions – have tried to ensure that they had friends in the House of Commons by sponsoring MPs or otherwise keeping in close touch with members who could speak for them when their interests were involved.[4] Normally sponsorship has meant that the supporting organisation will make provision for the electoral expenses of its chosen candidates, and the group may further support the MP with an annual retainer or other material assistance, such as office space or secretarial help.

Sponsored status is only one form of association which an MP may have with outside bodies. Many MPs are associated in some way with such bodies without being sponsored. They may merely be members of the body, former employees, or part of professional groups, such as the bar. Whether an MP is sponsored by or simply associated with an extraparliamentary group, he is frequently expected to speak on its behalf in the House of Commons.[5] For its part, the House welcomes such activity because it helps to keep Parliament in touch with the life of the country. There is only one major restriction – the MP should not be under contract with some organisation to achieve specific goals in the House. According to a resolution adopted by the House of Commons on 15 July 1947: 'It is inconsistent with the dignity of the House, with the duty of a Member to his constituents, and with the maintenance of the privilege of freedom of speech, for any Member of this House to enter into any contractual agreement with an outside body, controlling or limiting the Member's complete independence and freedom of action in Parliament or stipulating that he shall act in any way as the representative of such outside body in regard to any matters to be transacted in Parliament; the duty of a Member being to his constituents and to the country as a whole, rather than to any particular section thereof.'[6]

MPs are expected to 'declare their interests' when taking part in the proceedings of the House. It was disquiet over this practice, and concern over the increased use of MPs as consultants to industrial groups, advertising agencies, and public relations firms, that led the House to appoint a Select Committee on Members' Interests (Declarations) in May 1969, whose report was published that December. This disquiet has contributed to the continuing suggestions that there should be some sort of public or semi-public register of Members' interests.[7] The organisational affiliation of the union-sponsored MPs, of course, is already a matter of public record in the reports of the annual conference of the Labour Party, but the 'interests' of other MPs (and some sponsored ones) are not always so public.

The role of a group spokesman in the House becomes very clear from any examination of parliamentary debates, if an exception is made for the division lists, where expectations of party loyalty normally take priority over everything else. Legislative spokesmen are one way to influence policy making in Britain. Other ways include various types of direct action, such as strikes, demonstrations, and mass lobbying. Still another pattern, that of consultation between the government and the concerned interest, has become increasingly important in the twentieth century as the state has become more involved in detailed regulation of all sorts of activities.[8] In a democratic society, where the authority of the government rests upon the consent of the governed, consultation is one device the government uses for gaining acceptance of its decisions. In terms of influencing policy making or of access to the central decision-making process, direct action, legislative spokesmen, and consultation can be viewed as three different points along a continuum. Direct action represents the least amount of access among the three, and consultation the greatest.[9]

III

The British labour movement provides an interesting illustration of the transition from one form of access to another. Since the nineteenth century direct action, in the form of strikes, has been a major technique used by the labour movement to secure its goals. The second phase evolved in the 1860s and 70s, when a considerable part of the British working classes first secured the right to vote and, starting in 1874, to return workers to the House of Commons. The recruitment function taken on by the trade unions provided an alternative means of entry into the British political elite.[10] This second, or electoral and parliamentary, phase of access for the unions has continued to the present day.

Securing legislative spokesmen led to an eventual split of the British labour movement into industrial and political wings. The industrial wing, represented by the trade unions and the Trades Union Congress (TUC), never abandoned the possibility of some form of direct action, such as strikes, even while it relied on the sponsored MPs. In addition, it began to bypass the MPs when it gained consultative status with the government, starting at about the time of World War I.[11] The political wing of the movement, represented by the Labour Party, had originally been sent into the House of Commons to act as spokesmen for the trade unions, but after 1906 it was gradually transformed into an alliance of socialists and trade unionists with a broader conception of its role. After World War I the role of the sponsored MPs in the House of Commons began to change, as they became symbols of the unions' consultative position and thus guaranteed that the unions' position would not be lost. The importance of this symbolic role increased after World War II.

As sponsored MPs came to be seen as symbols rather than the substance of the unions' access to the government, there was a decline in the number of top union leaders elected to Parliament. The larger unions tended to prohibit top officials from serving in the House of Commons. But until the 1960s the unions insisted that sponsored MPs should be veteran union members who were still in touch with and able to speak on behalf of, their sponsoring organisations.

Consolidating their consultative status during World War II and the 1945–51 and 1964–70 Labour governments, the unions began to see sponsorship as simply one more means of aiding the Labour Party. Increasingly in the 1960s and 70s some unions began to sponsor MPs with a minimum of experience within the union movement. The increasing importance of 'professional representatives' was further emphasized by the decreasing number of sponsored MPs from traditional groups such as the miners. But the leftward turn of major unions such as the TGWU and the AEF accompanied by the rise of the white collar unions, helped to make the sponsored MPs more of a threat to the Parliamentary Labour Party leadership than they had been in the past.

IV

The existence of trade union MPs has raised problems since their entry into the House of Commons a century ago. The first revolves around their traditional cooperation with middle class MPs in the House, first in the Radical wing of the Liberal Party and later in the Labour Party. This alliance has been strained by class conflict over the years, as the trade unionists have resented their more articulate and better educated colleagues who lacked intimate knowledge of working class life. The sponsored MPs, tending to regard the party as *their* party, have resisted efforts by other Labour MPs to move it from the course laid down by the trade unionist founding fathers.

The non-sponsored MPs, predominantly middle class in background, often spoke with scorn of the poor intellectual training and lack of social graces found among union-sponsored MPs. The Fabian heritage of many middle class labour MPs, with its emphasis on intellectual ability and disdain for those lacking such ability, has not encouraged easy relationships within the Labour Party. Mutual resentment between sponsored and non-sponsored MPs has been a fact of life within the Parliamentary Labour Party (PLP) throughout its history. But whether the scorn shown to sponsored MPs is deserved has never been systematically examined. Except for occasional references in the press or in the memoirs of retired political figures, little is known about their role within the PLP. One objective of this study is to examine the activities of the trade union MPs over the years to see whether the attacks directed at them have been warranted.

The second problem these MPs face is related to the first – that of the proper role of sponsored Members in the House of Commons. More specifically, it involves what Wahlke and his colleagues term their 'representational role', or how to define the group which they represent or serve in the House of Commons. [12] Originally elected to the House to defend their unions and their class (a possible source of conflict in its own right), the sponsored MPs were exposed to demands that they should pay primary attention to their constituencies, to the nation as a whole, to the House of Commons, and to a particular political party. An MP had to reconcile all these expectations with his own conscience, and with the very practical realization that failure to satisfy one of these clienteles could lead to the end of his career.

The dominant set of clientele expectations has changed with the changing relations between trade unions and government. The original assumption that a sponsored MP was primarily the servant of his union gradually developed into expectations of loyalty to the Labour Party, after the unions acquired confidence in their consultative status. But the sponsored MPs have not been able completely to ignore expectations of loyalty to their unions in the years since 1945. While their voting behaviour is largely determined by party considerations, in other forms of activity in the House of Commons, such as Debate and the Question Hour, they are more flexible. Here class, constituency, union or other loyalties can significantly determine an MP's behaviour. The second major objective of this study is to examine the role confusion of sponsored MPs over the years, as the various sets of expectations confronting them have changed.

The study of representative institutions can focus on any of three aspects of representation: the procedures by which representatives are chosen; the relation between the behaviour of the representative and those whom he is said to represent; or the degree to which the representative has characteristics similar to or typical of those whom he is said to be representing.[13] Some have suggested that representation in the third sense may help to maintain support for representative institutions, because the public may be more willing to accept decisions if they feel that people like themselves were involved in making them.[14] It will be a third objective of this study to illustrate how the sponsored MPs have helped to make the British House of Commons more typical or representative of the British population. In so doing, they may have played a major role in generating working class support for the institutions of parliamentary democracy. British labour problems in the 1970s and the leftward drift of many major unions may be partly a response to the increasingly middle class makeup of the Parliamentary Labour Party and the disappearance of 'the man in the cloth cap'.[15]

Final evaluation of the trade unionists' role in the House of Commons is difficult because students of British politics lack a clearcut appreciation of the variety of their roles and of the kind of behaviour appropriate for each role that contributes to the efficient functioning of a legislative body. Is the Fabian emphasis on intellectual excellence, with its ministerial and bureaucratic bias, the only standard for evaluating the work of an MP? Is the MP aspiring to a ministerial career more important than the Member who merely says that his

constituents will not stand for some policy or other? [16] Remembering
Bagehot's distinction between the efficient and the dignified parts of
the Constitution, and the contribution of each to the larger political
system, can one say with complete confidence that the routine
procedures of the House or of the Whip's office are less important
that those of the Prime Minister? And how shall we evaluate 'system
overload'? Given the limited number of ministerial positions, the
reality of party politics, and the length of parliamentary careers,
what would be the effect on the House and on government if every
MP aimed exclusively for a place in the government? One need look
no further than the French Fourth Republic to see some possible con-
sequences of such ambition among legislators in a parliamentary
system.

V

This is not a study of all trade unionists who have sat in the House of
Commons. Because Labour Party rules and practice make union
membership common, to include all MPs who have been trade union
members would destroy any distinction in the term 'sponsored MP'.
We are studying union-sponsored MPs, not simply trade union MPs.
For this study, a sponsored Member is defined as one whose
parliamentary candidature was financially supported or guaranteed
within the Labour Party under the terms of the Hastings Agreement.
For the period before the adoption of the Agreement, a trade-union
supported MP is defined as one whose candidature was financially
supported by his union or whose salary was paid by the union while
he sat in the House of Commons. It must be admitted, however, that
the identification of union-supported MPs in the nineteenth century
and early decades of the twentieth century is at best an approxima-
tion.

The three chapters in Part I are essentially a chronological treatment of changes in union representation since 1874. The two
chapters in Part II contain a more detailed analysis of the activity of
sponsored MPs in the PLP and in the House of Commons since 1945.
The three chapters in Part III analyse the nature of the links between
the unions and their MPs, with particular attention to situations
where the MPs have found themselves in conflict with the expectations of their unions. [17]

Part I: Changing Patterns of Trade Union Representation

Chapter I

General Secretaries and Parliamentary Representation

The British trade union movement was 'definitely anti-political' from the fall of the Chartists until the 1860s and 1870s.[1] But during the last quarter of the nineteenth century it became increasingly concerned with political questions. For example, the South Wales Miners' Federation, created in 1898, sought among its stated objectives: 'To provide funds wherewith to pay the expenses of returning and maintaining Representatives to Parliament and other Public Councils and Boards, and to request them to press forward by every legitimate means all proposals conducive to the general welfare of the members of the Federation'.[2] Increased union interest in politics can be dated either from the passage of the Reform Act of 1867, which enfranchised part of the working class, or from the election of Thomas Burt and Alexander MacDonald, both miners, to the House of Commons in 1874. The election of these two men initiated the seating of trade-union supported or 'sponsored' Members of Parliament in the House of Commons.

In these early years, we define a trade-union supported MP as a Labour (or Liberal-Labour) Member with known trade union links, and there seem to have been about sixty known trade unionists among the eighty-one Labour MPs who served between 1874 and 1910.[3] As an estimate of direct union representation this figure is too high because it includes such Labour pioneers as James Keir Hardie, whose connections with trade unions during his parliamentary career were tenuous at best. Hardie had deliberately broken his official ties with various Scottish miners' groups in the early 1890s to give himself greater freedom of action. Sir William R. Cremer, winner of the Nobel Peace Prize in 1903 and a former leader of the Amalgamated Society of Carpenters, was another early Labour MP whose parliamentary career occurred after his close association with a trade union had ended. Exclusion of individuals such as Hardie and Cremer merely strengthens the conclusions drawn from the following discussion. Additional ambiguities in identifying the early trade-union supported MPs are suggested by the position of individuals such as David Randall, legal adviser to the Tinplaters' union, who was elected to the House of Commons in 1888. No one considers Randall a Labour Member, let alone a union-supported one, and MPs like him have not been dealt with in this study.

The Trade Union General Secretaries

Joint Industrial and Political Leadership

Of the sixty early Labour MPs with identifiable trade union links, over half had previously held union office at one time or another. Nineteen had served as general secretary or chief executive officer of their unions, and they were sent to the House of Commons to act as spokesmen for their individual unions and for the working class as a whole. The nature of union representation in Parliament and its overlapping with union positions can be seen in the careers of these nineteen general secretaries, as shown in Figure 1.

This combination of political and industrial leadership was also to be seen in the TUC, whose executive body between 1869 and 1921 was called the Parliamentary Committee. The committee usually included a number of MPs: at its height in 1906 there were nine MPs among its thirteen members, and the complex state of Labour representation is suggested by the fact that six were members of the new PLP while the other three were 'Lib-Labs.[4] The Miners' Federation of Great Britain (MFGB) showed a similar concentration of industrial and political leadership at both the national and regional levels. The national executive of the MFGB included the leaders of its regional components, and these men were generally MPs.[5] Similarly, in the South Wales Miners' Federation, the four top positions of president, vice-president, secretary and treasurer were generally held by MPs.[6]

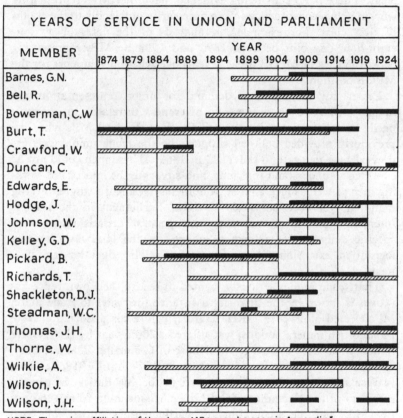

YEARS OF SERVICE IN UNION AND PARLIAMENT

MEMBER	YEAR 1874 1879 1884 1889 1894 1899 1904 1909 1914 1919 1924
Barnes, G.N.	
Bell, R.	
Bowerman, C.W	
Burt, T.	
Crawford, W.	
Duncan, C.	
Edwards, E.	
Hodge, J.	
Johnson, W.	
Kelley, G.D	
Pickard, B.	
Richards, T.	
Shackleton, D.J.	
Steadman, W.C.	
Thomas, J.H.	
Thorne, W.	
Wilkie, A.	
Wilson, J.	
Wilson, J.H.	

NOTE: The union affiliation of the above MPs may be seen in Appendix I
KEY: ▬▬▬ Parliamentary service   ▨▨▨ Union service as general secretary

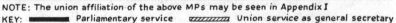

Fig. 1 Overlapping careers of Union General Secretaries first elected to Parliament in 1910 or earlier,

Rationale of Parliamentary Representation

The rationale of trade union parliamentary representation is not clear. There is no convincing evidence that other MPs representing working class constituencies were necessarily unfriendly to the claims of that class. For example, an analysis of the votes on various eight-hour-day bills between 1892 and 1908 by MPs representing constituencies in MFGB areas reveals overwhelming support for the MFGB position.[7]

Underlying the increased demand for union representation was mainly a class consciousness or awareness unrelated to objective need. Dissatisfaction with the middle class, Radical MPs who had previously provided political support for the trade unions was expressed by a delegate to the TUC in 1869: 'These men could not be expected to understand the wants and advocate the interests of working men so well as men chosen from themselves. Not a single working man had yet been permitted to enter Parliament in the Labour interest'.[8] But associated with this general dissatisfaction were specific demands for reform or change of the land laws, mining legislation, extension of the suffrage, free public education, and payment of MPs.

That trade unions seriously wanted to secure their own representatives is shown by the financial assistance they gave to trade union MPs elected after 1874.[9] Keir Hardie, before his dissociation from the Scottish miners' unions, was offered £200 a year by the Ayshire miners if he were elected to the House of Commons. Thomas Burt, the Lib-Lab Member for Morpeth from 1874 until 1918, received two salaries from his union, the first for his duties as general secretary of the Northumberland Miners' Association from 1865 until 1913, and the second for his parliamentary duties. The two salaries totalled £400–500 a year. Other miners' MPs, such as William Crawford and John Wilson, also received such support. Non-mining unions followed a similar practice. Richard Bell was paid a parliamentary salary of £200 annually by the railwaymen after his election to the House in 1900, and the gas workers gave Will Thorne and Peter Curran £150 a year each in addition to the salaries that went with their union jobs. Many of the early union-supported MPs would have been unable to serve without financial assistance from their unions or from the Liberal Party, because the state did not pay any MPs before 1911. Once public salaries did begin, however, some unions such as the miners required their MPs to turn over the £400 to the union and to receive only £350 in return.[10] The miners raised their MPs' salaries to £600 in 1919 and to £700 in 1920.

Interest representation was not the only reason for sending union leaders to Parliament. Election to the House of Commons also provided a way in which the unions could honour their leaders. As Figure 1 shows, most union leaders were sent to the House of Commons only after they had been in their union positions for some time. The House of Commons was recognised as one of the best clubs in Europe; in a highly deferential society what better way for the working class to reward their leaders?

A third factor contributed to the support for early trade union parliamentary representation. To accept working class representatives in the House of Commons indicated a symbolic acceptance of the importance of the working classes within the nation as a whole. At a meeting following the election of Thomas Burt to the House of Commons in 1874,

> Robert Elliott, the poet of the contest, was in the chair, and the speech with which he opened the proceedings is not without historic interest. They had met, he said, to celebrate the return of the first veritable working man to the British House of Commons. They had struck a blow at snobbery and sham respectability. The miners of the North of England – or England generally – had been looked down upon and despised by the other classes of society; but they might depend upon it that in the future they would be looked up to with greater respect. [11]

Beatrice Webb, commenting on the participation of Labour ministers in the World War I coalition, also recognised the symbolic importance of working class representation:

> The ordinary "rank and filer" is as muddleheaded as the ordinary Trade Union official. "We have our men in the Government", they argue, "and one of them is in the innermost Cabinet, that must be an advantage to us". And they are genuinely elated by this fact – they enjoy the vicarious glory of the Labour Cabinet Minister being among the rulers of the earth – a man whom they address by his Christian name and who sits and smokes with them. They cannot see that their

representative may be a mere tool in the hands of men who
have been hardened oppressors of their class. [12]

The acceptance of the MPs by the House of Commons and their appointment at least to minor government posts helped the working
classes in their continued willingness to accept the legitimacy of these
established institutions. Yet another factor which stimulated their
desire for direct parliamentary representation was the success of their
foreign counterparts, especially in Germany and Australia, in gaining such recognition.

All these reasons played a part in furthering early union representation in Parliament, but they were never of sufficient strength to
bring about the election of large numbers of trade unionists, even
after the 1880s when Britain moved towards universal adult male
suffrage. Trade union representation never rose above fifteen MPs
until 1906, and most of those early MPs were general secretaries.
Only the miners initially had the strength to force the nomination and
then secure the election of their candidates. [13] Other unions lacked
financial resources; their membership was too small or scattered to
overcome the opposition of other groups until after the turn of the
century; or else they were unwilling to oppose sitting Liberal MPs. [14]

The Reception of Union Leaders by the House of Commons

The major difference between the new trade union MPs and their
parliamentary colleagues lay in their educational and occupational,
i.e. class, background. The trade unionists, self-educated at best, had
usually not progressed further than elementary school in their formal
education; and such a background was not calculated to give them
the social graces of their middle class and aristocratic colleagues.
However, these trade unionists brought to the House an awareness of
a way of life – that of the working classes of Britain – little known to
their colleagues.

Union representation in Parliament preceded both the organisation of a separate Labour Party and the rise of socialism in England.
The first trade unionists were elected as Liberals and came to be
known in the House of Commons as Lib-Labs. Because of their
Liberal sympathies and support from Liberal organisations outside
the House, it was not too difficult for them to fit into that party's

parliamentary organisation and, through it, into the House as a whole. 'Classed among the Liberals, they followed them in everything according to the ethics of parties.'[15] It was not until the election of Keir Hardie in 1893 that 'the man in the cloth cap', who was unwilling to conform to the prevailing modes of gentlemanly conduct, appeared on the scene. The behaviour of 'agitators' such as Hardie or the early John Burns led some to comment favourably on the 'respectable Liberal trade unionists' who had preceded them.[16]

But even the Lib-Labs had social problems. The House of Commons was not accustomed to their lack of financial resources. Charles Fenwick needed special permission to second the Address in Reply to the Speech from the Throne in 1892, and he did not receive the traditional invitation to the Speaker's dinner afterwards because of his lack of formal clothes.[17] Lack of money also made it difficult for them to use the House of Commons restaurant, until reforms initiated by W. R. Cremer made it possible 'to dine inside the House of Commons as cheaply as outside'.[18] The increase in the number of Labour MPs after 1900 changed some of the conventions of the House. Pipes appeared in the smoking room, and Philip Snowden used to show up in a straw hat.

Generally, the early union-supported MPs were well received in the House of Commons. Thomas Burt, writing in *The Fortnightly Review*, described their reception:

> The Labour members cannot complain of their reception by the House. Whatever its faults and failings may be – and it has many – that assembly is, so far as its own members are concerned, thoroughly democratic. It believes in, and practises, equality, and is free alike from condescension and from arrogance. Let a member know in substance what he is talking about – let him talk straight at the House, not up to it, still less down to it – and the House will accord him a fair hearing, and will make generous allowance for his bluntness and inaccuracies of speech. Probably there is no place in the world where social position counts for less than in the British House of Commons. It may be unfair in its judgment of a man; but it never measures him by a mean standard. It estimates him by his character and ability, and not by the extent of his possessions, and cares just as much or just as little for a peasant as for a lord.[19]

Outside Parliament the country squires and businessmen in the House of Commons might have nothing to do with working class leaders such as Joseph Arch, but upon election, they became colleagues and deserved the respect and courtesy due to all MPs. [20]

Even the creation of the Labour Party did not significantly alter the reception accorded the early union-supported Members. Following the 1906 election, Sir Edward Grey and Winston Churchill were led to comment on the stability and dignity of the Labour MPs, and an anonymous writer described their treatment by the House as follows: 'During the early months of the Session [1906] the Labour Party received from all quarters in the House an amount of deference that would have been described as sycophantic if it had been directed toward an aristocratic instead of towards a democratic group'. [21]

The early trade union MPs had their critics, however. For example, one commentator thought that Alexander MacDonald was both ill at ease in the House and rather amusing. [22] In 1894 Joseph Chamberlain attacked the trade unionists as 'mere fetchers and carriers for the Gladstonian party'. And in 1900 he declared: 'When they come into Parliament they are like fish out of water; their only use is as an item in the voting machine ... Not one of these gentlemen had even initiated or carried through legislation for the benefit of the working classes, though occasionally they had hindered such legislation'. [23] Other critics included Charles Bradlaugh, who 'was hardly able to repress the scorn and indignation with which he beheld the appearance on the scene of men like Mr. Burt, Mr. Fenwick, and Mr. Broadhurst claiming to be heard on behalf of the working classes'. [24] Even within the Labour party after 1906 the trade unionists were subjected to the scorn of middle class Labour supporters like Beatrice Webb, and sometimes the scorn of other union MPs: in the report of the PLP to the Labour Party conference in 1911, for instance, George N. Barnes criticised their general inactivity in the House. Outside Parliament the acceptance of union-supported MPs also had limits. Some newspapers were willing to tolerate the appointment of Arthur Henderson to the World War I coalition Cabinet only because it was a national emergency and experiments were necessary. [25]

Not until the 1920s did it become clear which political party would secure most working class support, and this acted as a restraint on criticism of trade unionists who sat in the House of Commons. For the Liberals, there was a very real possibility that new Labour MPs would continue to join them. It was not until after World War I that the Liberals ceased to expect and appeal for working class support. [26] Many of the Lib-Labs, including Burt and William Brace, continued to support the Liberal Party; they were joined by others such as Barnet Kenyon in 1913 and Samuel Galbraith in 1915. A union which was later to become part of the National Union of General and Municipal Workers permitted one of its officials, A. J. Baily, to stand for Parliament as a Liberal in 1910. [27] The South Wales Miners' Association and other unions also showed some official support for Liberal candidates in the years preceding World War I. [28]

At the same time it tantalised the Conservative Party to think that the working classes might yet realise the Tories had their best interests at heart. And Conservative governments were prepared occasionally to pass legislation favourable to the workers, such as the Conspiracy and Protection of Property Act, 1875, which led Alexander MacDonald to comment: 'The Conservative Party has done more for the working man in five years than the Liberals did in fifty'. [29] This favourable attitude towards the Tories was furthered by the party's deliberate attempts to create distinctly Conservative organisations for the workers. For example, between 1890 and 1901 an 'Ilkeston Conservative Miners' Association' was organised among the Derbyshire miners to oppose the Liberals, but it never had more than two hundred members. [30] The Conservatives at that time received considerable working class electoral support as they still do. Some workers followed the Tories because of deferential attitudes. The support of others, especially in areas like Lancashire with a high proportion of Irish immigrants, tended to reflect hostility to the Roman Catholic Irish. [31] Whatever its basis, this support was not generally strong enough either to bring about union endorsement of Conservative candidates or to compel local Conservative constituency organisations to nominate working class candidates. The major exception occurred in 1899 when James Mawdsley, a leader of the Cotton Spinners (in Lancashire) and a member of the TUC Parliamentary Committee, stood as a 'Conservative-Labour' candidate and was defeated by Lib-Lab intervention. In 1906 Sir Fortescue Flannery stood for election as a Conservative with the support of his union, the Engineers, but he was defeated by a Liberal. [32]

The Activity of Union Leaders in the House of Commons

The Representative's Role Confusion

The early union-supported MPs were subjected to pressures from a variety of clienteles. On the one hand they had been put into the House of Commons to further and protect the interests of their respective unions. In addition, they frequently saw themselves as representing the entire working class. Within the House of Commons, however, they were expected to accept the Burkean view of the representative's function: that he should be responsible to no outside body except his constituency, and that he should consider the good of the entire nation rather than sections of it (including his constituency) when making decisions on public policy. [33]

The problems were simplified in some respects by the nature of the constituencies which the new MPs represented, for these were largely working class areas. A mining area, for instance, was dominated by one industry. But an examination of Hansard, together with the biographies and autobiographies of most of the first union MPs, suggests that the specific question or issue at any given moment usually overrode any longterm consistency with some general theory of representation.

The way in which an MP could respond to different clienteles at different times is shown by the comments and behaviour of Henry Broadhurst. In his autobiography he appears to have a constituency or general community orientation, specifically rejecting an exclusive working class loyalty. For example, he refers to his success in having Hanley, a town in his constituency, made a Quarter Sessions town, and then goes on to say: 'I took great pleasure in my success in this direction, which entirely disproves the theory that a labour representative could be of no service to the general and commercial interests of his constituency, and would confine his attention to voicing the desires of the working classes only.' [34] On the question of legal reform he writes: 'The reform of the criminal law was by no means a solitary example of the way in which the efforts of the Parliamentary Committee [of the TUC] were exerted, not merely for the working classes, but on behalf of the community at large.' [35]

In Hansard, however, his working class orientation seems far more important. For example, he spoke in favour of Sunday funerals in a debate on a burial bill in 1880, because that was the only day on which the working class could attend funerals. [36] Likewise, his comments in the House of Commons on the subject of law reform appear to have been far more oriented towards the working class than were the references in his autobiography. [37] In 1902, for instance, he was speaking out for greater working class representation on local school boards. [38] Finally, Broadhurst also appeared in the role of spokesman for the TUC, by supporting its petition for additional Factory Act inspectors. [39] Another MP with a divided role was John Burns, who often spoke in the House about the virtues of his constituency, Battersea, a predominantly working class district. [40]

A constituency orientation was supported only by a minority within the trade union movement. The TUC defeated a resolution in favour of it in 1892. [41] The class orientation suggested, in Broadhurst's legislative activity, on the other hand, was supported by the testimony of other MPs. For example, Will Thorne wrote: 'During all the years that I have been a Member of Parliament I have consistently tried to get legislation enacted that would improve the lot of the working class. I have been associated with Bills of all kinds, from nationalisation to cheap workmen's trains; I have introduced deputations to Prime Ministers and Cabinet Ministers.' [42] And this view was supported by the TUC in 1875 and 1876, in spite of opposition by the two miners, Burt and MacDonald. [43] The TUC's position was restated in 1902, when Richard Bell called for representation of the entire labour movement rather than of individual unions. [44]

Even those who opposed the working class orientation of the TUC could appear to support it elsewhere. For example, in 1879, Thomas Burt, only three years after opposing such an orientation in the TUC, could be heard in the House of Commons to call for greater working class representation on local governing boards. [45] In 1898 another miner, Charles Fenwick, protested in the name of the working class against a section of the Common Employment Abolition Bill. [46]

Others saw their representative roles in a still different light, holding that their primary function was to further the interests of their specific unions or industries. Joseph Arch, leader of the agricultural labourers, wrote, 'Now I hoped soon to be in the House of Commons to give the landlords a word or two about the periodical increases of rent and a few other things.' [47] When William E. Harvey was asked to stand for the South Staffordshire Division by the Cannock Chase miners, he replied: 'No, unless I can go to Parliament to represent the men whose servant I am, I will never go to Parliament at all.'[48] Shortly afterwards he was elected to the House from Northeast Derbyshire. Another miner, William Abraham, better known by his Welsh name of 'Mabon', took a similar position in his first election manifesto in 1885.[49]

Identifying a consistent role orientation is difficult. Fenwick, though he defended the working class interest in 1898, also took positions which suggest a constituency, a union, or even an industry orientation. In June 1898, for example, he unsuccessfully urged the Royal Navy to purchase additional Northumberland coal instead of the coal from South Wales which the Navy traditionally used.[50] Another miner who spoke in defence of the men who had sent him to the House of Commons was Thomas Burt; and the seamen's leader J. Havelock Wilson frequently defended the interests of his union in the House.[51] Some MPs who neglected their unions' interests were threatened with the loss of their union salaries.[52] Union demands on an MP's loyalty acquired critical importance in the decade preceding World War I, the old Lib-Labs were expected to transfer their allegiance from the Liberal to the Labour Party.

Clearly a basis existed for conflict between the expectations of different unions. For example, John Hodge of the Steelsmelters refused to join an effort by the Shop Assistants' union to secure PLP support for special legislation regulating the hours of shop assistants; but he had been willing to seek special legislation for the iron and steel industry. An attempt by the Groton Trades Council to censure him for not following the edict of the Shop Assistants' union actually resulted in a vote of confidence, when he pointed out the conflict among the Steelsmelters, the Shop Assistants, and the local cotton unions.[53] A similar point of view emerged in the 1899 annual report of the MFGB: 'I should like to ask why we as a Federation should be called upon to join an Association to find money, time or intellect to focus the weaknesses of other Trade Unionists to do what you are doing for yourselves, and have done for the last fourteen years.'[54]

Most of the early union-supported MPs resolved their confusion of roles by changing priorities according to the question before them. Of those who solved the problem by combining their clienteles, perhaps the best example was John Wilson, the general secretary of the Durham miners. Wilson, who served as an MP from 1884 until 1886 and from 1890 until 1915, saw no grounds for conflict between the expectations of the working class and the Liberal Party;[55] but it is indicative of his real loyalty that he dissociated himself from the Miners' union when it became affiliated to the Labour Party in 1909. To the end of his political career he continued to give his allegiance to the Liberal-Labour alliance. Similar sentiments were expressed by Thomas Burt.[56]

General Effectiveness in the House of Commons

The early union-supported MPs varied in their effectiveness within the House of Commons. One recent study describes several of the trade unionists as being unable to impress their colleagues. William Crawford 'is alleged never to have opened his mouth in the House'. William Abraham (Mabon's) 'oratory was designed for the Welsh valleys' rather than the Palace of Westminster. Even Benjamin Pickard, for all his extraparliamentary ability as the leader of the MFGB, 'was a failure as a parliamentarian. His interests were narrow; his speeches rare, bad, and sometimes muddled'.[57] Charles Duncan was reported to have had little impact on the House.[58] Other commentators have given some of these MPs a more favourable rating. On the death of Crawford, W. J. Davis wrote: 'The value of Mr. Crawford as a Trade Unionist and as a Labour representative in the House of Commons was far too well known to need recapitulation'.[59] Mabon's main concern was with mining legislation, but he was also interested in general questions facing Wales and in the fight to disestablish the Church of England in Wales. He was active in committees of the House of Commons and was a member of several royal commissions.[60]

Thomas Burt was one of the more respected early union-supported MPs and a strong advocate of class collaboration. Although he never achieved high office, he did become parliamentary secretary to the Board of Trade in 1892-95. One contemporary writer described him as being 'so modest that the House is apt to forget that he is Secretary to the Board of Trade'.[61] Burt was prepared to admit his own doubts when speaking in the House, especially in a ceremonial role, as, for instance, when seconding a no-confidence resolution in 1892.

> He spoke but seldom in the House, but when it was known that the member for Morpeth was on his feet, interest was immediately aroused. His name is associated with many reform measures, such as the Employers' Liability Act (1880), factory

and workshop legislation, amendments to the Trades Union Acts, and improved Mines Acts for the greater safety of miners.[62]

Burt also served on a number of royal commissions, including the Royal Commission on Labour in 1894. In the latter part of his parliamentary career he was honoured by being the first living politician to have his portrait hung in the Reform Club, and he finished his parliamentary career as Father of the House.

More effective than Burt as a political leader was Henry Broadhurst, the generally acknowledged leader of the early trade union MPs. Broadhurst was the secretary of the TUC Parliamentary Committee from 1875 until 1890 and served in the House of Commons from 1880 until 1906. While serving in this dual capacity between 1880 and 1890, Broadhurst often introduced legislation drawn up by the Parliamentary Committee and spoke in its behalf in the House. In 1886, as under-secretary to the Home Office, he became the first working class member of the government.

Other early union representatives of unquestioned ability included David J. Shackleton, who left Parliament in 1910 for a long and important career in the Civil Service; Arthur Henderson, who provided much of the organisational skill that was to make the Labour Party a successful mass party in the fifteen years after World War I; and John Burns of the Gasworkers, who was the first member of the working class to enter the Cabinet, when he became president of the Local Government Board in 1906. Burns had achieved some reputation as a backbencher following his first election to the House in 1892,[63] but he was not considered a success in his eight years in the Cabinet. Despite the achievements of these and other individuals among the first union-supported MPs, there seems little evidence to dispute V. L. Allen's assertion that they 'were now respectable members of the Liberal Party, fit to be given subordinate Ministerial positions (where incidentally, they held very little influence...)'.[64]

Basically, the main concern of the early union-supported MPs was to present the interests of the working class and of their respective unions to the nation assembled in Parliament. At times this sort of representation could be very elementary. For example, when the miners of England were accused of taking improper advantage of the prosperity which followed the Franco-Prussian War,

Mr. Burt made one of his earliest successes in the House of

Commons ... by replying to Sir John Holker, who told an amazed assembly how the miners fed their bull pups on mutton chops from the loin. He [Burt] was able to show that the miners of Northumberland, at any rate, did not keep bull pups. If they were doggy, their tastes ran to greyhounds and whippets. He was able to show elsewhere that in the year 1872, the average wage in the Northern coalfields was seven shillings a day, which was comfortable but by no means splendid.[65]

If they did nothing else, the trade union MPs enlightened their colleagues about living conditions among the working classes.

As was to be expected, industrial problems frequently claimed the attention of these MPs. For example, when in 1901 the government imposed an export tax on coal to help pay for the Boer War, the miners' MPs protested. They led a delegation to a meeting with the chancellor of the Exchequer, but were unable to persuade him to reverse the policy.[66] When speaking on industrial topics, the MPs frequently referred to their union associations and declared their interests. For example, William Brace, when speaking to Parliament in 1911 about an industrial dispute in South Wales, said: 'I represent the colliers. I am kept by them. I am paid by them and they are a body whom I am proud to represent. I do not for one moment think that they are guilty of the charges levelled against them, and, in common honesty, we are entitled, to ask in their name for the fullest investigation.'[67] Brace had also called attention to the union ties of the two preceding speakers. With the exception of a few trade unionists whose constituencies were concerned with defence industries or overseas trade, this group of MPs did not concern themselves with foreign affairs.

The eight-hour day. The early union-supported MPs were hampered in their legislative effectiveness by their own internal divisions. Nowhere did this become more apparent than in the struggle over the eight hour day. An eight hour work day was agreed to be desirable, but there was conflict over the means by which it could be achieved. The two major alternative methods (not mutually exclusive) were political and industrial action. On the one hand, the new unionists of the 1890s, as well as socialists, Radical Liberals, and even some Tory Democrats favoured state action or legislation to secure the reduced work day. On the other hand, old unionists, Liberals, and those

Conservatives who accepted the dominant liberal economic theories of the day were opposed to any sort of state action affecting the economic sphere. Those in the latter group who favoured the eight hour day felt that it should be secured through industrial action, i.e. by the trade unions acting against the employers. In addition to these divisions based on economic doctrine, the dispute was aggravated by rivalry and bickering among different unions and between unions and their leaders. This parochialism of the unions was most obvious in the dispute between the MFGB and various independent regional miners' unions.

In the late 1880s most union leaders opposed any idea of legislation which would enforce the eight hour day. In 1887 Henry Broadhurst spoke in the House of Commons in the name of the TUC against an eight-hour-day amendment to the Mines Regulation Act. [68] At the 1889 meeting of the TUC, the leaders of the MFGB joined with the majority of delegates from other unions to defeat a socialist--inspired resolution demanding a general eight-hour-day law. Having thus prevented action which might have affected the entire working class, the leaders of the MFGB turned about and staged a successful appeal to Congress for its support of an eight-hour-day bill for the miners. [69] Broadhurst drafted such a bill with the assistance of R. B. Cunninghame-Graham.

But the miners' struggle had only begun. The major obstacle to securing the desired eight-hour-day law was the failure of many miners to support the proposed legislation. The MFGB, led by Benjamin Pickard, was the major source of support for the eight-hour-day legislation. A number of the regional or county mining unions, however, were of quite a different frame of mind. South Wales, which did not join the MFGB until 1898, gave ambiguous support to the federation on this question, and its chief parliamentary spokesman Mabon, while supporting the idea of an eight hour day for the miners, did not always work in conjunction with the federation. [70] The Durham and Northumberland miners' associations, not part of the MFGB, were opposed to the idea of securing the eight hour work day through political action. From the start of the active parliamentary campaign in 1890 until the early years of the twentieth century, these two associations and their MPs led in *opposing* any attempt at legislating for an eight hour day. [71]

The parliamentary representatives of the Durham and Northumberland miners, Thomas Burt, Charles Fenwick, and John

Wilson, worked consistently with the mine owners and others to oppose passage of eight-hour-day legislation. Their position was sum-
med up by Burt, when he told the Eighty Club in December 1890: 'I
am against, strongly against, the fixing of the hours of adult men by
act of Parliament'.[72] Among MPs associated with unions other than
the miners, Henry Broadhurst, who retired from his TUC position in
1890, also opposed the legislation.

Throughout the 1890s the opponents of eight-hour-day legislation
came under increasing pressure. Broadhurst's defeat at West Nottingham in 1892 was widely blamed on his opposition to the
proposal.[73] The miners were secure in the support of their local unions, but they could be attacked elsewhere. Fenwick, for example,
had succeeded Broadhurst as secretary of the TUC Parliamentary
Committee in 1890. In the miner's federation campaign for an eight
hour day, the conflict between the committee's support for, and
Fenwick's union's opposition to, the bill led to repeated attempts to
remove Fenwick from his position with the Parliamentary Committee, which finally succeeded in 1894.[74]

The Durham miners were willing and able to communicate their
feelings about the eight hour day to all the MPs from Durham.
Liberals like John Morley opposed this legislation in the early 1890s.
And over a decade later, in 1905, Arthur Henderson was still opposing it in response to pressures from the miners. Even after the
adoption of eight-hour-day legislation in 1908, the Durham miners
were unhappy about it and prepared to use their influence to punish
its supporters. Thus in January 1910 they defeated a fellow miner
and officer of their association, John Johnson, because of his support
for the legislation.

The divisions within the union movement were only one aspect of
the struggle. Another was the prominence of non-trade-union supported MPs, especially those who depended on friendly Radical MPs
for assistance in supporting legislation. For example, R. B. Cunninghame-Graham drafted the first miners' eight-hour bill introduced by the MFGB leaders in Parliament in 1890. Throughout
most of the 1890s Sir Charles Dilke was active in support of the
legislation, and in 1898–1900 James Alfred Jacoby acted as floor
manager for the MFGB.[75] This dependence on middle class MPs
reflected on the legislative ability of the men sent into the House of
Commons by the miners' unions.

Opposition by the Durham and Northumberland miners'

associations and their MPs to the eight hour day lessened after 1900. Finally in 1908, after over fifteen years of parliamentary struggle, a miners' eight-hour-day bill was enacted as law, when the government adopted the proposal as its own.

Trade union law: the Taff Vale *decision.* The struggle over the eight hour day emphasised the internal divisions within the trade union movement and its contribution to the role confusion of the early union-supported MPs. These divisions were less obvious in the reaction to the *Taff Vale* and *Osborne* decisions. The *Taff Vale* case arose out of a railway strike in South Wales in 1901, and the decision of the House of Lords jeopardised the right of unions to strike. Summing up the decision, the Webbs wrote:

> After elaborate argument, the Law Lords decided that the Trade Unions, though admittedly not a corporate body, could be sued in a corporate capacity for damages alleged to have been caused by the action of its officers, and that an injunction could be issued against it, restraining it and all its officers, not merely from criminal acts, but also from unlawfully, though without the slightest criminality, causing loss to other persons. [76]

As early as May 1902, before the final decision was known, Richard Bell, general secretary of the Amalgamated Society of Railway Servants (the union directly involved in the case) and MP from Derby, was acting on behalf of his union when he introduced a bill to reverse the House of Lords' ruling. Designed to permit peaceful picketing, his bill had to be withdrawn in the face of government hostility.

Realising the seriousness of the situation, the unions began to take an increasing interest in parliamentary politics. After the full impact of *Taff Vale* became known, the number of trade unions affiliated to the new Labour Representation Committee (LRC) almost doubled between February 1902 and February 1903. With the increase in the number of affiliated unions, the LRC was in a better financial position to support additional candidates at the next election.

The TUC also sought to enlist political help wherever possible. Union-supported MPs would certainly support legislation to reverse the decision, but additional parliamentary support was needed to devise legislation that would restore the privileges and protection which the trade unions believed they had possessed since the 1870s.

The TUC made extensive use of friendly Radical MPs, such as Sir Charles Dilke.[77] The majority of trade union MPs lacked legislative skills, and only two of them, Richard Bell and David J. Shackelton, played a prominent role in the struggle.

The Liberal government approached the subject of trade union law with mixed feelings. It did not oppose a ruling that would ensure the political ineffectiveness of the new Labour Party, but the individual MPs who composed the Liberals needed to consider their constituencies and the forces that had brought about their election. 'The new Government had attempted to temporize over the annulment of the Taff Vale decision, but to its discomfort member after member from its own benches rose to explain that he had only been elected upon the specific promise of legislation to cancel that decision. The promises had to be fulfilled forthwith . . .'.[78] The initial proposal of the Campbell-Bannerman Government was not acceptable to the TUC. To force the issue, Walter Hudson (a former president of the Railway Servants' union and now one of its official parliamentary representatives) introduced the Parliamentary Committee's bill on 28 March 1906, and its progress through Parliament was directed by Dilke and Shackleton. When the degree of Liberal support for the bill became apparent, Prime Minister Henry Campbell-Bannerman, without Cabinet consultation, announced on the floor of the House that the government would take over the bill as its own.[79] When the Trades Dispute Act of 1906 became law, the trade unions thought that their right to strike was once again protected.

Trade union law: the Osborne *decision.* Even before reversal of *Taff Vale,* a new threat to the trade unions' political activity was emerging. Once again the union principally involved was the Amalgamated Society of Railway Servants. The secretary of one of the union's branches, W. V. Osborne, objected to the use of union funds to support the Labour Party, and to the attempts made by the union and the party to prevent Richard Bell from working with the Liberals in the House of Commons. The final decision, handed down by the House of Lords in 1909, prohibited a union from using its funds for any political purpose, since such functions had not been included in the list of objectives in the Trade Union Amendment Act of 1876.[80]

Different judges used different rationales, but the results were clear: the Labour Party's source of funds was to be cut off and some twenty union-supported MPs faced the elimination of their principal financial support.[81] To alleviate the immediate difficulties caused by *Osborne*, and to ensure Labour Party support for his National Insurance Programme, David Lloyd George, then chancellor of the Exchequer, introduced the state payment of MPs in 1911, with an annual salary set at £400.

What the unions regarded as larger problems – that of protecting their political activities and the Labour Party's financial base – had not been dealt with. Once again the Liberals were not particularly disturbed by the discomfiture of the new party. The Labour MPs were forced either to support the Liberal government or to face the possibility of the Conservatives' being returned to power, in which case the prospects of reversing *Osborne* would become even more remote. Finally the Liberal government enacted the Trade Union Act of 1913, which allowed trade unions to establish separate funds for political purposes after taking a vote of the membership. But the act restored only part of what the unions felt they had lost in *Osborne*. Specifically it authorised the political funds to be used for the maintenance of 'any Member of Parliament or other holder of public office', and 'the selection of a candidate for Parliament or any public office'. This is the legal basis for the modern form of union parliamentary representation.

Two results of *Osborne* greatly affected the future development of the Labour Party and the entire labour movement. First, the decision solidified the unions' attachment to the Labour Party and opened the way for it to become a national mass party. After *Taff Vale* there were enough unions affiliated to the Labour Representation Committee to make it a successful pressure group. But many trade unions gave only lukewarm support to the new political organisation and some refused to support it at all. There was still a strong Liberal sentiment to be found among the members of many unions and their MPs. All the trade unionists initially elected with the support of the LRC showed a definite tendency to work closely – sometimes, as with Richard Bell, too closely – with Liberals; and the situation was not helped when the fourteen miners' MPs joined the new Labour Party in 1909. This support for the Liberals weakened because one of the judges in *Osborne* was a former Liberal MP, and also because the Liberal government failed to take immediate steps to reverse the decision. The impact of this disenchantment could be seen in the way the number of Lib-Lab MPs declined while those of the Labour Party grew. 'By the time the spate of litigation over the *Osborne* case ceased, only three Lib-Lab MPs survived whilst there were fifty MPs accepting the Whip of the Labour Party.'[82]

Second, *Osborne* opened the way for the eventual separation of the entire labour movement into two quite distinct wings, one mainly industrial and the other political. As long as the union-supported MPs depended on their unions for a livelihood, serious disagreement between them was unlikely. As long as the unions continued to send their top personnel to the House of Commons, there was little possibility of a serious split between the industrial and political sides of the movement. But with the state payment of MPs enacted in 1911 as a reaction to *Osborne*, both these conditions for working class political unity began to change. The union-supported MP now found himself with a guaranteed source of income independent of his union. No longer did he have to fear withdrawal of financial support if he disagreed with his union. More important, pressure began to increase from other sources for the MP to devote more of his time to parliamentary duties. The trade unions began to realize that being a MP was potentially a fulltime job incompatible with the demands of a regular position within the union. The unions thus began to find it increasingly less useful to send their top personnel into the House of Commons.

Evaluation. The failure of the early trade union MPs to achieve greater success must be viewed against the background of British politics in the late nineteenth and early twentieth centuries. First, the union-supported Members were never more than a small minority within one of the two major parties of the time. Even the Labour Party, which came into existence in 1906, was forced to function more as a pressure group within the House of Commons than as an alternative government. Only with the Trades Disputes Act of 1906 did it bring any real power to bear on the government, and this was due more to electoral pressures on the backbench Liberals than to the number of Labour MPs. Even the accession of the miners to the Labour Party in 1909 did not give it enough MPs to make it a major force in the House.

The interests of the early trade union spokesmen may have been shared by a number of middle class Radical Members of Parliament, but the Radicals were only a minority within the Liberal Party, and the union MPs' ability to attract all-party support for their proposals was eroded by the gradually increasing importance of party discipline within the House of Commons as a whole, and especially in the division lobbies.[83] As one trade unionist expressed it, 'As session succeeds session the opportunities for initiating legislation open to private Members grow less and less. Except in the case of absolutely non–contentious measures, the private Member has not the remotest chance of success'.[84] And of course all Labour Party MPs were private Members.

Second, the legislative effectiveness of the early union-supported MPs was lessened by their role confusion, by their lack of unanimity on the question of the clientele to which they should respond. Because of the differences in behaviour resulting from this confusion, the trade union spokesmen frequently seemed more interested in safeguarding the interests of their particular unions than those of the working class as a whole. This parochialism was reflected in the struggle over the eight hour day and in the failure to create any sort of separate organisation within the House of Commons until the late 1890s, when a subcommittee was organised to deal with labour questions which came before the House of Commons and to appoint a group whip.[85] Not only were there divisions among the various trade unions, there were also divisions between the trade unionists themselves and those Labour supporters who were committed to socialism. This split was most evident in the struggle over the National Insurance Act of 1911. The trade unions welcomed the act as a means of strengthening their position, while the committed socialists generally opposed it as a device copied from imperial Germany and aimed at introducing the 'servile state'. [86]

The parochialism of individual unions remained a major factor in labour politics until the entire movement was engulfed by the rising tide of British socialism, which Beer has called the 'Socialist generation'.[87] The labour movement's gradual adoption of a common ideology meant that the union MPs were confronted with a somewhat different set of expectations concerning their role as legislators. Instead of the earlier parochial positions of unions such as the miners' or textile workers', which saw no particular need for intra-class or intra-union cooperation,[88] the trade union MPs were increasingly confronted by a new set of expectations calling for cooperation with the Labour Party as it grew during the first decades of the twentieth century. While it would be incorrect to say that the interests of individual unions came to be ignored because of this ideological and institutional development, the unions did need to adjust their expectations of their MPs' roles to fit the newer and broader frame of reference offered by the Labour Party. [89]

A third difficulty for the union-supported MPs was their continual dependence on middle class MPs for votes, for parliamentary skills such as the drafting of legislation and debate on the floor of the House of Commons, and for guidance on the general parliamentary code of behaviour. Here the working class characteristics of the trade union MPs put them at a great disadvantage, as shown in the case of Keir Hardie, who refused to cooperate with MPs of other parties in Parliament and found it very difficult to learn the skills required for a successful legislative career. He might use the House of Commons as a public platform, but that was not the same as securing legislation favourable to the working classes. As one contemporary commentator expressed it, 'There is no doubt that Mr. Keir Hardie in his House of Commons relations has turned out a failure.' [90] The trade union MPs did not appreciate the importance of the more routine work of the House of Commons and tended to neglect committee work. This meant that middle class Radicals such as Charles Dilke or, after the turn of the century, Labour MPs like J. Ramsay MacDonald would be forced to provide leadership. [91]

This basic pattern of dependence on non-trade-union leadership continued after the establishment of the Labour Party. Even as early as 1910, when the proportion of non-trade unionists in the PLP was still very low, it was J. Ramsay MacDonald and Philip Snowden who were gaining parliamentary ascendency. [92] The experience of these early trade union spokesmen suggests that the qualities necessary for adequate and even great union leadership were not those which contributed to parliamentary success. [93] The union leaders who dominated union representation during World War I offered no examples of exceptional parliamentary effectiveness. The evaluation offered by Elie Halévy effectively sums up the situation: 'The new Labour members, men who owed their political education to long years of trade union negotiation, flattered by their membership of the first Parliament in the world and the courteous reception they received, felt almost overawed as they listened to the discussions of questions of general policy which transcended their professional competence'. [94]

Dependence on their Radical allies was transformed by the rise of the Labour Party into an alliance between working class votes and money and middle class intellectual power. The conflicts in this alliance have continued to bedevil the Labour Party to the present.

Chapter II

Retirement Home or Consolation Prize: The Second Phase of Union Representation in the House of Commons

The second and third decades of the twentieth century witnessed a gradual separation between the political and industrial functions of the British labour movement. The Labour Party increased its share of the popular vote and its number of seats in the House of Commons until it emerged as the official Opposition (after 1922) and then the government (as in 1924 and in 1929–31). In this development the relative importance of the trade unions in the party declined. In numbers, however, the unions were growing: from about one and a half million members in 1893 to over eight million in 1920. While there was a gradual decline throughout the 1920s and early 30s, there were still more than four million members at the low point of 1933.[1] This increase in membership gave the unions added industrial and financial strength.

The split in the labour movement was reflected in the Labour Party's standing orders which prohibited simultaneous membership of the Party NEC and the TUC's Parliamentary Committee after 1918. The split also contributed to the establishment of the TUC's General Council, which superseded the Parliamentary Committee in 1921. And the split was apparent within individual unions, as they increasingly adopted the custom of appointing fulltime political officers. For example, the National Union of Railwaymen (NUR), which had been created in 1913 after a merger of the Railway Servants' with several other railway unions, decided in 1919 to create separate posts of industrial general secretary and political general

27

secretary. The latter job went to J. H. Thomas.

At the turn of the century, 'we must remember, the work of both a
general secretary and a Member of Parliament was less heavy than it
is now'.[2] The increasing size and responsibilities of the trade unions
in the twentieth century meant that union leaders now had more
work to do in their union positions, while the Labour Party was expecting MPs to devote more time to the House of Commons. As the
union-supported MPs were preoccupied with union matters, the
relatively few non-trade unionists in the early PLP, men such as
Philip Snowden and J. Ramsay MacDonald, were doing more than
their share.

But after World War I the union-supported MPs could not completely ignore their parliamentary responsibilities. As a result many
unions, including the Nottingham miners, the Steelsmelters, and the
Footplatemen, found that their own organisations were suffering.[3]
The absence of union officials from their union jobs because of
parliamentary duties did not go unnoticed by the union rank and file,
it was one of a number of criticisms levelled at miners' officials in a
pamphlet, *The Miners' Next Step*, published in 1911.

Increasing demands on the time of union officials also came with
the growth of consultation between the government and unions, starting with World War I.[4] The symbol of the trade unions' growing
stature was the establishment of the Ministry of Labour in 1916; a
trade unionist, John Hodge, was appointed the first minister of
labour, and a former trade union MP, David J. Shackleton, became
the first permanent secretary. Given the opportunity to further their
interests through public or behind-the-scenes consultation, union
leaders saw less need to represent their unions personally in the
House of Commons.

The Passing of the General Secretaries

As a result of these developments union leaders, especially the
general secretaries, no longer tended to serve as MPs. In a number of
unions their withdrawal was encouraged by the adoption of rules
that required union officials to work fulltime at their union jobs.
Men such as James Griffiths, Frank Hodges, and Stephen O. Davies,
who all desired a political career, were forced to relinquish their union jobs.[5]

A major exception to this development was provided by the

General and Municipal Workers (NUGMW). Their leadership was weakened during the 1930s when some of their top officials served in Parliament, but the NUGMW did not prohibit such dual service until 1950.[6] The Union of Postoffice Workers (UPW) was another exception, although the MPs it supported were technically not sponsored because the union was barred from affiliation to the Labour Party by the Trades Disputes Act of 1927. To avoid legal difficulty, the union created a Direct Parliamentary Representation Society, whose membership coincided with that of the union; it was the society that supported the MPs. The union's major leaders did not serve in the House, but it could still defend the practice of having other officers there.

> Many of the advantages of having Union officers in Parliament are obvious. Trying to utilize other MPs (even ex-officers of the Union) is less advantageous. For one thing, these MPs naturally have many other matters that occupy them and the Union cannot trespass on their time excessively. It cannot maintain daily contact with them as it can with its own officers who are MPs.
>
> Again the MP who is not actually working for the Union is at a disadvantage. It is essential that he should be right up to date with his information and know in detail what problems are pressing, and the way in which the staffs are affected. The PMG [Postmaster General] is briefed with the latest information, and can always score off a critic who is not fully informed of all the details.
>
> One small but important illustration is the asking of questions. We can brief a friendly MP to ask a question of the PMG, but often the real value of questions is in the supplementary question put in directly the PMG answers the original question. The PMG may give a misleading or evasive answer, and only the Union officer who is an MP can be well enough informed to expose this at once. If the opportunity is missed it may not come again.[7]

Of course, the withdrawal of the major union leaders was not abrupt. Those who had already entered the House of Commons continued to serve, but henceforth major union leaders would only enter the House in exceptional circumstances; examples are Ernest Bevin's entry during World War II and the abortive experiment with Frank

Cousins in 1964–67. Even if the general secretaries and other major leaders had not gradually disappeared, their impact would have been lessened by their decline relative to the gains made by other segments of the party. Table II–1 shows the growth of the Labour Party since 1900. While almost all the members of the PLP received direct financial support from a trade union in the earliest years, the proportion fell to only half by the 1920s, and has remained at about one-third of the PLP in the elections since 1935.

TABLE II – 1
LABOUR PARTY GROWTH, 1900–1974*

Election	Candidates		Members of Parliament		Union Sponsored MPs as a % of all Labour Party MPs	Union Sponsored MPs as a % of all Union Sponsored Candidates
	All Labour Party	All Union Sponsored	All Labour Party	All Union Sponsored		
1900	15[b]	?	2[b]	1	50.0	?
1906	50[b]	35[a]	30[b]	21[a]	70.0	60
1910–I	78[b]	?	40[b]	38[a]	95.0	?
1910–II	56[b]	?	42[b]	39[a]	92.8	?
1918	361	163	57	49	85.9	31
1922	414	?	142	86	60.6	?
1923	427	?	191	102	53.4	?
1924	514	?	151	88	58.2	?
1929	569	139	287	115	40.1	83
1931	491	132	46	32	69.5	24
1935	552	128	154	79	51.3	62
1945	603	126	393	121	30.8	96
1950	617	140	315	110	34.9	79
1951	617	137	295	105	35.6	77
1955	620	129	277	96	34.6	75
1959	621	129	258	93	36.0	72
1964	628	138	317	120	37.9	86
1966	622	138	364	132	36.3	95
1970[c]	624	137	287	114	39.7	83
1974–I[c]	627	155	301	127	42.2	82.7
1974–II[c]	626	141	319	129[d]	40.1	91

* There is occasional disagreement among various authorities for the actual number of candidates supported by the Labour Party or sponsored by a trade union. This problem is especially acute for the years prior to 1929.
Sources: Except where otherwise noted, the above table is based on data derived

from: F. W. Craig (ed.), *British Parliamentary Election Statistics, 1918–1968* (Glasgow: Political Reference Publications, 1968), p. 54.

[a] H. A. Clegg, Alan Fox and A. F. Thompson, *A History of British Trade Unions Since 1889,* Vol. I: *1889–1910* (Oxford: Clarendon Press, 1964), pp. 384, 387, 420–422.
[b] David Butler and Jennie Freeman (eds.), *British Political Facts, 1900–1967* (Second edition; Macmillan, 1968), pp. 141–144.
[c] Labour Party, Annual Conference Reports (1970 and 1974).
[d] Based on correspondence with the Labour Party and detailed analysis of the information given in the Annual Report of the Labour Party for 1974.

Had the top union leaders remained in the House of Commons, they would have been surrounded by an increasing number of rank and file trade unionists, for whom a parliamentary seat was frequently a kind of consolation prize, as well as by a growing number of middle class Labour MPs. This change in the pattern of Labour representation is described by Guttsman:

> From then [1918] onwards, however, the character of Labour representation changes and widens. It becomes a national party and contests a growing number of seats. No longer exclusively active in constituencies predominantly working-class in character, it works through local party organizations open to individual members of all classes of the community. Accordingly, it begins to draw its parliamentary candidates from outside the working class. While 'safe seats' still tend to be held by trade union candidates, and while their chances of success are thus great, the expansion in the number of Labour MPs is largely accounted for by candidates with other backgrounds. The total number of seats fought by trade union sponsored candidates fluctuated within comparatively narrow limits throughout the period from 1918 to 1955 and the trade union bloc found its strength within the PLP almost inversely related to the magnitude of the Labour Party's victory. Not all TU sponsored candidates were union officials. Some were rank-and-file members while others had been active members, but had left manual work altogether while keeping their Union Membership card. But on the whole, the trade union sponsored MPs tended to be men of working-class origin, even if some had moved away from the working-class occupationally and possibly socially, even before they entered the House of Commons.[8]

The New Members of Parliament

After World War I it becomes easier to identify trade-union-supported or sponsored MP, although some confusion persists into the 1920s.[9] Not all trade unionists in the House of Commons were necessarily financed by a union. Emanuel Shinwell, who worked for the Seamen's union, was not; nor was F. W. Jowett, a member of the Bradford and District Power-Loom Overlookers' Society.[10] While Shinwell received some financial assistance from his union, neither was officially sponsored by a trade union and both are excluded from the analysis.

A different kind of confusion arises with those individuals who changed their status from time to time. For example, J. R. Clynes was sponsored by the Independent Labour Party (ILP) in his first three elections, but from 1918 onwards he received backing from the NUGMW. Two better known examples are the Clydesiders, David Kirkwood and George Buchanan. Both men were prominent in the Maxton ILP group in the House of Commons during the 1920s, but they were sponsored by trade unions for most of their careers, Kirkwood by the Engineers and Buchanan by the Patternmakers.[11] Other trade unionists associated with the ILP, usually before World War I, included Peter Curran of the Gas Workers, Ben Tillet of the Dockers and Transport Workers, George N. Barnes and Tom Mann of the Engineers, G. J. Wardle and Walter Hudson of the Railwaymen, and T. F. Richards of the Boot and Shoe Makers. All have been treated here as union-supported MPs, along with Clynes, Kirkwood, and Buchanan.

Sometimes the changes in union representation were compounded by events within the unions. For example, when the creation of the Transport and General Workers' Union (TGWU) in 1922 resulted in a surplus of top officials, Ernest Bevin found it convenient to encourage such men as Ben Tillett, Harry Gosling, and James Sexton to enter the House of Commons, which he thus used as a retiring ground for officials who did not fit into the new union.[12]

It might be argued, of course, that this practice of retiring officials to the House of Commons had gone on earlier to some degree. The general secretaries and other union leaders who represented the unions in the House of Commons before World War I were usually elected only after they had held their union positions for some time, and they frequently continued to serve in Parliament after they had retired from active work in the unions. In the 1920s and later, this practice gained sophistication. By the late 1930s it was a commonplace among students of Parliament that the unions were using it as a retirement home;[13] the miners came in for the harshest criticism on this score. But because of early retirement ages and the lack of adequate pensions, sometimes a seat in Parliament was the only way to support former officials in their later years. The career of Harold Neal of the Derbyshire miners is an example. Neal had held various positions with the Derbyshire miners and was a candidate for the position of general secretary in 1942. Following his defeat he stood successfully for Parliament. Once in Parliament, Neal was able to satisfy his constituents and local CLP, so that when the miners adopted a retirement age for MPs which barred Neal from further sponsorship in the 1966 General Election, he could still be renominated and elected. Another case is Bernard Taylor (now Lord Taylor of Mansfield), who became a vice president of the reunited Nottingham miners in 1937. 'At the end of the [initial] two year period I was [re]elected each year until 1941 when I retired and became Member of Parliament for the Mansfield constituency, thus ending my active association with the Union.'[14]

This use of the House of Commons as a retirement home or consolation prize was slow to change, because of the electoral fortunes of the Labour in the 1930s and its unexpected victory in 1945. Thus the authors of the first Nuffield election study could write: 'Against the Labour Party it has been alleged that too often a senior and undistinguished Trade Union official has been chosen to the neglect of the younger and more active trade unionists, that, as the critics put it, the unions retire their officials to the House'.[15]

Role Definition

The union-sponsored MPs who have served in the House of Commons since World War I can be regarded primarily as a visible sign of the increasing public and behind-the-scenes consultation between the unions and the government. With this growth of consultation, the unions no longer have the same need for direct representation as before World War I, and parliamentary spokesmen have increasingly become simply a guarantee against a future loss of consultative status.

But the unions did not immediately alter their expectations of their MPs. Between the wars the MPs were still expected to work on behalf of their unions, and these expectations sometimes conflicted with their own perceptions of their roles. There were a number of groups, including party, class, constituency, the trade union movement, individual unions, and even the House of Commons, to which the MPs might look for cues regarding their behaviour. And, of course, all these group expectations had to be balanced against the Members' own consciences and their conception of the national interest. While party and the House of Commons generally took precedence over the others in determining actual behaviour, MPs were aware of expectations from other sources. The working class orientation of some sponsored MPs is reflected in J. R. Clynes' words on his initial parliamentary candidacy: 'It had become obvious to me that the only effective way in which Labour could control and improve conditions for the working classes was by going to Westminster.' [16]

Conflict between class and individual union representation was magnified by some who identified one or the other with the union movement as a whole. The ambiguities in this viewpoint were clearly indicated in the comments of Walter Smith (sponsored by the Boot and Shoe Operatives until he lost his seat in 1931) to his union conference in 1932:

> The fundamental basis upon which any political movement can be built up in this country is the Trade Union movement, and the man who does not recognize his responsibility to his trade organization does not understand his Labour movement. It is the first fundamental expression of working class opinion towards the interest of themselves and their class. [17]

There was agreement within the party that the sponsored MPs had special claims to speak on behalf of the union movement. For example, in the years immediately following World War I the party's NEC sought to help MPs by providing members of the PLP with materials on various questions 'not connected with trade unionism'. [18] The most notable of those claiming to represent the union movement as a whole was Ernest Bevin, who wrote: 'Employing interests – the railway interests, the docking interests – are powerfully represented in the House . . . The Trade Union *has* to come in or the workers' interests go by the board.' [19] Even after he entered the House of Commons in 1940, Bevin continued to claim to represent all the unions. During 1943, when he became embroiled in a dispute with the Labour Party over the Beveridge Report, he is alleged to have said that 'if he were expelled from the Party, he would continue to act as Minister of Labour, having entered the coalition in the first place as a representative of the trade unions, not of the Labour Party'. [20]

In contrast to an orientation toward the working class or toward the trade union movement as a whole, allegiance to a particular union was suggested by J. H. Thomas when he wrote: 'Throughout the whole of my life I had never done anything but work on the railways for the railwaymen. My life was dedicated to their interests.' [21] Thomas's point of view was echoed by George Tomlinson and George Edwards, [22] as well as in union expectations of this kind of orientation. According to the historian of the Typographical Association (TA), for example: 'The elected member, moreover, was not merely a Labour Party member and MP for West Bromwich; he was in a real sense the TA Parliamentary Representative and was expected to support its special interests in the House of Commons; he had to keep in touch with his constituents in the TA as well as in West Bromwich.' [23] This orientation is only slightly modified by the fact that the union generally supports the Labour Party. A union bias was also expressed by the historian of ASLEF: *'For the first time in the history of our Society, we were represented in Parliament.'* [24]

This union orientation caused critical comments from those who disliked the sponsored MPs. David Kirkwood (sponsored at times by the Engineers but usually associated with the ILP Clydeside group) justified his support of MacDonald and Snowden (before 1931) on the grounds that they were not limited by sectional interests, whereas the trade unionist 'was restricted in his political outlook by the fact that his chief interest was in his union and his first loyalty was to his own section'. [25]

Rejecting all the above loyalties, Aneurin Bevan claimed to give emphasis to his own constituency:

> *I do not represent the FBI [Federation of British Industries] or the TUC [Trades Union Congress]. I happen to represent constituents in Ebbw Vale. When I go back to my constituents I expect them to hold me to account for what I have done, and I do not expect if they disagree with anything I have done to be able to explain it away by saying that I did it on the instructions of some outside body.* [26]

The congruence of class, constituency, and union pressures in mining constituencies could account for Bevan's comments, and even among

the miners' MPs he was noted for the high degree of personal support
which he had within his constituency.

Sponsored Members and the House of Commons: The Parliamentary Labour Party

Within the PLP the union-sponsored MPs were organised in the
Trade Union Group, whose membership after 1924 was restricted
to 'persons whose candidatures were promoted by Trades Unions'. [27]
The Group gave a central focus and organisation to the trade union
element, and there seemed little disagreement that this part of the
party had to be listened to with patience. [28] But the Group seldom
acted as a cohesive pressure bloc within the PLP, and never tried to
establish itself as an independent force alongside it. It had no
authority to compel its members to support a particular line of
policy; agreement, when it came, derived from a common
background and experience in factory or mine, and unanimity was
never assured. On the other hand, groups of union-sponsored MPs
frequently played key roles in the inner workings of the party, as in
the contest for the PLP leadership in 1922.

The 1922 Leadership Fight

The leadership fight in 1922 can only be understood in terms of a
rivalry between the ILP and the union-supported MPs that began in
the 1890s. While the internal politics of the PLP cannot be reduced
solely to this split, because of the overlapping between the two groups
and because of other currents within the Labour Party [29] the
leadership fight does illustrate the role of the trade unionists in the
PLP.

As early as 1906, when the PLP elected its first chairman, there
was competition between David Shackleton of the trade union wing
and Keir Hardie of the ILP wing. Hardie's success in 1906 indicated
that some trade unionists had voted for him. [30] The attitudes of the
trade unionists and ILP supporters toward World War I emphasised
the differences between them: for the most part the trade unionists
went along with the mood of national patriotism and supported the
war while the more active ILP MPs opposed it. When the war was
over, the conflict between the two wings of the party did not disappear. The ILP, including MacDonald, were highly critical of the
leadership of the union-dominated PLP. In 1919 MacDonald dubbed

J. R. Clynes 'the Hobbes of representative government . . . more servile to authority than the Whigs'.[31] ILP's dissatisfaction with trade unionists was not reduced by the fact that some of them were former members of the ILP. (Clynes had broken with the ILP over the war. Margaret Bondfield had quit in 1918 because 'I could not be as useful in the ILP at this stage as in the larger Movement'.)[32] Indicative of the PLP's attitude toward Macdonald was their rejection of his offer of aid on parliamentary tactics and strategy following the 1918 General Election.[33]

The chairman of the PLP had been customarily elected at the start of each parliamentary session, until 1921 when the PLP decided to elect him at the end of a session to serve during the next one. Operating under these rules, the PLP elected Clynes as chairman for the 1922 session of Parliament. The 1922 General Election tripled the number of Labour MPs and shifted the balance between the trade unionists, now relatively weaker, and the ILP, which, joined by the 'Clydesiders', beame the stronger of the two groups. Many of the new MPs wanted a voice in deciding who would lead the PLP.

Despite an endorsement by the ILP MPs, MacDonald came to the meeting of the PLP as an underdog. It was reasonable to assume that Clynes, the incumbent and a trade unionist, would have the support of most of the other union-sponsored MPs. When the votes were counted, however, MacDonald emerged the winner, with a majority of less than six votes. One reason for Clynes' defeat was the absence of some twenty union MPs, whose union duties prevented them from attending the meeting.[34] But even had these MPs been at the meeting, there seems to be some question whether Clynes' replacement by MacDonald would have been delayed by more than a year, since some of the trade unions were becoming unhappy with Clynes' leadership.[35] Once MacDonald was elected leader and chairman of the PLP, he received the traditional loyalty of the trade unionists. This made it possible for him to defeat George Lansbury in a leadership contest in 1925.

The First Labour Government

Union-sponsored MPs played a secondary role in the first two Labour governments. In the 1924 government they had only seven out of the twenty seats in the Cabinet, although they comprised over half of the PLP. They did somewhat better in positions below Cabinet level, but were nevertheless unhappy.[36] Reasons for the low union repre-

sentation in the 1924 government varied. One was Mac-
Donald's well-known dislike of the trade unions. [37] Another was
his fear that sponsored MPs would be restricted by their union ties.
When, for example, Emanuel Shinwell objected to being offered a
position in the Mines Department, saying that a miner should have
been appointed, MacDonald replied, 'It would be wrong to put a man
in the job who could not take an impartial view.' [38] Shinwell agreed
to take the job only after consultation with the miners' MPs. A third
reason was the refusal of union leaders to relinquish their union jobs
in order to serve in the government. For example, Robert Smillie
turned down the government post offered to him because 'he was too
old to learn a new trade'. [39]

But the basic reason for the low union representation seems to
have been the poor quality of MPs available for service. As Lyman
observes: 'No one of the trade unionists made a distinguished record
as Minister.' [40] Willie Adamson is the best illustration of their
parliamentary weaknesses. Adamson, a Scottish miner, served as
secretary of state for Scotland in the 1924 government. When
answering supplementary questions during the Question Hour, his
stock reply was: 'Muster Speaker, I'll gie the matter ma due conseederation.' When asked if he could give any other answer, he would
reply: 'Muster Speaker, I'll gie tha' matter ma due conseederation as
weel'. [41] Another trade unionist, Frank Hodges, was described by
Sidney Webb as follows: 'He did not justify his appointment . . . and
he failed . . . to "get the hang" of his administrative duties, whilst he
seldom spoke to advantage in the House; and did not do any ap-
preciable useful service outside'. [42] And Mrs. Webb could echo this
with her usual deprecating remarks about trade unionists in the
Whips' office. [43]

In the social revolution represented by the Labour government the
new ministers had their personal problems and experiences. Beatrice
Webb describes Lord Haldane, an ex-Liberal and a member of the
Labour government, carrying off Stephen Walsh, an ex-miner, the
night before he was to receive his official appointment as minister of
war, in order to instruct him how to behave with the army generals
and to see that he was properly dressed for the official ceremony. [44]
And in a story told by Jack Lawson, he and Clement Attlee were
visiting the officers' mess in Woolwich as members of the Army
Council. 'That great chandelier must look fine when lit up', Attlee
commented, 'Yes, it does', replied Lawson. 'Have you been here

before'? 'Yes'. 'When'? Attlee asked. 'The last time I was here', replied Lawson, 'I was serving these tables as officers' orderly on fatigue, after stables.'[45] The story sent Attlee into a fit of laughter, since he had served as an officer during his own wartime duty.

The government experienced more serious difficulties with its union supporters. When the miners' MPs introduced a bill to nationalise the coal mines and place them under the joint control of the government and the MFGB, the government refused to support the bill and Sidney Webb and Shinwell had to make the best of a bad job in defending the government in the House.[46] The unions also resented government interference in the settlement of several important labour disputes.[47]

The General Strike

Greater attention to industrial action after the fall of the first Labour government led first to 'Red Friday' (31 July 1925), when the miners were able to secure substantial concessions from the government through the threat of a general strike, and then to the General Strike of 1926, which attempted to force the government to accept the miners' proposals for the coal industry.

These two events provide an interesting study of the role confusion of the union-sponsored MPs. For one thing, the unions expected little help from the MPs. In the negotiations leading to Red Friday in 1925, and during the course of the General Strike itself, the MFGB failed to enlist the aid of its parliamentary representatives or specifically requested that they do nothing.[48] When the union-sponsored MPs did speak up about the strike in disagreement with the union leaders, they were attacked by Ernest Bevin, who 'made it perfectly clear that this was a trade union show and that the politicians had better keep out'.[49] The only Labour MPs to play important roles in the events of 1925 and 1926 were the four leaders of the PLP: J. Ramsay MacDonald, Arthur Henderson, J. R. Clynes, and J. H. Thomas. For Thomas and Clynes, it was their union positions, rather than membership of the House of Commons, which led to their involvement.[50] Other MPs, such as Frank Varley, also acted because they were primarily union officials.[51]

It was clear that union leaders looked on the MPs as delegates, who should only raise questions when asked to do so by the unions. The confusion resulting from the lack of communication among different unions caused further problems, as indicated in an exchange between Bevin and Thomas at a meeting of union officials on 29 April 1926. The meeting 'heard Ernest Bevin make a savage attack on the Parliamentary Labour Party for its cowardice in failing to make a statement in the House of Commons about miners' wages. ... Thomas defended the Parliamentary Party on the ground that they had been specifically asked by the miners not to interfere in an industrial dispute'.[52]

Equally important, if not more so, were the sponsored MPs' perceptions of a clientele's expectations. Some of course sought to represent their own unions or other unions during the dispute. For example, Joshua Ritson (sponsored by the Durham miners) was bitter after the strike because the MFGB had failed to make use of their MPs.[53] When they did seek to speak out on behalf of their unions, the miners' MPs found obstacles placed in their way by parliamentary manoeuvring. When the House of Commons debated a Soviet offer of aid to miners during the strike, for example, not one of the miners was able to 'catch the Speaker's eye', despite a considerable commotion in favour of allowing an MFGB-sponsored Member to speak. Likewise after the strike the protests of the miners in the House against victimisation were generally ineffective.[54]

On the other hand, some sponsored MPs, including Thomas and Clynes, disagreed with their unions and were disapproving of the General Strike. Clynes was quite explicit in recognising a responsibility to the nation as a whole when he wrote, 'Labour MPs did all they could to counsel moderation, and not only keep the men within the law, but advise them to have a care for public convenience and national well-being.'[55]

The Second Labour Government and the 1931 Crisis

Threatened by the Trade Disputes Act of 1927, the unions reacted with increased political efforts which contributed to the Labour Party success in the 1929 General Election. Once more the party was called upon to form a government, albeit a minority one. Once more there was an opportunity for the union-sponsored MPs to demonstrate their effectiveness.

The top leadership of the PLP in 1929 consisted of J. R. MacDonald, Philip Snowden, Arthur Henderson, J. H. Thomas, and J. R. Clynes. The last three were trade unionists and held major positions in the second Labour government, but this could not conceal the low proportion of union MPs in the government. Despite

Snowden's warning about overlooking the trade unions, sponsored MPs held only twenty-one of the fifty-four major appointments. [56] MacDonald's antipathy to the unions had not decreased since 1924. Indeed, one participant in the events of 1929–31 suggests that MacDonald was deliberately trying to discredit the union MPs by refusing to appoint more of them to office, or by deliberately appointing men such as Ben Turner to positions for which they were not qualified. [57] On the other hand, the prime minister may have appointed Turner and other trade unionists to Cabinet positions because of their stature as trade unionists, and because the party could not completely ignore the unions regardless of the calibre of the men who represented them. Two examples of this latter practice were the appointments of Stephen Walsh and Tom Shaw as ministers of war in the first and second Labour government respectively. Such symbolic appointments helped to maintain the image of the Labour Party as the workers' party among its trade union supporters.

The major problem facing the second Labour government was the worldwide depression and the domestic unemployment resulting from it. Trade unionists in the House of Commons tried to have policy towards the unemployed softened by removing a restriction on receiving unemployment insurance. Rather than withholding insurance if the unemployed were 'not genuinely seeking work', they believed that 'the sole ground for disqualification should be the [labour] exchange's proof that a claiment was "definitely offered suitable employment and had refused it" '. [58] Arthur Hayday, who, like the Minister of Labour Margaret Bondfield, was sponsored by the NUGMW, attempted to get the Morris Committee on Unemployment Insurance to recommend the elimination of the 'not genuinely seeking work' provision. When his efforts failed, Hayday carried his appeal to Bondfield and then, in a letter from the entire Trade Union Group, to the prime minister, who agreed with the Group's position. [59] As a member of the general council of the TUC, Hayday also sought to have the proposed unemployment insurance bill drawn up in consultation with the TUC. Again Bondfield was unwilling to agree and merely cooperated in the establishment of a committee to watch the bill's passage through Parliament.

At the same time the sponsored MPs, in conjunction with the more militant ILP Members were trying to increase unemployment insurance benefits. When Hayday placed an amendment on the Commons Order Paper which would do this, Snowden appeared before the Trade Union Group and persuaded them to rise above their union and class loyalties to consider the needs of the nation as a whole, by withdrawing the amendment. [60]

Bondfield's refusal to consult with the TUC over the 1929 unemployment insurance bill was echoed in late 1930 when the government appointed a Royal Commission on Unemployment Insurance. The TUC eventually refused to have anything to do with the commission, and 'Hayday [Chairman of the General Council in 1930] went so far as to say that "the Labour Government have not been as fair as some of the other Governments" '. [61] On the other hand, some government departments were willing to consult with the unions. A biographer of J. Maxton comments that the Coal Mines Act pushed through by the Labour government in 1930 'was the first industrial Bill in the history of Great Britain in which the Trade Unions, the representatives of the workers concerned, were consulted at every stage'. [62]

The second Labour government undertook one attempt at nationalisation and thereby pointed up another source of conflict between the party and the unions. The London Passenger Transport Bill, in the form introduced by Herbert Morrison, would have created a board of independent experts to run public transportation in London; yet Morrison specifically rejected the demand by Ernest Bevin of the TGWU that provision be made for the direct representation of workers on the board. Morrison's bill set the pattern for the nationalisation proposals adopted in the years after World War II.

The attitudes of the 1929–31 Labour government and of many sponsored MPs toward industrial questions were hardly calculated to please the trade unions. The final blow came just before the fall of the government in 1931, when the Cabinet voted to approve cuts in welfare payments as a step towards solving the continuing economic crisis. Three of the six trade unionists in the Cabinet, J. H. Thomas, Margaret Bondfield, and Thomas Shaw, voted for the cuts. [63] Had it not been for MacDonald's resignation and his decision to form a 'National' Government, this vote would have caused even more anger in the trade unions.

The 1920s and the experience of the first two Labour governments were a lesson to the trade unions. They were beginning to realise that union representation at the highest levels of decision making was not the same as securing favourable decisions. Allen describes their experience: 'Trade union influence in the Governments was negligible, for even the Ministers who had been union leaders did their utmost to forget their past.'[64] As the Labour Party adopted attitudes and policies more in keeping with its national responsibilities, the importance given to the particular interests of trade unions was correspondingly reduced.

The 1930s

The PLP was decimated in the General Election of 1931. Most of the successful Labour candidates were union sponsored, but even their number had been sharply reduced. Only one Labour minister, George Lansbury, remained on the Opposition benches. Numerically the miners' twenty-six MPs were able to dominate the PLP, but their opposition to the national government was not effective. Nor was Lansbury, who had become leader and chairman of the PLP by default, able to provide strong leadership. Finally forced by Bevin to resign before the 1935 General Election, he was succeeded by Clement Attlee, who had been a junior member of the second Labour government.

The 1935 General Election tripled the number of Labour MPs there had been in 1931. J. R. Clynes was initially offered the post of leader and chairman, but he declined on account of his age. A three-way contest among the incumbent Attlee, Herbert Morrison, and Arthur Greenwood then developed. For the first time since the party had been created, no sponsored MP was a candidate for the leadership. Trade union support on the first ballot was divided between Greenwood and Attlee. When Greenwood withdrew, Attlee inherited much of his support and became the new leader.[65]

Another example of crucial trade unionist activity occurred in the late 1930s in a dispute over the party's attitude towards military rearmament. Hugh Dalton led a successful attempt to stop the PLP from voting against the Service Estimates in 1937, and the union-sponsored MPs provided the bulk of Dalton's support.[66] In describing the attempt by his opponents to reverse the PLP's decision, Dalton writes:

> After the vote there was very violent feeling among the minority. Some of the South Wales Miners, led by Jim Griffiths and Arthur Jenkins, pushed about trying to convene a special miners' meeting and to commit its vote in a block against the majority decision. Gordon Macdonald of Lancashire, the

secretary of the Miners' Group, who was on my side, refused, saying, quite correctly, that the decision had been taken by the only body competent to take it. The South Wales Miners then signed a requisition to him asking him to call a meeting. Thereupon he incited other miners, chiefly from Lancashire and Durham, in the total more numerous than the South Wales group, to sign a counterrequisition against such a meeting, and none was held. [67]

Ernest Bevin

The crisis brought about by British entry into World War II finally destroyed Ernest Bevin's reluctance to serve in the House of Commons. His service as minister of labour and national service in the World War II coalition government headed by Winston Churchill encouraged a massive growth in the process of consultation. [68] 'Instead of trying to play safe, Bevin boldly asserted his claim to be, in a special sense, the representative of the trade unions and the working class in the Cabinet and the spokesman of the Government to organized labour.'[69] He had been brought into the Cabinet to ensure trade union support of the war effort. He more than satisfied the demands for workers throughout the war and became an indispensable member of the inner War Cabinet within five months of joining the government.

Despite his achievements, Bevin did have weaknesses. Bullock writes:

> Many members, without distinction of party, admired his strength of personality and were impressed by the confidence which he conveyed; most of them were ready enough to be convinced, but they were disappointed by his parliamentary performance. The natural ease with which he spoke to audiences outside the House deserted him in the Chamber. There he was awkward, either reading out an official brief in pedestrian fashion, or when he spoke impromptu, often losing the thread of his argument and failing to catch the mood of the House. The formalities and procedure of parliamentary debate irked him. Criticism which a practised parliamentarian accepted as the common form of debate without allowing it to ruffle his temper, goaded Bevin to anger. He took it too personally and was too fierce in rebutting it. [70]

Bevin's difficulty in adjusting to the House of Commons is partially explained by his age: he was comparatively old (fifty-nine) when he entered the House, and he did not have time to acquire the parliamentary skills and graces which young men could cultivate. [71]

As a major leader of the Labour Party within the wartime coalition, Bevin was also active in the internal politics of the PLP. He was completely committed to Attlee's retention of the party leadership and protected him from attack. In particular, he distrusted Herbert Morrison and used his influence within the party to keep Morrison from becoming too important. In 1943, for example, he persuaded the TGWU to vote against Morrison, who was then a candidate for party treasurer. [72]

The General Election of 1945 saw a Labour majority returned to the House of Commons and the creation of a Labour government not dependent on other parties for votes. It marked the first peak in Labour's rise to power, which would not be matched again until 1966, when once again Labour would be returned with a large parliamentary majority. The changes in trade union parliamentary representation and the role of the union-sponsored MPs after World War II will be discussed in the following chapters.

Evaluation

Making allowance for such exceptions as Clynes, Thomas, Henderson, and Bevin, the best overall evaluation of the trade union MPs between the wars is given in V. L. Allen's analysis of the capabilities of trade union officials in general: 'The mere entry of trade union leaders, however, into the circle of Government did not automatically make the Government more democratic in practice; though it did give it a more democratic facade. What happened in practice depended upon the contribution which union leaders were able to make in the determination of detailed policy.' [73] And in trying to determine detailed policy most sponsored MPs were not effective.

Chapter III

The Symbolic Role of the Professional Representative

Background of Changing Sponsorship

Educational Reform

Momentous domestic changes in Britain during the first half of the twentieth century have had a major impact on the patterns of union sponsorship of MPs. Perhaps the most basic of the five to be discussed here has been an extension of the educational system, so that more formal education is available to an increasing segment of British society. The proportion of fourteen-year-olds receiving a fulltime education rose from two per cent in 1870 to one-hundred per cent in 1962; and in 1972 the school-leaving age was raised to sixteen. The proportion of nineteen-year-olds still attending school increased from one per cent in 1870 to seven per cent in 1962. [1]

The importance of this development can be overstated, for increased opportunity has not been available equally to all sections of the population. One report in the 1950s indicated that while only twenty-five per cent of the children of professional and managerial fathers left school by the age of fifteen, the figure for the children of skilled workers was seventy-eight per cent, and for unskilled workers ninety-two per cent. The obverse of these figures can be seen in the proportion of children who remained in school after the age of seventeen. For the professional and managerial fathers it was thirty-four per cent, for the skilled workers four per cent, and for unskilled workers one per cent. [2]

At the secondary level the distinctions among the public schools, state-supported grammar schools, and state-supported secondary modern schools are also very great and widely recognised, with class differences dividing the children who are able to take advantage of each type of school. This is most obvious in the case of the privately supported public schools with their high tuition fees, but it is also true among the state-supported schools; the grammar schools tend to have a large number of students from the middle class, and the secondary modern schools draw their students mainly from the working class. The development of comprehensive schools is only partly changing this picture.

Clearly the working class has benefited least from the increase in educational opportunity; yet:

By the later Fifties some of the first fruits of this educational revolution were discernible. (If many other factors were involved, the schools certainly played a substantial part in the change.) Hitherto the British working classes had been largely a "secret people", with their own language, ways of thinking, codes. Theirs was a world which remained – in the south at least – largely impenetrable by any person from the middle classes. In print and on the stage – since working-class writers were rare – representation of them was condescendingly "anthropological", from the outside looking in – the comic chars of *Punch,* Noel Coward's adenoidal naval ratings, the stoic idealised workers of Orwell's *Wigan Pier.* As for the working classes themselves, there appeared to be only two alternatives to the traditional "not-for-the-likes-of-us" self-segregation: the political attitude of class-conscious challenge of the earnest, lonely, self-conscious, rather over-awed, attitude of the small body of working-class seekers after Knowledge and Culture.

Now it seemed that more normal two-way communication might at least be opening up. In many of the working-class children who left the new schools was to be noted a new sort of social assurance, a new disposition to speak their minds – in accents and idiom of a new universality. Doors, which had been closed, were seen to be open. There were moments when it seemed that the Age of the Common Man – so long overdue in Britain – might yet be ushered in by the Age of the Common Boy.[3]

The social assurance described by Hopkins implies that new union MPs might soon be able to challenge other MPs on the basis of verbal and social skills, instead of relying on the spectre of the strength of their sponsoring unions.

Trade Union Growth and Decline

Of more immediate concern to the working class and the unions are the changes within the trade union movement. There was continued growth in the years after World War II, and in 1971 the TUC had a total membership of just over ten million. But since 1919 there has been a longterm decline in the number of unions affiliated to the TUC, despite the overall increase in membership. By 1972 the number of affiliated unions fell to 132, the lowest number since 1888.

This pattern has been accompanied by significant changes in the relative size of various unions. Such old stalwarts as the miners and the railwaymen have rapidly lost members. By 1966 the National Union of Mineworkers (NUM: the successor of the MFGB) had only half the number of members it had had in 1920, and the decline has continued. On the other hand, the general unions and the white collar unions have been growing. These changes become even more significant when we realise that declining unions are usually found in industries where there are few unorganised workers, while the growing unions, especially the white collar ones, are normally in industries with large numbers of unorganised workers. [4]

Unions such as the Clerical and Administrative Workers (CAWU), the National Union of Public Employees (NUPE), the Association of Scientific, Technical, and Managerial Staffs (ASTMS), and the Draughtsmen's and Allied Technicians Association (DATA) are rapidly increasing in size. These unions are not to be counted among the giants of the movement, though their rapid growth suggests that they might become powers of the future. The white collar unions became a significant component of the TUC when the National and Local Government Officers Association (NALGO) joined in 1964 and the National Union of Teachers in 1972. The proportion of TUC membership classified as white collar rose from 13.2 per cent in 1948 to 19.5 per cent in 1964, and has continued to increase since then. [5]

The increase in the number of white collar employees in the TUC does not mean that they automatically support the Labour Party. On the contrary, white collar union members are less willing to support the party than are their colleagues in heavy industry.[6] NALGO, for example, has refused to become involved in this type of politics. One indicator of party attachment is the amount of money the union is willing to pay in affiliating to the party. Each union must pay a per capita fee based on the number of members it wishes to affiliate, and this determines the union's votes at the Labour Party conference. The unions may use a membership figure in affiliating to the party which is either greater or less than the number in the union who pay the 'political levy'. The party does not question whether there are actually people to back up the funds it receives. Compared with the six largest unions sponsoring MPs, the white collar unions are generally either less willing or less able to affiliate as high a proportion of their TUC membership to the party. The NUM, for example, has frequently had more members affiliated to the party than to the TUC. Four other large unions, the AEF, the NUGMW, USDAW and the NUR, seldom fall below having 70% of their TUC membership affiliated to the party, and only the TGWU frequently was under that figure. On the other hand, the Musicians and DATA affiliation figure was almost always under 45% in recent years and even the militant ASTMS usually ranged between 50 and 60%.[7] Nonetheless, the white collar unions are making an important contribution to the changes in the types of unions sponsoring MPs and types of MPs being sponsored.

In the 1960s and 70s this shift in the kinds of unions sponsoring MPs has been accompanied by changes in the political orientation of some of the unions, the TGWU and the AEF in particular. In both cases the union leadership has taken a turn to the left. Hugh Scanlon of the AEF and Frank Cousins or Jack Jones of the TGWU are of a very different political persuasion from that of their predecessors in these unions. As one writer described Jack Jones, he 'most vigorously reminds us of those deep, inarticulate needs of the industrial workers that even the best wage-packets do not satisfy, and who testifies that striking workers are usually trying to assert themselves as men in industries where they are still regarded as hands'.[8] The traditional working class orientation suggested here was reinforced when the 1964–70 Labour government tried to reform industrial relations along lines laid down in the White Paper 'In Place of Strife.' But most unions were clearly unhappy with the Labour government's proposals, as indicated by Victor Feather's comments to the 1970 National Union of Teachers' conference: 'I can knock on the door of

Iain Macleod as well as I can knock on the door of Roy Jenkins and get an equally friendly response. I can knock on the door of Robert Carr and get a more friendly response than I got from Barbara Castle.'[9] One doubts, of course, if Feather would have said this after the Tories produced their own proposals for the reform of industrial relations in 1974.

The implications of the changes in the AEF are still not clear, because Hugh Scanlon was only elected to the presidency of the union in 1967, in succession to the late Lord Carron and until early 1974 he shared top authority with the union's general secretary James Conway, who was much more conservative in the Labour Party context. In addition, Scanlon's control of the AEF is limited by the union's highly developed democratic procedures and the divided political affiliations they reflected.[10] These divided political attitudes, plus the reliance on relatively objective selection by examination of the AEF's panel of potential parliamentary nominees, reduced the immediate impact of the change in the union on its sponsored MPs. (For a fuller discussion of unions' nominating procedure, see pp. 56–60 below.)

The implications of the changes in the TGWU, on the other hand, are far more obvious, in part because Cousins and his successor Jack Jones have had almost two decades to influence and direct the union. In addition, the TGWU has always had a much more centralised and less democratic leadership than that of the AEF.[11] The Transport Workers allow the union executive to decide whom to sponsor, without the limitations imposed by the AEF's examination system or USDAW's electoral procedures. In any event, the changes in the orientation of the TGWU were first made clear in 1967, when the union's conference adopted a resolution calling for a review of its panel of sponsored MPs. This action was reaffirmed in 1969, and in 1971 the TGWU called specifically for a review of MPs' political activities and ideological viewpoints in deciding whom to retain on the union's parliamentary panel. The TGWU's actions in a number of cases will be discussed below, but clearly the change in the union's leadership, accompanied by the increased importance of white collar unions and the changing background of sponsored MPs, will have a major impact on the Labour Party in the next decade.

Consultation

Yet another domestic change which has an impact on the sponsorship of MPs is the continuing development of consultation between unions and government. The basis for this is indicated by Eric Taylor:

> Every new Act that is passed, in a highly developed society such as ours, is bound to interfere with someone's happiness and peace of mind, and to trample upon established interests somewhere. Sectional interests have to be consulted, if possible met, or, failing that, soothed. No one, not even the Government, can afford to ignore or trample upon these various groupings or opinions. There is always the new general election to be remembered. So there must be endless negotiations, deputations and interviews, before even the form of the Bill is settled.[12]

Consultative status gives many groups more or less direct access to the bureaucratic establishment of the Civil Service, which is charged both with the original formulation of legislation before it is submitted to Parliament by the Cabinet, and with the implementation of that legislation after it has been approved by Parliament. It was one of Ernest Bevin's major achievements as minister of labour and national service and as a member of the War Cabinet to establish a broad network of consultative bodies aimed at ensuring the cooperation of government, labour, and management in the British war effort. In the third Labour government, formed in 1945, Bevin served as foreign secretary, but he continued to look after the trade unions' interests in the domestic sphere, ensuring that the new network of consultation was not allowed to wither away.[13] The eventual return of a Conservative government in 1951 did little to alter the overall procedures which has been developing since 1940 for use in consultation, and the Labour victory in 1964 accentuated the more or less permanent and continuous nature of these links between government and organised labour.[14]

The primary agency for recruiting labour representatives to consultative bodies is the TUC; indeed the government's recognition of the TUC as the primary voice of organised labour in the National Economic Development Committee (NEDC) after 1963 was a major factor in NALGO's decision to join the TUC in 1964. Individual unions have also secured consultative status on matters of particular concern to them. For example, NUM leaders frequently meet with the National Coal Board and the minister of power to discuss the state of the coal industry. Similarly, the Amalgamated Engineers (AEF) have representatives on the Ministry of Supply's Joint Industrial Council, which is concerned with the Royal Ordnance factories and potential unemployment.[15] The government retains the right to decide who will be consulted in cases such as these and, of course, the TUC or the unions retain the right to reject invitations when offered. For example, the unions rejected an invitation to serve on the National Incomes Committee (NIC) between 1963 and 1965.

Consultation does not guarantee that a group's views will be accepted and followed. A story that appeared in *The Times* shortly after the return of the Labour Party to power in 1964 illustrates the implications of an MP's ties with a group. 'The old civil servant watched the new minister studying a file. "I think I ought to warn you, Sir", he said, "that we don't take that organisation very seriously".' To which the minister amiably replied: '"I think I ought to warn you that I am a member of this organisation." '[16] This story was fictional, but there is evidence to suggest that it bears some relation to reality. In 1967, for example, during the conflict over the Labour government's economic policy, it was announced that in future the TUC General Council would have the right of direct access to the prime minister; the chancellor of the Exchequer would also be more accessible.[17]

When policy decisions are announced in the House of Commons, the responsible minister will usually indicate if proper consultation with interested groups has taken place. The decision in 1946 to end wartime labour controls was announced with the words: 'After consultation with my Right Hon. Friend the Minister of Fuel and Power, who has been in touch with the employers' and workers' organisations concerned, my Right Hon. Friend the Minister of Labour has informed them that the Essential Work (Coalmining Industry) Order, 1943, will be revoked with effect from 1st September next.'[18]

Along with consultation has gone the continued willingness of governments to appoint leading trade unionists and union-sponsored MPs to various public boards: thus John Benstead, former general secretary of NUR, was appointed to the British Transport Commission; Alfred Robens, a former USDAW-sponsored MP, was made chairman of the National Coal Board as Lord Robens of Woldingham; Richard Marsh, formerly sponsored by NUPE, became head of British Rail; and five or six union officials or sponsored MPs were made members of the Prices and Incomes Board (PIB) between 1965 and 1971. As well as these official appointments, of course, seats in the House of Lords have often been conferred on trade union figures. The unions have generally been interested in securing more positions on public bodies for their leaders. [19]

A second effect of consultation is the change noted earlier, in Chapter II: the growing separation of the political and industrial wings of the labour movement, which is widely recognised by both MPs and union leaders. As Hugh Gaitskell expressed it to the 1959 meeting of the TUC: 'We are part of the same great Labour Movement. We are comrades together, but we have different jobs to do.' [20] Clement Attlee had expressed similar views when he wrote: 'The Labour Party, although it originated as a group of Trade Unionists sent to Parliament with the specific objective of supporting organised Labour by action on the political field, is not a mere political expression of Trade Unionism. Trade Unions are the backbone of the movement, but the Party represents something more than the needs of organized Labour.' [21] Harold Wilson's attempt to broaden the base of the party in the late 1960s and 70s to transform it into Britain's 'natural' governing party, did little to end the split between unions and party. [22] After all, if the Labour Party did not remain true to its social base in the trade unions and the working class, why should they continue to support it?

Awareness of the split is generally found among union leaders, who resent and resist attempts by politicians to interfere in the industrial sphere. [23] This was one reason why the unions (and many of their sponsored MPs) were so unhappy with the proposals contained in 'In Place of Strife'. Industrial relations were felt to be a matter that the political wing of the movement should avoid.

But there are exceptions even to this. When consultative status is denied or the unions refuse to take part in consultation, they find it necessary to rediscover their Members of Parliament. This was the case following the 1970 General Election, when the Conservatives attempted to reform industrial relations and to reject the unions' demands for autonomy in that area. As the Industrial Relations Bill was working its way through the House of Commons, union leaders were in active and frequent contact with their MPs (and with the remainder of the Labour Party, of course) on the best means to oppose the bill. As David Wood expressed it in *The Times*, the Trade Union Group in the PLP became the union movement's 'one hope'. [24] With this sort of challenge confronting both the unions and the party (since the bill was sponsored by the Tories), the political and industrial sides of the Movement could draw closer together for the moment.

The more general nature of the split within the labour movement can be seen elsewhere. Major industrial disputes are seldom commented on by sponsored MPs in the House of Commons. [25] Most unions continue to be unwilling to allow fulltime officials to enter the House. Even the NUGMW finally decided to follow this policy in the late 1940s when it 'came down firmly and finally in favour of the view that trade unions and the Parliamentary Labour Party are distinct if complementary bodies requiring separate leadership'. [26] When Walter Alldritt was chosen to become a regional secretary of the union in 1971, he had to give up his seat in the House of Commons. [27] The lack of fulltime union officials in Parliament is paralleled in the industrial wing of the movement by the absence of MPs from union delegations to the TUC or even to the Labour Party conference.

Their consultative status and the resulting split within the labour movement means that unions frequently bypass their sponsored MPs when dealing with the government, which can lead to resentment among the MPs. [28] To counter this, the MPs are frequently heard to urge closer ties between the unions and the party. [29] But the continuing lack of major trade union officials among the sponsored MPs makes it difficult to achieve these closer ties and to reconcile the diverse goals of the industrial and political wings of the labour movement. The stresses inherent in this relationship are bound to continue as the British government attempts to deal with industrial problems in the future.

Party Reforms

A fourth source of change in sponsorship is the effort of the Labour Party to exert more control over sponsoring procedures. The basis for party regulation of sponsorship exists in the Trade Union Act of 1927, which in effect reduced the unions' political funds. [30] Replacing 'contracting out' by 'contracting in' meant that the apathetic were less likely to pay the political levy after 1927 and the unions would have less money for political purposes, including sponsorship.

After the disaster of the 1931 General Election this problem was aggravated by tremendous competition for the few available seats. The 1933 by-election at Clay Cross, for example, witnessed a mad scramble for the candidature, as a number of unions, including the Miners', the TGWU, and the NUR, all placed nominees before the CLP.[31]

At Hastings in 1933 the annual conference of the Labour Party adopted certain regulations covering the amount of financial support a union could offer to a CLP in exchange for its adopting the union's nominee as a candidate. Initially the union maintenance grant to a CLP was limited to £150 a year in borough constituencies and £200 a year in county constituencies. Gradually increased, these figures now stand at £350 and £420 respectively. In addition to the annual maintenance grants paid to a CLP, unions were permitted to pay up to eighty per cent of the election expenses within a constituency. Two aspects of these payments should be emphasised. First, they are the maximum payments that can be made and many sponsoring unions do not pay the maximum. The Simpson Committee's inquiry into party organisation in 1966–68 reported that the maximum was reached in only 59 out of 151 cases.[32] Secondly, these payments are given to the local CLP, not to the MP, and should not be confused with the personal financial aid which some unions give to some MPs.[33] Thus the arrangements under the Hastings Agreement were beyond the scope of Parliament's Select Committee on Members' Interests, whose report was published in late 1969.

The Hastings Agreement aimed specifically at regulating the role of union money in the adoption of parliamentary candidates. The more general problem of local party organisation was studied by the Wilson Committee, established after the 1955 election defeat. This committee issued a highly critical report urging that the local affiliation fees of both individuals and groups should be increased to encourage the financial independence of CLPs. Sponsorship was seen as a threat to the financial independence of the local party organisations.[34] It was hoped that greater financial independence would enable the CLPs to be more selective in the candidates they adopted. The continuing poor state of local Labour Party organisation, however, raises questions about the validity of the Wilson Committee's assumptions, especially in the light of changes in the type of candidates being adopted by CLPs.

Union Recruitment Procedures

While the above factors have an indirect effect on union representation in Parliament, the internal procedures used by the unions to certify individuals whom they are willing to sponsor are even more important. As the unions are in competition with one another and with the Co-operative Party for available and especially, winnable constituencies, and as they are under pressure from Labour Party headquarters to sponsor the best qualified people possible, it is not surprising that a major change is underway in their certification procedures.[35] Certification generally involves two separate steps. First, the union creates a panel of possible parliamentary nominees, whose names are usually but not always included on the party's list of approved candidates. Secondly, the union decides which of these people will actually be nominated for a particular constituency. Union nomination does not guarantee that the CLP will adopt the individual, but that aspect of the process does not fall within the scope of this study.[36]

Elections. Unions generally follow one of three procedures in deciding who will be placed on their panel of possible parliamentary nominees. The first is the traditional democratic method of election. Using a variety of techniques, including a mail ballot of all union members, voting at branch meetings, or voting by delegates to the union's conference, the union members share in deciding whom the union will certify for sponsorship. Unions that use some form of election include USDAW, some components of the NUM, TSSA, CAWU, UPA, ASLEF, NUTGW, and the NGA.[37]

Among the leaders and rank and file members of many unions, however, there is considerable dissatisfaction with these methods because they fail to produce a panel of possible nominees that CLPs find attractive. In USDAW, for example, there is particular concern over the age of its panel members. Until 1969 the union selected its parliamentary nominees according to seniority on the panel of potential nominees. This rule was formally modified to allow the USDAW executive to choose any member of the panel without regard to seniority. The selection of the most senior panel member for a candidature in late 1969 indicates that changes in rules do not necessarily result in changes in behaviour.[38]

Even in the NUM there is increasing discontent with electoral procedures, as miners' nominees before CLP selection conferences are less frequently adopted than are those of other unions. For example, only one of the five miners retiring in 1970 was replaced by a miner. The primary authority in the NUM for certifying potential nominees is exercised at the regional level, but in recent years the national NUM conference has been confronted with demands for a national panel consisting of candidates who would prove more attractive than those on the existing regional panels. So far these resolutions have not produced any action. [39]

Until 1959 the NUVB chose its parliamentary panel through an election by all those members paying the political levy. After H. P. H. Gourlay's success in the 1959 General Election, the union eliminated the electoral procedure and allowed its executive to sponsor any two NUVB members adopted by the CLP as candidates. [40] After the NUVB's merger with the TGWU in 1973, these procedures were superseded by those of the Transport Workers.

In any event, electoral procedures seldom guarantee that a person will be nominated for a parliamentary candidature. They only certify that he or she is eligible for such nomination. The union executive must still decide whether it wants to nominate a particular individual at a particular CLP selection conference. The only exceptions to this executive discretion were found in USDAW before 1969 and in some of the regional components of the NUM today, where local union branches in mining constituencies decide which individual from the region's panel will be nominated.

Examinations. The second procedure used by unions to certify possible nominees is a written and oral examination. This is a more recent development, little used before World War II. [41] In explaining the change from election to examination, one union general secretary has written:

> Before this procedure [certification by examination] was introduced in April 1964, members were elected to the Parliamentary Panel by a vote of all members of the Society paying the political levy. This was changed because the procedure had led to a progressive reduction in The Society's parliamentary representation and it was believed that the new procedure would ensure more adequate representation. In other words, the membership did not necessarily elect those persons

who were most likely to be adopted as candidates by local constituency parties, and election was replaced by selection. [42]

Certification by means of examinations has been pioneered by the
AEF and is now used by a number of other unions, including UPW,
ASW, DATA, NUPE, and BISAKTA. The AEF's 1966 examination
consisted of ten parts designed to cover various aspects of an MP's
work. The major portion of the exam consisted of written and oral
presentations evaluated by people outside the union for the most
part. Only 10% of the exam was concerned with the union and its
history and policy. Additional training in public speaking is provided
to those successful in the examination. [43]

The change from the traditional method of certifying possible
nominees to the use of examination is not always smooth. In the
UPW there was a struggle at the annual conference in 1962 when the
union leadership supported a successful attempt to introduce the examination procedure. Rank and file opposition was led by Denis
Hobden, who feared that political bias might now determine the union's selection. Several years earlier Hobden had had difficulty in
securing approval from the Labour Party NEC for his inclusion on
the Party's list of possible parliamentary candidates; thus he was
acutely aware of the threat that the change in procedure might pose
to those who did not always agree with the union leadership. [44] He
feared that the leadership might take advantage of the change to
punish him for his activities in the Campaign for Nuclear Disarmament, which the leaders of the UPW had opposed. Hobden's opposition did little to halt the change by the union, and he was appointed
to the new panel of potential nominees. [45] Elected to the House of
Commons in 1964, he was finally accepted by the UPW as a sponsored MP before the 1966 General Election.

Executive appointment. The third procedure for certifying possible
nominees is handled entirely by the union's executive council or other
top leadership body. Here the first step of the process and the second,
the decision on which possible nominees to place before a CLP selection conference are combined. Thus the Union leaders can certify
almost any member of the union as eligible for nomination; the only
rank and file participation might be a preliminary suggestion of
possible names. Assigning both steps of the certification stage to the
top union leadership occurs in the TGWU, NUGMW, the NUR, and

the NUVB. With a few exceptions almost all unions permit their leadership discretion in deciding whether to submit a name on its panel of possible nominees to a CLP selection conference. Initial certification by election or examination limits this discretion but does not eliminate it. Since this second step is repeated before each general election, it is the point where unions seem most likely to try to influence an MP's legislative activity, by threatening to withdraw their sponsorship in successive elections, or by promising to add him to their list of sponsored MPs. We will discuss some of the resulting union–MP conflicts in Part III below.

Retirement rules. In some unions the rules require that sponsorship of an MP cease after he has reached a certain age, usually about sixty-five. Unions with this rule include the NUR, the Durham and Derbyshire miners of the NUM, ASLEF, and TSSA. Such rules vary in their impact and in their political implications. Adoption of such a rule is sometimes an attempt to remove a sponsored MP whom the union dislikes: this appears to have happened when, before the 1955 General Election, the Durham miners adopted an age limit for sponsored MPs and forced the retirement of J. D. Murray; [46] and it may have played a part in the Derbyshire adoption of a similar rule following the 1964 election.

Loss of sponsored status because of retirement rules or because of union unhappiness about an MP's age does not necessarily mean that he will give up his seat in the House of Commons. In fact, if they have adequate local support, it is not unusual for these MPs to continue in the House. For example, Alfred Balfour, sponsored by the NUR in 1945 and 1950, passed their retirement age before the 1951 election but was nonetheless re-elected to the House in 1951 and in 1955 without official union support. Walter Monslow passed the ASLEF retirement age before the 1964 election but was successfully re-elected; two other recent examples include Charles Mapp of TSSA and Harold Neal of the Derbyshire miners in 1966. But perhaps the best recent example of the importance of local support was Stephen O. Davies' successful election as an Independent in 1970, over the opposition of both his local Labour Party and the South Wales miners.

Union retirement rules are not a new development, but they have become more common since World War II. However, while party leaders may be interested in securing the election of younger MPs, the unions are not rushing to adopt retirement ages for sponsored

MPs. A proposal to retire all MPs at the age of seventy was defeated at the USDAW conference in 1960,[47] and a similar one placed before the 1963 NUGMW congress, to compel MPs to retire at sixty-seven, was treated lightly and rejected.[48]

Constituency selection. Unions are concerned with the kinds of constituencies for which their nominees are proposed, wanting to place them in 'safe' seats where victory for the Labour Party is practically assured. As one union official expressed it, 'We want a good return on our investment.'[49] – of time, money, and energy. Thus efforts by militants among the rank and file to persuade their unions to pay greater attention to marginal seats have not always been very successful.[50] The result of the unions favouring of safe seats can be seen in Table II-1, p.30.

Changing Patterns of Union Representation

All the factors discussed above have some impact on the type of person sponsored by the unions in the House of Commons, although precise relationships cannot always be identified. What will become clear in the following pages is that the years since 1945 have witnessed a major change both in the type of union sponsoring MPs and in the background of the individuals being sponsored.

Even since 1945 the group of sponsored MPs in Parliament has not necessarily included all MPs associated with the trade union movement. Examples of those who were not officially sponsored and thus fall outside the scope of this study include Hilary Marquand, an industrial adviser to the Blastfurnacemen, who received a retainer from the union while he was in the House of Commons; Sir Barnet Stross, honorary medical adviser to the Pottery Worker's Society and the North Staffordshire Miners' Federation; James Callaghan and Douglas Houghton of the Inland Revenue Staffs' Association; Edward Redhead of the Society of Civil Servants; and Robert Edwards, general secretary of the Chemical Workers Union. There are also a few MPs who have lost their sponsored status, usually because of retirement rules, but remain in the House without official union support. Further confusion in identifying sponsored MPs is caused by the fact that some unions make small contributions to CLPs which have adopted any of the unions' members. In the NUGMW, for example, in addition to the sponsored MPs there are two groups of assisted MPs who are not sponsored: those in one group receive a small election grant from their union; and the others, whose association with the union is mainly political, are given a nominal sum.[51]

Unions that Sponsor MPs

With these complexities in mind and using the party conference reports as our chief source of data, we may now ask which unions sponsor MPs.

The changing pattern of union representation in Parliament can be seen in Table III–1. Such old stalwarts as the textile workers, the boot and shoe operatives, and the woodworkers are disappearing from the Palace of Westminster. Among the railroad unions, the NUR and ASLEF, which include the bulk of the railways' manual employees, are being replaced by the TSSA, which organises the clerical and white collar workers. Other unions that are gaining ground include USDAW (until 1974), the general workers' unions (especially the TGWU), and the AEF. The increased parliamentary representation of these unions is paralleled by the emergence of new unions organising clerical and service occupations. Unions such as ASTMS, NUPE, CAWU, and DATA have been actively seeking to increase their representation.

Increased representation of the TGWU and AEF (which is taking on the appearance of a general union as it extends the groups it is willing to organise) is an exception to the general shift away from heavy industry. However, these gains must be viewed against the particular background of each union and the types of men they sponsor. Both have used either examination or executive certification, rather than election, in making up their panels of potential parliamentary nominees.

In the case of the TGWU, the development of an aggressive policy towards sponsorship dates from the election of Frank Cousins as general secretary in 1956, with no apparent change under his successor Jack Jones. Under their leadership the union has sought to adopt as many sponsored MPs as possible, which since 1959 has included a number of sitting MPs such as Anthony Greenwood, Anthony Probert, Dr. Jeremy Bray, and Leslie Huckfield. By 1966 the union had a total of twenty-seven MPs, replacing the miners as the union sponsoring the largest group of MPs. While the TGWU fell behind the miners in 1970 (in part because of the decision to review

TABLE III – 1
UNION REPRESENTATION IN PARLIAMENT, 1918–1974
(in numbers of MPs)

UNION TYPES	DATE OF GENERAL ELECTION																
INDIVIDUAL UNIONS**	1918*	1922*	1923*	1924*	1929*	1931	1935	1945	1950	1951	1955	1959	1964	1966	1970	1974–I	1974–II
UNSKILLED																	
Miners (MFGB/NUM)	25	41	43	40	41	23	34	35	37	36	34	31	27	26	20	18	18
Railwaymen (NUR)	1	3	4	3	8	1	4	12	10	9	8	5	6	7	5	6	6
BISAKTA	–	2	1	3	4	–	1	2	2	2	2	2	1	1	2	2	1
UTFWA	4	3	3	2	4	–	–	3	2	1	1	1	1	1	–	–	–
Agricultural Workers (NUAW)	–	–	1	–	–	–	–	2	1	1	1	2	1	1	–	–	1
NUTGW	–	–	–	–	–	–	–	–	–	–	–	1	–	–	–	–	–
Seamen	–	–	–	–	–	–	–	–	–	–	–	–	–	–	1	1	1
Subtotal	30	49	52	48	57	24	39	54	52	49	46	42	36	36	28	27	27
GENERAL																	
TGWU	3	6	9	8	13	2	7	17	16	14	14	14	21	27	19	23	21
NUGMW	4	4	5	4	6	2	6	8	6	4	4	4	9	10	12	13	13
Engineers (AEF)	1	7	4	4	3	1	3	3	8	7	6	8	17	17	16	17	16
Subtotal	8	17	18	16	22	5	16	28	30	25	24	26	47	54	47	53	50
SKILLED																	
Woodworkers (ASW)	1	1	3	2	6	1	2	4	3	3	2	1	1	1	1	1	1
NUBSO	1	2	1	–	2	–	1	4	1	1	–	1	1	1	–	–	–
ASLEF	–	–	1	1	1	–	–	1	2	2	3	3	1	–	–	–	–
Boilermakers	1	1	2	2	1	1	–	1	1	2	–	–	1	1	3	3	–
ETU	–	–	–	–	–	–	–	1	1	1	–	–	1	1	3	3	3

																		Subtotal
NGA	—	1	—	—	1	—	—	2	1	1	1	—	1	—	2	—	1	1
Blastfurnacemen	—	1	—	—	1	—	—	1	—	—	—	—	—	1	1	—	1	1
Fire brigades	—	—	—	—	—	—	—	—	—	—	—	—	—	—	—	—	—	2
AUBTW	—	—	—	1	—	—	1	—	—	—	—	—	1	—	—	—	—	1
Constructional Engineers	—	—	—	—	—	—	—	—	—	—	—	—	—	—	1	—	—	1
NUVB	—	—	—	—	—	—	—	—	—	—	—	—	1	—	1	—	1	1
Pattern Makers (UPA)	—	1	—	1	1	—	1	—	1	1	—	—	1	1	2	—	—	—
London Compositors	2	2	—	2	2	—	2	—	1	1	—	1	—	—	—	1	2	2
Post Office Engineers	—	—	—	—	—	—	—	—	—	—	—	—	—	—	—	—	—	—
Subtotal	3	4	10	8	11	3	7	17	8	9	21	20	18	7	10	9	10	11	13
CLERICAL, TECHNICAL & WHITE COLLAR UNIONS																			
SOGAT	—	1	—	—	—	—	1	1	1	1	1	—	—	—	1	—	—	—
TSSA	—	1	—	4	7	6	9	7	7	5	5	5	7	5	4	3	3	3
Shopworkers (USDAW)	—	3	3	4	1	1	5	6	8	8	9	9	10	10	9	6	6	5
Postoffice Workers (UPW)	2	3	—	2	—	—	—	—	1	2	2	2	2	4	2	2	2	2
Public Employees (NUPE)	—	—	—	—	—	—	—	1	2	2	2	2	5	6	6	6	6
CAWU	—	—	—	—	—	—	—	1	1	1	2	1	3	4	3	4	6	6
Draughtsmen (DATA)	—	—	—	—	—	1	1	—	—	—	—	—	—	2	4	4	4	4
ASTMS (formerly ASSET)	—	—	—	—	—	—	—	—	—	—	—	—	1	1	2	3	9	12
Musicians	—	—	—	—	—	—	—	—	—	—	—	—	1	—	1	—	—	1
Insurance Workers	—	—	—	—	—	—	1	1	—	—	—	—	—	—	—	—	—	—
Subtotal	2	8	14	10	17	5	12	17	20	21	20	18	27	31	29	37	37	37
OTHER UNIONS	8	14	14	10	17	3	5	5	1	1	—	—	—	—	1	1	1	1
Total	8	49	86	102	88	115	32	79	121	110	105	96	93	120	132	114	127	129

Sources: Labour Party Conference *Reports* (1918–1974) and Labour Party Library Records.

* The figures for General Elections prior to 1931 are not precise. The Party Conference *Reports* only list candidates and sitting MPs for the early years without always showing the financing or sponsoring body.

** The names of the unions are those used in 1970. The number of sponsored MPs includes all Members sponsored by unions that have merged with or into one of the above unions with the exception of 1974. Unions that merged between 1970 and 1974 are shown under their 1970 name.

the sponsored status of all its MPs, after which four were dropped from the panel), they once again moved into the lead in the two elections of 1974, with twenty-three MPs in the first and twenty-one in the second. The prestige of having the largest group of MPs is one fringe benefit for Britain's largest union.

The background of the newer TGWU MPs is not without its social and political significance. Officials of the Transport Workers' union are usually drawn from among its rank and file members, but the MPs are increasingly drawn from professional and white collar groups. This difference has attracted unfavourable comment from some of the rank and file members, which was to no avail until 1970 and of little impact even then.[52] Reflecting the political orientation of Cousins and Jones, the newer TGWU MPs are more likely to be found on the left wing of the PLP, in organisations such as the Tribune Group, and they may represent an effort by the TGWU leadership to compel the PLP to accept Labour Party conference decisions by packing the PLP with individual MPs who accept the conference's authority.

The AEF has also emphasised the desirability of increasing its parliamentary representation since the 1950s. Disdaining the TGWU's practice of 'buying' Members,[53] the AEF has undertaken an extensive and expensive programme to train rank and file trade unionists for parliamentary careers. The reasons for this action are not clear, although one possibility is the increasing importance of governmental action in the engineering, automotive, and aircraft industries. More significant was the initial support of Fred Lee, who encouraged the change even though his own selection as an AEF MP occurred by means of an election within the union. In addition, the late Sir William (later Lord) Carron, who served as union president from 1956 until 1967, was an active proponent of the new system, using it as a device to keep Communists within the AEF from gaining greater recognition. It is still not clear if Carron's successor Hugh Scanlon will make any significant changes in the AEF's system, which stands in sharp contrast to the electoral procedures found elsewhere in the union.[54]

Unlike the newer TGWU MPs, the Members sponsored by the engineers are far more likely to be veteran and active union members, closer in spirit to the traditional trade-union sponsored MPs. The success of the Labour Party in maintaining a working class image will largely depend on the success of the AEF and other unions in using certification procedures to produce well qualified and sponsored trade union MPs in the next decades.

The other side of the changing pattern of union representation is to be seen in the history of the miners' MPs in the House of Commons. Traditionally the NUM (the MFGB before 1945) has had the largest single group of sponsored MPs in the House. As it pioneered parliamentary representation, this seemed only right and proper. It is difficult to conceive of the Labour Party without the miners, but they are a declining force, as indicated by the data in Table III–1 (p. 62 above) and Figure 2. Allowing for the debâcle of 1931 and the gradual recovery from it, we can see a decline in miners' representation which dates back to the 1920s. By 1974 the number of NUM-sponsored MPs had fallen to eighteen, the lowest since before World War I; and the miners no longer constituted the largest group of sponsored MPs in the House.

The miners' decline reflects the shrinking coal industry, a loss of union membership in the NUM, and the continued insistence on traditional certification procedures within the union's regional components. Even more important is a general disenchantment with the Labour Party and with its sponsored MPs, as indicated by the increased militancy of the union since 1970. The unwillingness or inability of Roy Mason to slow the decline of the industry when he served in the 1964–70 government merely strengthened the militants in the NUM and heightened their scepticism of all politicians.[55] Indeed, were it not for the concentration of the coal industry in particular areas and the closeknit communities that have characterised the industry and contributed to the miners' unwillingness to attack those who once served them, the number of NUM-sponsored MPs might have dropped even more precipitously than it has.

MPs Sponsored by Unions:
'A Lot of Damned Constituents'[56]

Union-sponsored MPs have traditionally been distinguished from other MPs, regardless of party, by their lower level of education, their particular occupational background, and their relatively older age of entry into the House of Commons. Their presence among the ranks of Labour MPs has validated the claim that the Labour Party is more representative or typical of the country as a whole, and has helped to assure the working class that the Labour Party is indeed the party of the workers. It is precisely this relative difference in

NUMBER OF MINERS

ELECTION	0	10	20	30	40	50
1874						
1880						
1885						
1886						
1892						
1895						
1900						
1906*						
1910**						
1918***						
1922						
1923						
1924						
1929						
1931						
1935						
1945						
1950						
1951						
1955						
1959						
1964						
1966						
1970						
1974 (I)						
1974 (II)						

Figure 2. MINERS IN THE HOUSE OF COMMONS, 1874–1974.
Sources: R. P. Arnot, *History of the Miners' Federation of Great Britain,* vol. I, pp. 295–96, 365–69; II, pp. 550–51; and Labour Party Annual Conference, *Reports* (1931–1974).

* The figure for 1906 includes five miners' MPs not covered by the Pickard scheme adopted by the MFGB in 1902.

** P. Arnot does not give separate figures for the two 1910 elections. J. H. S. Reid (*The Origins of the British Labour Party* [Minneapolis: University of Minnesota Press, 1955], p.118) claims that 10 miners were successful in the first election and 17 in the second. Thomas Burt, Charles Fenwick, and J. Wilson, who had not signed the Labour Party Constitution in 1909 and thus lost further official MFGB support, are included in the figure given above.

*** The figures after 1910 include not only those miners' MPs officially supported by the MFGB or its successor the NUM. Lib-Labs such as Thomas Burt, elected in the years immediately preceding and following World War I, are excluded, as are other Independent miners, such as S. O. Davies, who was re-elected to the House of Commons in 1970.

Labour MPs' backgrounds which has begun to change since the 1950s. 'Workers by brain' are beginning to replace 'workers by hand' even among the sponsored MPs. Jeremy Bray (an MP of the TGWU between 1964 and 1970), with a Ph.D. in mathematics from Harvard, was merely an extreme example of this development. Another was Anthony Greenwood (now Lord Greenwood of Rossendale). Unions are able to find such men because individual members of the Labour Party must belong to a union in order to qualify for such membership. With the general and the white collar unions defining their potential membership in very board terms, many middle class individuals are able to join one. This requirement and the general expectation that union membership lends respectability to an individual within the Labour Party sometimes lead to absurdities, as prospective parliamentary candidates search for a union to join. [57]

The changing background of the sponsored MPs is augmented by the willingness of many unions to add sitting MPs to their list of sponsored Members. The TGWU and the NUGMW both engage in 'buying' Members, but it is most noticeable among some of the smaller but rapidly growing white collar unions such as ASTMS and CAWU. Their action in 1974 meant that such long-serving MPs as Ian Mikardo (ASTMS) and Shirley Williams (CAWU) suddenly became sponsored MPs. If the number of individuals sponsored by the general and white collar unions continues to increase, and if the certification procedures followed by such unions as the AEF fail to produce a large number of sponsored MPs in the late 1970s and 80s, there will be few who can quarrel with the reporter who wrote about 'The Death of a Hero': the man in the cloth cap. [58]

Statistics can help illustrate the extent to which the type of person sponsored by the unions is changing. Tables III–2 and 3 below show selected differences between the union-sponsored MPs elected in 1945 and in 1966. These two elections both yielded large Labour victories, and the twenty-one years between them bred a new parliamentary generation. By 1966 only thirteen of the MPs sponsored in 1945 remained in the House in that status. The defeat of the Labour Party in 1970, its plurality in February 1974, and its narrow majority in October 1974 mean there has been no massive shift among the Labour MPs since 1966, and the changes apparent then have been marginally increased.

TABLE III – 2

AGE DISTRIBUTION OF SPONSORED MEMBERS
ELECTED IN 1945 AND IN 1966

AGE GROUP	1945		1966	
	No.	%	No.	%
Under 30	2	1.7	–	–
30–34	1	0.8	1	0.8
35–39	6	5.0	14	10.5
40–44	7	5.8	25	18.8
45–49	23	19.0	16	12.0
50–54	15	12.4	19	14.3
55–59	28	23.1	25	18.8
60–64	15	12.4	20	15.0
65–69	7	5.8	8	6.0
70–74	7	5.8	2	1.5
75–79	2	1.7	1	0.8
80 and above	–	–	1	0.8
Unknown	8	6.6	–	–
Total	121	100.0	132	100.0
Mean Ages	53.9		51.1	

Source: Calculated from *The Times Guide to the House of Commons* and other standard biographical sources.

Age. Our expectation that the 1966 union-sponsored MPs would be younger than the 1945 groups, because of the changes suggested earlier in this chapter, is borne out by the data presented in Table III–2. In particular, the number and proportion of trade-union sponsored MPs who were under the age of forty when elected increased greatly.

It has been suggested that for sponsored MPs the House of Commons is frequently a consolation prize following failure in the union. If this is the case, newly sponsored MPs would be expected to be older than new fulltime union officers, and we can test this hypothesis by comparing the ages of newly sponsored MPs with those of new union officers. In 1945 the mean age of the fifty-five newly sponsored MPs was 49.0; in 1964 it had fallen to 44.1 for forty-one new sponsored MPs; and in 1966 it fell to 41.7 for thirteen new trade union MPs. Despite this decline, the MPs had a higher mean age than that of the union officials, whose mean starting age for selected unions between 1945 and 1958 was 40.7; but the gap was closing. [59] Sponsored MPs start their careers later than fulltime union officers, but the differences are decreasing. Thus it can still be argued that the newer MPs are less likely to be frustrated union officers.

The lower mean age of new sponsored MPs is at least partly explained by the declining number of MPs sponsored by the miners' union. The miners traditionally sent older men into the House, and individuals such as Aneurin Bevan, Tom Fraser, Roy Mason, or Eric Varley, who were elected around the age of thirty, were extremely unusual. Miners' candidates in 1950, for example, had a mean age six years higher than that of all sponsored candidates. [60]

TABLE III – 3

EDUCATIONAL BACKGROUNDS OF 1945 AND
1966 UNION-SPONSORED MPs

Educational level	1945		1966	
	No.	%	No.	%
Elementary only	37	30.8	25	18.8
Intermediate	57	47.0	74	55.6
University	6	5.0	32	24.0
Unknown	21	17.4	1	0.8
Total	121	100.0	132	100.0

Education. A second major background variable is education. As indicated above, the national increase in educational opportunity might be expected to lead to an increase in the overall educational level of MPs. Table III–3 attempts to categorise the educational backgrounds of all union-sponsored MPs in 1945 and in 1966. Given the nature of the educational system and the information available about some MPs these figures are at best approximations. The major change has come in the two extreme categories: the MPs with only elementary school education and those with some sort of university training. The stereotype of the union-sponsored MP, with only an elementary school training, is being threatened by the newer breed who have attended university. At least in terms of education the traditional cleavage within the PLP is being reduced.

The changing social background of sponsored MPs has attracted the attention of many who are committed to the tradition and stereotype of the union MP in the cloth cap. As one sponsored Member wrote in the late 1950s, 'Still it is a fact that something will go out of our movement if we fail to keep up our quota of trade union Members of Parliament, of those who have dirtied their hands, done the hard jobs in the factory, on the railway, or in the mines; who have used the tools, earned the rate for the job, walked the stones in unemployment or on strike.'[61] These sentiments are echoed in an article by Frank Allaum, 'Wanted – More Trade Union MPs', which was reprinted in a number of union journals in 1966.[62] To make it precisely clear what he wanted, Allaum cited Ellis Smith (who retired before the 1966 General Election and died in 1969) as a typically traditional working class MP. Yet another warning was issued by John Leonard, president of the Amalgamated Union of Building Trade Workers, regarding the increasing proportion of professional men to be found in the PLP.[63] Even Labour Party officials could call for 'the strongest possible contingent of trade union candidates in the Commons'.[64] In a 1969 *Tribune* article, Roy Hughes, M.P. made explicit the rationale for an increase in working class representation:

> Admittedly the number of people receiving higher education today is certainly greater than it was pre-war, but the proportion as a percentage of the overall population is still very small indeed. The fact is that for many years to come there will be millions of people doing mundane jobs in factories, mines and docks, and in our transport undertakings, and it is my contention that *true political representatives of these people can only come from their own ranks.*
> If parliament is to be a true forum of the nation it cannot be otherwise, and it was for this purpose that the trade unions formed the Labour Party at the turn of the century. (Emphasis added)[65]

The transformation in the social background of sponsored MPs is reflected in the experience of Frank Cousins and his family.

Cousins, like so many of the older generation of trade unionists, came up the hard way. If the playing fields of Eton are the traditional training-ground for Conservative statesmen, the asphalt playgrounds of the elementary school have been the nursery slopes for most Labour leaders. Times have changed and nowadays, among the post-war generation, one finds many with a grammar school and university education. One of Cousins' own sons, Michael, went to Cambridge. [66]

It was even seen in a family where both father and son served as sponsored MPs. Arthur Moyle, now Lord Moyle, had been sponsored by NUPE between 1945 and 1964 and served with credit as parliamentary private secretary to Clement Attlee in the late 1940s and early 50s. His secondary school background can be contrasted with that of his son, R. D. Moyle, who attended the University of Cambridge and then entered the House of Commons under NUPE sponsorship in 1966.

The implications of these changes will be discussed in greater detail in later chapters, but several points can be made now. First, sponsored MPs with only minimal industrial ties with their unions are far more open to political pressures than were the former union officials, who had been retired to or honoured with a seat in the House of Commons. [67] Second, the newer sponsored MPs are less likely to be the traditional bulwarks of party loyalty and discipline within the union movement. And third, it will become more difficult for the Labour Party to continue to appear as the party of the working class if it no longer has the traditional cloth-cap figures among its top leadership. Partial recognition of this problem by party leaders was a major reason for including Frank Cousins in the 1964 Labour Cabinet, in spite of his lack of parliamentary experience. [68]

Rationalisation and Justification of Sponsorship

Union sponsorship of MPs has come under attack from various sources in the mid-twentieth century. In 1964 public opinion was very clearly divided on the subject with thirty-seven per cent opposed to sponsorship, thirty-three per cent in favour and thirty per cent undecided. [69] The growth of consultation led the TUC, at last, to reduce its emphasis on sponsoring. 'The sponsoring of candidates for Parliament is . . . of secondary and quite limited importance.' [70]

The leaders of a number of unions within the TUC have taken quite a different stand. They continue to see value in sponsoring MPs but their reasons differ from those of their predecessors. Union leaders see four major reasons for sponsoring MPs in the mid-twentieth century. The first and most common is utility: sponsored MPs are seen as a major aid in gaining acceptance for union policies. As the secretary of the UTFWA expressed it: 'The reason we sponsor candidates is to ensure that policies decided upon at our annual congress are pursued at the highest level and pressure brought to bear in an attempt to improve the standard of living of those whom we represent.'[71] Similar views are given by the TGWU, USDAW, NUGMW, the AEF, the Durham miners and ASLEF. Unions such as the Furniture Makers, who have lacked parliamentary representation for most of the years since 1945, felt that their interests were not being adequately taken care of.[72] Union-sponsored MPs such as Mark Hewitson, Jack McCann, and Charles Pannell joined in defending the utility of their position.[73]

In part, of course, this defence of sponsored MPs on the grounds of utility, either to their union or to their class, is simply an appeal to tradition. The unions have been sponsoring MPs for a century, and in a tradition oriented society such as that of the British working class this in itself is sufficient cause for continuing the practice. Lacking vocal opposition, it continues as a result of inertia. Many union rulebooks seem to require such activity, which simply makes it seem more legitimate.[74] Justification on the grounds of both tradition and utility have grave implications for the sponsored MPs and their legislative roles. These will be given greater attention in Part III.

A third justification for sponsorship often cited by union officials is aid to the Labour Party, i.e. a means of providing additional funds for the party over and above affiliation fees. The MPs, once elected, are Labour MPs and the union has little or no special claim on them; only in a symbolic sense could they be said to represent the union.[75] Some union rulebooks support this claim by requiring the sponsored MPs to accept the Labour whip. On the other hand, if enough unions sponsor enough MPs of a particular political persuasion, perhaps they can effectively influence the direction taken by the PLP and the policy to be supported by the whip. If the party conference is unable to coerce the PLP, perhaps there is another way.

A few union officials regard sponsorship as a matter of prestige and honour for the union. Since comparable unions sponsored MPs, it was felt that they should also do so.[76] This would seem to provide a partial explanation for the willingness of unions such as the TGWU to sponsor MPs with very limited experience within the union or in industry. Related to the element of prestige is that of status. 'There can be no doubt that confidence is still felt in sponsored MPs and the unions feel that without them their position would be weaker. *It is their status they fear for, not the loss of opportunities for group representation'.*[77]

The practice of sponsoring MPs is not just an occupation for union leaders. It is also a matter of real concern to some rank and file members. Repeated resolutions at union conferences urge the continuation of parliamentary representation or an increase in the number of MPs sponsored by the union. Both sentiments were summmed up in the following resolution adopted by the Amalgamated Society of Woodworkers in 1967:

> Conference regrets the failure of the Trade Union Movement to achieve more effective numerical representation in the House of Commons.
>
> Conference believes that the situation must result in a reduction of trade union influence within the Parliamentary Labour Party.
>
> Conference calls upon the EC and general membership to do all in their power to mobilise support for ASW and TU sponsored candidates aspiring to Parliamentary office. [78]

Similar resolutions have been introduced at other union conferences, although they were not always adopted. [79]

Nevertheless, rank and file union members have little awareness of their sponsored MPs' activity, [80] partly due to a widespread apathy towards their unions' general political activity. This means that the sponsored MPs lack real support from the mass membership of the unions. But it also means that they have little or no active opposition, and union leaders can preserve the *status quo* at little cost. Because of the political apathy of rank and file unionists, efforts by militants to insist that sponsored MPs should be responsible to the unions that sponsor them may continue to receive little support.

Evaluation

What can be said about the general pattern of recruiting sponsored MPs in the years since 1945? First of all, there is a continuing desire for this form of political activity within the union movement. Despite critics, there are few who want sponsorship eliminated. Second, in simple numerical terms sponsorship has been healthier in the late

1960s and 1970s than ever before. The 1966 General Election saw more sponsored MPs elected to the House of Commons than ever, and the 1964 and 1970 results were not far behind. Third, numbers conceal the fact that the new sponsored MPs are not the traditional 'workers by hand', but a new breed of 'professional representative' first foreseen for the labour movement by Sidney and Beatrice Webb in *Industrial Democracy*.[81] (One may question, of course, whether such professional representatives were the goal of the men who originally demanded trade union representation in the House of Commons.) Fourth, the new sponsored MPs are younger and less likely than their predecessors, to use the House of Commons either as a retirement home or as a consolation prize for failures in union politics. In the next chapters these professional representatives' activities in the House of Commons and in the PLP will be discussed.

Part II:
Sponsored MPs in the House of Commons, 1945–1975

Chapter IV

Trade Union MPs in the Parliamentary Labour Party in the Mid-Twentieth Century

The focus of this and the following chapter will be the parliamentary activity of union-sponsored MPs since 1945. Attention will be given to the Trade Union Group, which is the institutional focus of union MPs in the PLP, and to the contributions of trade unionists to the leadership of the PLP, both in government and in Opposition. Chapter V will analyse the relationship between various characteristics of the sponsored MPs (such as their sponsoring union, age, and education) and their participation in Debate, the Question Hour, and certain Commons committees.

The Trade Union Group

The sponsored MPs, composing over one-third of the PLP since 1945, have their own organisation, the Trade Union Group, which leads a dual existence. On the one hand it is one of the formally recognised backbench study groups found in both parties, which seek to educate MPs about particular problems. In this role the Group is the PLP's study group on industrial relations and labour problems, open to all interested MPs and Labour peers. In its second role, however, it is a private organisation, not fully recognised by the PLP, with membership restricted to those sponsored MPs whose unions are affiliated to the Labour Party. As the lineal descendant of the first trade unionists who sat in the House in the nineteenth century, the Group views itself as the corporate representative of the modern trade unions.

Constitutional Status

The formal position of the Trade Union Group within the PLP is regulated under the terms of a constitution adopted by agreement between the whips of the PLP and the officers of the Group. The main points of this agreement, as listed by the Group, are:

(a) It is impossible that the Trade Union Group has the right to mandate its members in any way or for any occasion.

(b) That we, as a trade union group, should discuss topical issues as they arise from time to time.

(c) That we ask the Parliamentary Committee to pass on to this Group, for consideration, any legislation or Statutory Orders likely to touch trade union interests or matters of labour relations.

(d) Arising therefrom we should, when appropriate, try to initiate debates in consultation with the Chief Whip on Motions to be tabled in the names of our members.

(e) That the officers be authorised from time to time to issue press notices.

The agreement attempts to clarify points (b), (c), and (e) by further stating:

(b) That no vote be taken at any meeting which was likely to be the subject of contemporary consideration by a meeting of the Parliamentary Party except where a Trade Union matter is under discussion.

(c) That in agreeing to pass on to this Group for consideration any legislation or Statutory Orders likely to touch trade union interests and matters of labour relations, it is agreed that this should be an open meeting to allow other Members of the Parliamentary Party not eligible for membership of this Group to be present while such matters are discussed.

(e) That in anything arising from the implementation of (c), i.e. when the Group is acting as a specialist group of the Party, no Press notice should be issued, the officers to undertake when in doubt to consult the Chief Whip about the issue of Press notices. [1]

Specialist Role

Functioning in its first role as a backbench study group, the Trade Union Group meets regularly to hear speeches from politicians and industrialists and to discuss with them the problems of an industrialist society. During the 1961–62 parliamentary session, for example, the Group was addressed by: Richard Beeching (then chairman of the British Transport Commission); Hugh Gaitskell (leader of the Labour Party); John Harris (public relations officer for the PLP); Gerald Crossdell (general secretary, British Actors' Equity); Paul Chambers (chairman of the board, Imperial Chemical Industries); John Beavan (editor, *The Daily Herald*); and Anne Goodwin (chairman of the TUC General Council in 1961–62 and general secretary of CAWU). In addition there were a number of other speakers on various topics.[2] The views expressed both by the speakers and by the members of the Group are conveyed to the PLP leadership by whips who usually observe these meetings.

The Group also discusses legislation before the House to help formulate the PLP's position. In 1962–63, for example, the Group held several 'open meetings . . . on the Contracts of Employment Bill. It was the general feeling of the Group that this Bill was mean and nebulous but that it could hardly be opposed on second reading'.[3] Frequent meetings between the Group and the PLP leadership during the struggle over prices and incomes policy in 1966–70 failed to produce any significant changes in the government's position. Clearly the party leadership is not bound by what the Group says or does, and the degree of influence it can exercise through these essentially educational activities is difficult, if not impossible, to determine. Such an evaluation would require far more information about the internal policy-making procedures of the PLP than is currently available, especially for the most recent period. Furthermore, the role of the Group as a backbench study group is not completely separable from its activity as a distinct organisation, more or less independent of the PLP, with membership restricted to sponsored MPs.

Corporate Representative of the Trade Unions

The second role of the Group follows from the fact that many of its members regard it as the corporate representative of the trade unions in the House of Commons.[4] When acting in this capacity the Group restricts itself to those MPs sponsored by unions affiliated to the Labour Party, yet there is considerable confusion over membership. The Group's list of members does not agree with the list of sponsored MPs maintained by the Whips' office of the PLP, nor with the list of union-sponsored MPs given in the annual report of the Labour Party conference following each election. If an MP is prepared to claim that he is sponsored by a union, the Group will not dispute that fact. Indeed, to the officials of the Group the crucial determinant of sponsorship appears to be whether the MP receives any sort of official recognition from a union, independently of sponsorship under the terms of the Hastings Agreement. [5]

In recent years the problem of membership has become somewhat more acute because of the changing social background of union-sponsored MPs. Men such as Anthony Greenwood, sponsored by the TGWU, were technically qualified for membership of the Group, and they frequently attended its meetings. But one rather more traditional member stated that there would be a great deal of resentment if they made any serious effort to become active participants in the Group's business. [6] The increasing heterogeneity of the Group in the 1970s will help to reduce the strength of such views.

In its second role the Trade Union Group poses the threat of becoming a party within a party, or a political faction, though this danger has all but disappeared in the last several decades. As *The Times* wrote in 1954: 'There was a time when the trade union group exercised a considerable influence, but since 1940 they have been a dormant force.' [7] The whips of the PLP recognise the potential threat but are not greatly concerned by it. [8] The traditions of the Labour Party, and especially of its trade union wing, discourage the formation of such factions. Repeatedly the annual reports of the Group refer to the fact that they are not a pressure group within the PLP. [9] Such denials are supplemented by an overlapping of leadership between the Group and the PLP as a whole. For example, from 1953 until 1964 George Brown was chairman of the Group. He was also an elected member of the Parliamentary Committee of the PLP from 1955 until 1958 and again in 1959–60, afterwards serving as PLP deputy leader from 1960 until 1970. The leaders of the PLP in the post have been well aware of the desirability of maintaining some trade unionists among themselves.

Sectarianism. Perhaps the most important factor preventing the Group, as a group, from becoming an independent force within the

PLP is its own heterogeneity. The sectarianism shown by the union MPs in the late nineteenth century has not disappeared in the twentieth century; few issues can elicit a unanimous response from the union-sponsored MPs. And as the composition of the Group becomes increasingly diverse in the mid-twentieth century, we may expect its internal policy differences to increase further.

The internal differences within the Group can be seen in a variety of ways. Perhaps the most obvious is its own leadership, which is influenced by currents of opinion affecting the PLP as a whole. For example, during the defence dispute in 1960–61, Fred Lee, a vice chairman of the Group, was a candidate for the deputy leadership of the PLP when Harold Wilson was seeking to defeat Gaitskell for the position of leader; at the same time two other members of the Group's executive committee, Ness Edwards and Walter Padley, were very outspoken in opposing Gaitskell's public disavowal of the party conference decision on unilateralism. As a result, all three were denied re-election to their Group positions at the start of the 1960–61 session of Parliament. Lee and Padley were again defeated at the start of the 1961–62 session. [10] The man chosen to replace Lee as vice chairman was David Griffiths, a miner from Yorkshire. His election, according to *The Yorkshire Evening Post*, could mean 'only one thing. The down-to-earth union men in the group – most of them Gaitskell supporters – are going to assert themselves and give the Left wing intellectuals something to worry about'. [11] The general reconciliation within the PLP following the death of Gaitskell was demonstrated in 1964 by the election of Edwards as chairman of the Group, following George Brown's resignation to enter the Wilson government.

In a similar fashion the conflict within the PLP over British entry into the Common Market had an impact on the Group's elections in 1971–72. The chairman during the 1970–71 session, James Tinn, and one of the vice chairmen, Robert Brown, had abstained on the 28 October vote in the House of Commons. When new officers were chosen in December for the 1971–72 session, both Tinn and Brown were defeated and replaced by sponsored MPs who had voted against entry. [12]

General Activity. The Group has shown signs of attempting to act as a collective force during some internal crises of the Labour Party, such as the Bevanite revolt of the early 1950s, the defence dispute of the 1960s, and the battle over industrial relations in the late 1960s and early 1970s. One example of its efforts occurred shortly before the 1951 General Election. The 1951 budget introduced by Hugh Gaitskell, then chancellor of the Exchequer, contained provisions, much resented by the sponsored MPs, for altering the pension system. As a result the MPs summoned Prime Minister Attlee to a meeting of the Group, but he sent Gaitskell instead. When the Group emphatically indicated that Gaitskell was unacceptable, Attlee finally attended; and when it was realised that the sponsored MPs might ally themselves with Aneurin Bevan, who had recently resigned from the government because of other aspects of the budget, Gaitskell's proposals were then modified. [13]

The union-sponsored MPs usually supported Gaitskell while he was leader of the PLP. One exception occurred in 1959, when he was seeking to repeal *clause iv* of the party constitution, which bound it to a policy of collective ownership. As one of them expressed it in a speech to the National Union of Railwaymen: 'The whole of the Trade Union Group in the House unanimously advised the leader of the shadow Cabinet to forget it altogether, that it was unnecessary, that it was pointless and would lead only to misunderstandings, and suspicions which we could well do without.' [14]

In the defence dispute, in addition to purging its officers, the Group adopted a resolution regretting 'the public attacks upon the elected Leader of the Party'; [15] and it circulated a list of twelve 'recommended' names for election to the Parliamentary Committee of the PLP. Thirty or forty of the union MPs who supported Gaitskell in the defence dispute resented the lack of support from other MPs. In the case of Anthony Wedgwood Benn, who resigned from the party's NEC in protest at Gaitskell's intransigence, the trade unionists refused to support him in the struggle to renounce his peerage in 1961–63. [16]

In contrast to the spate of activity during the defence dispute, the Group sought to avoid involvement in the election of a new leader in 1963 following the death of Gaitskell. The two chief contenders were Harold Wilson and George Brown, who was then chairman of the Group and acting leader. The Group actually ceased to function during the struggle, [17] but this did not prevent individual trade unionists from taking sides in the contest.

Regarding the working conditions of employees of the House of Commons, the Group has maintained the traditional interest begun by early trade union MPs. Following several meetings with the chairman and secretary of the Group in 1959–61, the speaker of the House of Commons conceded, for the first time, the right of the staff to organise and bargain collectively. [18] Within the House the Group has also sought to increase the frequency with which the minister of labour can be first in line to answer questions during the Question Hour.

The ETU. From time to time the Group engages in extraparliamentary activity, as for example during the 1960–61 session, when it was interested in the conflict revolving around the Electrical Trades Union (ETU). This union, one of Britain's largest, had allegedly come under Communist control as a result of the apathy of its members and corrupt elections. After a bitter dispute the ETU was finally expelled from both the TUC and the Labour Party, because of the irregularities in its internal operations and its Communist domination. The Group held three 'open' meetings to discuss the problem and to hear speeches by John Byrne (non-Communist general secretary of the ETU), George Woodcock (general secretary of the TUC) and Lord Citrine (formerly general secretary of the TUC and onetime assistant secretary of the ETU). Another Group meeting was held 'for private discussions among members regarding "next steps".' [19]

When the Communists on the union's executive committee were forced from office by legal action initiated by Byrne, and when new elections were ordered, the Group's executive committee issued a statement urging all ETU members to vote. [20] The general distrust of politicians by the industrial wing of the labour movement and the Marxist sympathies of many of the non-Communist leaders of the ETU were reflected in the response of the union's executive committee, which told the Group in effect to mind its own business. [21]

'In Place of Strife'. In June 1968 the Royal Commission on Trade Unions and Employers' Associations (the Donovan Commission) issued its report on British industrial relations. This report was discussed at a June meeting of the Group, at which Victor Feather indicated some of the TUC's reactions. Five months later Barbara Castle, who was secretary of state for employment and productivity, met with the Group but 'was extremely "cagey"', and, despite searching questions, little was learned about future Government legislation'. [22]

The members of the Group were clearly uneasy about the government's intentions, but the only satisfaction they had was a two-hour preview of the 'In Place of Strife' White Paper on 17 January 1969. The proposals contained in the White Paper would have eroded some of the traditional autonomy of the unions, by requiring a formal vote before a strike, a cooling-off period before a strike could begin, and changes in rules affecting closed-shop contracts. In addition, wildcat or unofficial strikes, which many felt had been a particularly heavy burden on British industry in recent years, were to be prohibited; and workers violating the main points of the White Paper and the legislation to be based on it would face the possibility of prosecution and fines or prison sentences if convicted.

A poll of the Group's members showed considerable internal differences on the proposals, but less than a third were willing to support legislation imposing penalties on trade unionists engaging in unofficial strikes. A meeting of the Group on 20 January suggested a much stronger line and far more unanimity in opposing the White Paper.[23] Outside Parliament the unions shared the Group's concern.

The Group continued to meet to consider its position on the legislation that would be based on 'In Place of Strife', and some of its members, led by Eric Moonman, organised an action committee to work within the PLP and the House of Commons to mobilise opposition to the government. Before the fight was over, Moonman's committee reported that sixty-one Labour MPs were ready to vote against any bill based on the White Paper, and when a government motion approving the paper was laid before the House on 3 March, fifty-three Labour MPs including twenty-six trade unionists, voted against the government, while another fifty Labour Members abstained or failed to vote.[24] With Tory help, however, the motion passed. During the same period other sponsored MPs, including Eric Heffer, Cyril Bence, and Ernest Thornton, were engaged in an abortive effort to call a special meeting of the PLP to depose Wilson as leader because of his support of Mrs Castle's proposals.

There was also conflict over 'In Place of Strife' in the Cabinet. Richard Marsh opposed the proposals from the start, and this was a factor in his dismissal from the government later in the year. The other trade unionist in the Cabinet was Roy Mason, a miner. He was less opposed to the proposals than was Marsh, but even he favoured some sort of compromise with the unions and the TUC. Neither Marsh nor Mason could hope to stop the prime minister and Mrs

Castle from going ahead. The man who might have been able to do so was James Callaghan, then home secretary. Callaghan was not a sponsored MP, but his long association with parts of the union movement, together with the opportunity to improve his own position within the party after the fiasco of devaluation, led him to oppose 'In Place of Strife'. His position was made clear on 26 March 1969, when he joined the majority of the party NEC in rejecting the White Paper. Callaghan's opposition earned him the support of many trade unionists in the PLP and led one author to claim that, in the absence of a leading sponsored MP in the Cabinet, 'Now he was the Keeper of the Cloth Cap.' [25]

While trying to encourage the trade unions to formulate alternatives to the White Paper's proposals, Victor Feather of the TUC stayed out of the internal struggle of the PLP, though he did make known his opposition to the paper. Some union leaders were less reticent. Hugh Scanlon of the AEF had spoken to the Trade Union Group about the deteriorating relations between the unions and the government, but he indicated that the independence of the AEF's MPs would be respected. In contrast, Jack Jones of the TGWU reminded his union's MPs that their 1967 conference had adopted a resolution requiring a review of its parliamentary panel before the next election. [26] Other union leaders, such as Tom Jackson of the UPW, were also active in encouraging sponsored MPs to oppose the government.

The crisis reached a climax on 17 June 1969, when the new chief whip, Robert Mellish, sponsored by the TGWU, rose at the start of a Cabinet meeting in an almost unprecedented manner to say that there was no way in which he could guarantee the votes of the PLP for the government's proposal, with the left wing and so many of the more moderate trade unionists in opposition. Following Mellish's statement, the Cabinet agreed to drop the matter and to repair the damage that had been done to party unity. [27]

The struggle over 'In Place of Strife' indicated that sometimes Mr Wilson and Mrs Castle seriously misunderstood the feelings of many MPs who were normally supporters of the PLP leadership. They 'undoubtedly misjudged the temper of the trade union MPs, [28] and their understanding of the trade union movement in general was little better. This lack of feeling or understanding is related to the increasing middle class domination of the Labour Party leadership. Not that some members of the 1964–70 Government were unaware of the problem. Richard Crossman, in a 1965 diary reference to Frank Cousins, wrote:

> 'He sounds like a terrible old blatherer, talking on every subject and usually saying the obvious thing. *But he does say it in a working-class way and that's important because nobody else talks in that way in this cabinet and we ought to be reminded of what sensible people think in the Labour Movement.'* [29] (emphasis added)

Without someone of the stature of Arthur Henderson, Ernest Bevin, Aneurin Bevan or even Frank Cousins to remind the Labour leadership of the original source of its support, it is not surprising that it should be so insensitive to the needs and desires of the union movement.

Conservative Industrial Relations. The Industrial Relations Bill introduced by the Conservative government of Edward Heath late in 1970 contained similar proposals to those of 'In Place of Strife'. But, as already indicated, the bill had been drawn up without the usual extensive consultation with the trade unions, who were forced to fall back on their MPs. As a result of the chief whip's invitation to the Trade Union Group in November 1970, sponsored MPs contributed twenty of the twenty-three members of a working party established by the PLP to oppose the Conservative bill. [30] The leader of this working party was Barbara Castle, who had been the minister in the previous Labour government responsible for 'In Place of Strife'. Despite protests from the sponsored MPs, who had serious doubts about her ability to lead the fight against the Tory bill, [31] she continued to head the Labour side although two sponsored MPs, Eric Heffer (ASW) and Harold Walker (AEF), were her chief assistants. The Trade Union Group had several meetings to discuss the bill and to plan strategy to assist Mrs Castle's working party. In December, for example, Victor Feather of the TUC spoke to the Group on the TUC's view of the bill.

Given the reality of party politics in the House of Commons, opposition was nearly hopeless if the intent was actually to block the government. 'What then were we trying to prove and to whom? Ultimately, I suppose, we were parading our virility, partly for self assurance and partly to show the trade unions outside that we hadn't gone soft.' [32] In so doing, the working party tabled over a thousand amendments to the bill and forced the government to invoke the guillotine to shut off debate. Led by Lord Blyton (formerly William Blyton, MP for Houghton-le-Spring from 1945 until his retirement in 1964, and sponsored in the House of Commons by the NUM), a number of formerly sponsored MPs were active in the unsuccessful effort to defeat the government when the bill was finally passed and sent to the House of Lords. Once the bill became law as the Industrial Relations Act of 1971, the fight shifted to the industrial and legal arenas outside Parliament. But for one brief moment, at least, the unions had again seen what sort of representatives they were supporting in the House of Commons.

The trade unions launched a massive effort of noncooperation with the new Industrial Relations Act and with the court it established.[33] Matters came to a head in 1974 when the court awarded damages against the AEF for some of its actions and then seized some of the union's assets to satisfy the judgement. On 2 May the AEF called a strike of its members to protest the action of the Industrial Relations Court, and temporary industrial peace was assured only after an anonymous donor(s) offered to pay the £280,000 judgement against the union.[34]

While this was going on the minority Labour government elected in February 1974 was formulating its own position. Michael Foot, the new secretary of state for employment, circulated proposals to the unions that called for the virtual repeal of the Conservatives' statute. These proposals were then included in a new Trade Union and Labour Relations Act which received the Royal Assent on 31 July. Unfortunately, the government's minority status meant that some Opposition amendments vehemently opposed by the unions remained in the act. Bitterly denouncing these amendments, Foot indicated that further legislation would be forthcoming in 1975 in an effort to preserve the 'social contract' negotiated between the unions and the Labour Party to ensure industrial peace for the country.[35]

Evaluation

By and large the Group's attempt to act as the corporate agent of the unions in Parliament has not been very effective. This does not mean the Group has been only a backbench study group for the PLP. As a private organisation of union-sponsored MPs, it became increasingly a social club, held together by nostalgia for a shared common experience in the factory or mine; less charitably, it has acted as a protective shell around the trade unionists in an otherwise foreign environment. [36] With this as the Group's *raison d'être,* its longterm prospects must be questioned. The increasingly heterogeneous background of its members before their entry into Parliament will make it more difficult for them to recall their 'shared common experience', though on the other hand it will make the environment of the House much less foreign for them. Sponsorship and the Group thus far have compelled the Labour Party to remember its working class roots on a day-to-day basis rather than only at times of financial need. In the not too distant future this may no longer be true.

Conscious of its roots, the Group has served to focus resentment of the increasingly middle class dominance over the party and the PLP. This was illustrated by union criticism of Gaitskell and the so-called 'Hampstead set' in 1959, and the opposition some of Wilson's associates in the middle 1960s. Sometimes its resentment has affected the internal politics of the PLP. For example, the defeat of Douglas Jay and Roy Jenkins, who had been officers of the PLP economic committee until the start of the 1959 session of Parliament, was 'interpreted at Westminster . . . as a part of the trade union group's campaign to assert itself in the party councils'. [37]

The sponsored MPs have in the past been more concerned with material things than with ideological questions. [38] In addition, on a number of issues between 1964 and 1970, such as abortion, capital punishment, homosexuality, and divorce reform, the sponsored MPs were more likely to vote against reform than were their non-sponsored colleagues. [39] The traditional working class orientation suggested by their positions on these questions will soon be a thing of the past if the changes already discussed continue.

The love-hate relationship between trade unionists and their middle class colleagues is related to, but very clearly not the same as, the sponsored MPs' opposition to the party's left wing. The left wing of the PLP may have been drawn predominantly from the non-union section of the party in the past, but this will be less true in the future.

Whatever problems they have encountered, the union sponsored MPs have contributed a touch of informality and earthy humour which would otherwise have been lacking in the dignified surroundings of the House of Commons. Although not loath to accepting seats in the House of Lords when offered, they carry over the traditional working class dislike of titles, preferring to be on a first—name basis so as not to revive memories of past master—man relationships.[40] The earthy quality of some of their humour is suggested in Jack Jones' reply to an attack by Lady Astor on the use of alcohol. "I have always enjoyed a glass of beer and I am willing to lay my stomach against the Hon. Lady's any day'.[41] The views of other MPs on such informality are reflected in this story told by Bevin in the House of Commons:

> When he and Churchill were watching the preparations for D-Day, a soldier called out: "See they don't let us down when we come back, Ernie". "Ernie"? asked a Conservative MP who was shocked at this disrespect for one of His Majesty's Ministers. "Yes, Ernie, that's what my people call me", replied His Majesty's Minister of Labour and National Service.[42]

Clearly the sponsored MPs collectively have represented a major force within the party which all leaders and aspiring leaders have had to take into account.[43] Acting sometimes as an organised force, at other times only as a latent influence, it has been there nonetheless, and part of the task of leadership has been to retain or secure its support. One major reason why Aneurin Bevan failed to attain leadership of the PLP was his failure to cultivate the Trade Union Group and to take much interest in its activities. In contrast, it was the support of the bulk of the trade unionists that contributed to Gaitskell's election as leader in 1955. At times Harold Wilson has also appreciated the importance of keeping in touch with feelings of sponsored MPs.

> It is one of Mr. Wilson's habits, when the political barometer is unsettled, to pace the corridors of the Commons. Obscure backbenchers have been startled to find themselves suddenly face to face with their chief, who emerges, as it were, from nowhere. Humble mining MPs have been flattered by his insistence on joining them over a bun and a cup of lukewarm tea, while genially encouraging them to chat. The Prime Minister does not take these strolls for exercise; neither is he desperate for company, nor, indeed, a bun. His aim – in these moments of uncertainty – is to find out for himself the trends of party feelings.[44]

Such attempts at seeking information and discovering the sentiments of the PLP backbenchers do not, of course, mean that a leader is unwilling to be highly critical of the MPs at times or that he will always understand their position.[45] (See, e.g., pp. 83–86 above.)

Party Loyalty and Discipline

In terms of party loyalty and discipline the union-sponsored MPs have played a major role within the PLP. During the Labour Party's history the trade unionists have acquired a reputation as the main bulwarks of party leadership, resisting any sharp shifts in the party's position either to the left or the right. Their union background has given sponsored MPs a strong sense of organisational loyalty, and they have usually been prepared to support the leadership of the PLP against attacks, especially from the ideologically oriented left wing. Traditionally only a few sponsored MPs have been found on the left.[46] As James Griffiths expressed it:

> I came to Parliament in 1936 after ten years as an officer, and for a period as President, of the South Wales Miners' Union. I had worked in the coal mine for seventeen years. Life in the mine is hard and perilous. It would be hell without the loyalty of man to man, and the fellowship of kindred spirits. To curry favour with the boss was a heinous crime, to betray a comrade an unforgivable sin. Loyalty became the supreme virtue. It was our rule never to argue with one another in front of the management. Policy and attitude would be settled in the privacy of the committee, and once settled called for one voice and one voice only. If this meant the sacrifice of personal liberty, then that was the price of survival. [47]

This loyalty was carried over into the House of Commons where it involved more than simply voting in the correct way or signing the proper motion: it also implied an active effort against those who did not share this conception of party loyalty and were willing to broadcast differences outside the PLP. This was the basis of the resentment felt by many sponsored MPs at the Crossman–Silkin policy of loosening the traditional rules of discipline in the PLP in 1966 and 1967. Once again, as the changing background of the sponsored MPs rapidly erodes the basis for their traditional loyalty, we can expect the newer sponsored MPs be far less automatic in their future support of the PLP leadership.

Evidence of a change in the behaviour of sponsored MPs is still difficult to find, but there is one very significant development. Within the PLP, the Tribune Group has frequently expressed leftwing criticism of the parliamentary leadership. For example, following the

1970 Election the Group published a pamphlet advocating that MPs should obey the rulings of the annual party conference, a proposal that would effectively have subordinated them to the dictates of a few union leaders.[48] With the TGWU and AEF already clearly moving to the left, the ideological intent of this proposal was obvious. But more important is the composition of the Tribune Group. By 1972 the sponsored MPs composed a larger proportion of its membership than they did of the PLP as a whole (see Table IV–1). Three-quarters of the sponsored MPs in the Group had been elected in 1964 or later, of the sponsored MPs who were not in the Group only half were of that vintage. Older non-Tribune MPs such as Austin Albu or Charles Pannell retired in 1974, but none of the trade unionists in the Tribune Group did. As a result, the sponsored MPs composed almost half the Group in May 1974 (48.8 per cent) and continued to be overrepresented there in proportion to their share of the PLP as a whole.

TABLE IV – 1

SPONSORED MPs IN THE TRIBUNE GROUP, 1972

	Tribune Group		Non-Tribune MPs		Entire PLP	
	No.	%	No.	%	No.	%
Union-Sponsored MPs	23	46.9	91	38.2	114	39.7
Other Labour MPs	26	53.1	147	61.8	173	60.3
Total	49	100.0	238	100.0	287	100.0

Source: *Political Companion*, No. 13 (October – December, 1972), pp. 61 – 4, 75.

The implications of this for the PLP are very important. First, to retain the support of these new MPs, the leadership may find it increasingly expedient to adopt policy goals favored by the left wing of the party. The vote on the United Kingdom's entry into the Common Market provided an early example of this. Despite the overtures made to the EEC by his Labour government in the late 1960s to negotiate its own terms of entry, Harold Wilson led the PLP in opposition to the terms negotiated by the Conservatives under Edward Heath. In the 28 October 1971 vote in the House of Commons, more than three-quarters of the sponsored MPs obeyed the party whip, while only fourteen went into the Government's lobby and ten abstained.[49] Other examples of party leaders adopting more left wing policies were the renewed discussion of nationalisation during 1973 and 1974, the publication of a bill for the nationalisation of ship–building and aircraft firms in May, 1975, and the details of Anthony Wedgwood Benn's 1975 Industry Bill.

Second, the union MPs' support for the PLP leadership will be less habitual and automatic in the future. And because of their lack of long-term trade union experience, it will be more difficult to retain the support of the newer sponsored MPs. Elections to the Parliamentary Committee when the PLP is in Opposition will be more volatile, and Harold Wilson or any other leader will have to spend more time seeking out obscure MPs to test sentiment. The Labour government first formed after the February 1974 election and confirmed in the October election postponed this development by giving Wilson the wealth of patronage available to any prime minister, and by allowing him to make stringent demands on party solidarity in face of Labour's tiny majority.

Trade Union MPs and Leadership of the Parliamentary Labour Party

The Leader and Deputy Leader

The position of leader of the PLP has not been held by a sponsored MP since the brief and unusual tenure of Arthur Henderson following MacDonald's defection in 1931. The position has fallen vacant twice since 1945. In 1955 Hugh Gaitskell was elected with the support of the sponsored MPs to succeed Attlee as leader; he defeated Aneurin Bevan, the only sponsored MP in the contest, and Herbert Morrison. When the leadership fell vacant again in 1963, following the death of Gaitskell, George Brown, chairman of the Trade Union Group, was one of the three candidates for the position. The failure of the sponsored MPs to vote as a bloc for Brown contributed to Harold Wilson's success.

The leader of the PLP has generally appointed a parliamentary private secretary drawn from the ranks of the sponsored MPs. Attlee had a series of sponsored private secretaries, with Arthur Moyle, known as 'Clem's Clam', being the best known.[50] This tradition was reasserted in 1968, when Eric Varley resigned as whip to become Wilson's parliamentary private secretary.

The position of deputy leader has been held by sponsored MPs for much of the period since 1945. James Griffiths defeated Bevan to win the job in 1955. Bevan was elected to it in 1959, and George Brown served as deputy leader from 1960 until 1970. Following Brown's defeat in the 1970 election, the position of deputy leader was filled first by Roy Jenkins and then, after his resignation in the dispute over the Common Market, by Edward Short. Neither was a sponsored MP, although Jenkins is the son of a Welsh miner and Short has connections with the National Union of Teachers.

The Labour Government, 1945–1951

The importance of union-sponsored MPs can be inferred from their positions within the government. In the Labour government appointed in late July and early August 1945, sponsored MPs held six of the twenty Cabinet-level positions and twenty-three more junior posts, ranging from ministers not in the Cabinet to whips (lord commissioner).[51] Dalton reports that within the PLP there was some discontent over the preference given to those who had attended public schools or were members of the railway clerks' union; but in light of the balanced representation of all segments of the party, the resentment hardly seems justified.[52] By 1951 the representation of sponsored MPs had dropped, and the decline of Ernest Bevin, who was exhausted by his ten years as a minister and nearing death, led Dalton to call for a trade unionist to succeed him at the Foreign Office so as to counter the intellectual Gaitskell at the Treasury. But Herbert Morrison wanted and got the job.[53] Attlee's willingness sometimes to ignore the sensibilities of the trade unionists was shown when the prime minister refused to accept Emanuel Shinwell's suggestion that a miner such as James Griffiths should be in charge of the fuel and power ministry to ensure continued union co-operation during the 1947 fuel crisis. Attlee felt that Shinwell still had the confidence of the miners.[54]

No quantitative analysis of union representation in the 1945–51 Labour governments can convey the absolute importance of one union-sponsored MP, Ernest Bevin, who served as foreign secretary for most of the period. Bevin was far from being a typical trade union MP. He had been the creator and leader of Britain's largest union, the TGWU, before his entry into the wartime coalition in 1940. He played a major role during World War II as well as in the Labour Government that followed, by developing and extending the practice of consultation between the unions and the government. Until his last illness he was the second figure in the government.

Opposition, 1951–64

The Parliamentary Committee. The executive committee of the PLP in Opposition is known as the Parliamentary Committee (not to be confused with the Parliamentary Committee of the TUC, which existed from 1869 until 1921). It has eighteen members – three from the House of Lords; the leader, deputy leader, and chief whip of the PLP elected by the PLP; and twelve other members elected by the Labour MPs. Of the fifteen members elected by the PLP, trade unionists held between three and six of the positions between 1951 and 1964. The trade unionists were underrepresented on the Parliamentary Committee except during 1957. This was only partly compensated for by the fact that the chief whip between 1942 and 1955 was a trade unionist, and that the deputy leaders after that time were trade unionists. But union-sponsored MPs lacked any sense of deprivation and made no attempt to increase their representation within the PLP.

Trade unionists seldom acted as a bloc in the committee itself. [55] The nine sponsored MPs, all men of ability, represented a variety of unions and of ideological positions and personal philosophies. Bevan and Lee were usually on the left wing of the party. Brown and Fraser were men of the right. Griffiths was the great compromiser. William Whiteley had been an effective chief whip, even though he waited too long before finally resigning. Three of them, Bevan, James Griffiths, and George Brown, went on to become deputy leaders of the PLP. Griffiths and Brown both secured major positions in the Labour government formed in 1964. And in 1960 a Conservative government appointed Alfred Robens deputy head of the National Coal Board, making him head the following year. Finally, Bottomley, Fraser, Lee, and Gunter were given important posts in the 1964 Labour Cabinet.

During the 1950s Aneurin Bevan was the trade unionist who had the greatest impact on the PLP. In the 1945 Labour government he had been appointed minister of health and played a major role in creating the National Health Service. In this undertaking he showed great skill as a negotiator in persuading the British Medical Association to accept and co-operate with the NHS.[56] Without such co-operation, the NHS would have been doomed to failure. Bevan's resignation from the government in 1951 over the introduction of charges into the Health Service and his opposition to the PLP leaders in the fight over foreign policy and defence questions in the early 1950s antagonised many in the PLP. As a result he was unable to take advantage of the change in the PLP leadership in 1955, when Gaitskell replaced Attlee. Only in the late 1950s, just before his death, did Bevan effect a reconciliation with Gaitskell to become the deputy leader in 1959.

Throughout his career Bevan remembered his origins, even though he went far beyond them. He maintained a strong loyalty to the working class, although occasionally he disagreed with some of its organisations, such as trade unions and the Labour Party. However unorthodox he may have been at times, few questioned his ability to serve as an advocate of what he felt to be the working class's interests. And it was this advocacy that he believed to be the real role of a political leader.[57] Bevan was a major working class political leader in the tradition of Thomas Burt, Arthur Henderson, and Ernest Bevin, even if his style differed from theirs. The social changes that began to affect the PLP in the 1950s and 1960s may have made him one of the last. *The Times* could note the predominance of professional men in 1959 and ask, 'Where are the experienced leaders with the sure common touch'? [58]

The Shadow Cabinet, 1955–1964. Since 1955, whenever the Labour Party has been in Opposition the leader has appointed a Shadow Cabinet composed of the Parliamentary Committee and other Members needed to provide coverage for most ministries. The leader has some flexibility in assigning people to cover the departments. It is politic, of course, to allocate all members of the Parliamentary Committee to major departments, but the committee is not large enough to cover all ministries. Additional flexibility is introduced by the practice of naming assistant shadow ministers among the younger members of the party. This power of appointment can be used judiciously to heal splits in the PLP and to integrate potential rebels into the power structure of the party. An obvious example of this was Aneurin Bevan's assignment to shadow the Foreign Office in 1959–60.

In the years between 1955 and 1964, sponsored MPs were respon-

sible for between six and eleven of the twenty-five to twenty-eight
Shadow Cabinet positions with the larger representation coming during the 1960s.[59] Numerically they were at least as well represented in
the Shadow Cabinet as they were in the PLP as a whole. Their underrepresentation in the Parliamentary Committee was compensated
for in the Shadow Cabinet.

The sponsored MPs were given particular responsibility for
shadowing ministries that worked closely with industry, with the ex-
ception of Transport. For example, Fred Lee shadowed Aviation;
Lee, Ray Gunter, and Tom Fraser followed Fuel and Power; and
Lee, Gunter, George Brown, and Alfred Robens looked after Labour.
Trade unionists also occupied several secondary Shadow Cabinet
positions affecting the industrial departments, with Harold Finch
and William Blyton assisting at Fuel and Power, Reginald Prentice at
Labour, Roy Mason at the Post Office, and Robert Mellish at
Transport.

The sponsored Members were not concerned only with industrial
questions. Several of them held positions which were far removed
from this area. Aneurin Bevan at the Foreign Office; George Brown
at Defence and the Home Office; Tom Williams at Agriculture;
James Griffiths shadowing Colonies or Wales; A. Bottomley charged
with watching Colonies and Commonwealth Affairs; and Fred
Mulley, who wrote about strategic problems, with responsibilities for
air, all demonstrate that the sponsored Members were not completely
insular in their outlook.

There were few complaints about the ability of the trade-union
sponsored Members in the Shadow Cabinet and their effectiveness in
debate. Some, such as the late Ness Edwards, were felt to be more
effective in Opposition than they had been in power.[60] One exception
was Fred Lee, who was occasionally criticised, but demotion would
have been difficult because of his membership in the Parliamentary
Committee (and, after Harold Wilson became the leader in 1963,
because of his long support for Wilson).

The Crossman affair. The major criticism of the trade unionists
was precipitated by a speech of Sir Tom Williamson to the NUM conference in 1957, in which he complained about the decline in the
number of sponsored MPs and called for more effort in this area.[61]
Williamson's complaint was answered by Richard Crossman's argument that the decline was due to the failure of the unions to put up

qualified people at constituency selection conferences. In fact, Crossman went on to say, 'Of the ninety-seven sponsored trade union MPs in Parliament today, only four – Mr. James Griffiths (Miners), Mr. Aneurin Bevan (Miners), Mr. George Brown (Transport Workers) and Mr. Alfred Robens (Shopworkers) – suggest themselves for key jobs'.[62] The fireworks began with this statement. The Trade Union Group protested against it in a letter to the party NEC.[63] And they had at least one defender in the political correspondent for *The Daily Telegraph*, H. B. Boyne, who argued that there were perhaps twenty-five sponsored MPs qualified for high office. Some of them, such as Austin Albu, were 'quite the equal of any "clever Dick".'[64] Certainly Crossman exaggerated a little. But others suggested that his major sin was either that of being indiscreet or of not being broad enough in his condemnation, which could apply to the entire PLP.[65]

Crossman's statement was not necessarily an indictment of the sponsored MPs. There are good grounds for having ordinary men in Parliament, to ensure both that it is representative of the entire population and that there are people in a position to tell ministers how ordinary people feel about this or that policy. Clement Attlee comments in his memoirs:

> You've got to have a certain number of solid people whom no one would think particularly brilliant, but who between conflicting opinions can act as middleman, give you the ordinary man's point of view. . . . You remember little George Tomlinson. I can remember a thing coming up which looked like a good scheme, all worked out by the civil service. But I wasn't quite sure how it would go down with the ordinary people so I said, "Minister of Education, what do you know of this." "Well," says George, "it sounds all right, but I've been trying to persuade my wife of it for the last three weeks and I can't persuade her."[66]

Is it possible that Fabian elitism might be carried too far? The union-sponsored MPs have long memories and did not forgive Crossman. In 1967 they used their influence to keep him from taking charge of a review of party organisation.

The Labour Governments, 1964–70

The General Election of October 1964 saw Labour returned to power with a very narrow majority, whereas the election of March 1966 produced a large Labour majority. In the government led by Harold Wilson from 1964 until the 1970 election, the sponsored MPs started off with a loud bang, but by 1970 they had been reduced to a mere whimper. The stages in this development can be seen by examining the makeup of the Cabinet in 1964, in 1966 following the election, and again in 1970 (see Table IV–2). Nine of the twenty-three members of Wilson's first Cabinet were union-sponsored MPs. The nine included George Brown as secretary of state for economic affairs and first secretary of state; Frank Cousins as minister of technology (following his co-option into the government after the election); Arthur Bottomley at the Commonwealth Office; James Griffiths as the first separate secretary of state for Wales; Anthony Greenwood at the Colonial Office; Ray Gunter at Labour; Fred Peart at Agriculture; Tom Fraser at Transport; and Fred Lee at Fuel and Power. All of the industrial ministers were trade unionists.

Following the 1966 election, the number of union-sponsored Cabinet ministers decreased by one, with Fraser and Griffiths eliminated and Richard Marsh being added, along with several shifts from one ministry to another. But Brown, Cousins, and Gunter, the top three trade unionists, were still in their original positions. Then the decline began, as first Cousins, then Brown and Gunter resigned and other trade unionists were dropped or resigned from the Cabinet. By 1970 the number of trade unionists in the Cabinet had been reduced to three.

There were those who viewed Brown's resignation from the Wilson government in early 1968 as the end of the era of the man in the cloth cap.[67] But it was Ray Gunter's television interview following his resignation in mid-1968 that really called attention to the declining representation of the sponsored MPs.[68] This disappearance of the old-style sponsored MP was resented by many traditionalists in the Labour Party, and it was curious that Gunter forced the matter into the open. He was associated with white-collar trade unionism in TSSA and had himself been criticised by a spokesman of the more traditional industrial unions, John Boyd of the engineers, before his appointment as minister of labour in 1964.[69] In fact, of course, as the figures in Table IV–2 indicate, the sponsored MPs were underrepresented in the Wilson government from its creation. Only in the Whips' office were they especially prominent.

Comparing the trade unionists prominent in the Wilson government in 1964 and in 1970 helps to show the impact of changing spon-

TABLE IV – 2

UNION-SPONSORED MEMBERS IN LABOUR GOVERNMENTS, 1964–1970 and 1974

TYPE OF OFFICE	1964			1966			1970			1974		
	Total Posts	Union No.	MPs %	Total Posts	Union No.	MPs %	Total Posts	Union No.	MPs %	Total Posts	Union No.	MPs %
Cabinet Ministers	23	9	39	23	8	35	22	3	14	21	6	28
Ministers not in the Cabinet	22	3	14	30	5	17	28	6	21	31	12	38
Junior Ministers	48	11	23	55	12	22	42	6	14	36	9	25
Whips	9	4	45	15	8	53	11	6	55	13	11	84
All offices in the Government	102	29	29	106	30	29	104	21	20	101	39	39

Sources: *The Times Guide to the House of Commons, 1964*, pp. 4 – 8; *Ibid., 1966*; pp. 4 – 8; *Ibid, 1974*, pp. 4 – 7; *Dodd's Parliamentary Companion, 1970*, pp. 640 – 44.

sorship patterns discussed earlier. Of the three chief trade unionists in the government in 1964, Brown had had a secondary education while Cousins and Gunter had attended only elementary school. Brown started his political career in his early 30s; Gunter entered Parliament in 1945 and then returned to his union for a period during the 1950s before re-entering the House of Commons in 1959. Cousins, in contrast, had spent his entire life working for the TGWU and entered the Wilson government and Parliament only after the 1964 Election.

The new sponsored MPs who came to prominence toward the end of the Wilson government have quite different backgrounds. Roy Mason started as a miner but went on to the London School of Economics and then into politics in 1953 at the age of twenty-nine. Richard Marsh was a Fabian and attended Ruskin College, Oxford, before his entry into Parliament in 1959. Before starting his political career he had been a NUPE official and was adopted as one of its sponsored MPs shortly after the 1959 election. Unfortunately for the Labour Party, he left Parliament after the 1970 election and eventually became head of the British Rail Commission. Peter Shore attended Cambridge and worked for the Labour Party before being elected to Parliament in 1964 at the age of forty. He was sponsored by the TGWU and was not untypical of the professional men on its panel of MPs. None of these three can be said to resemble the 'man in the cloth cap', who has been part of the Labour Party's tradition and image since its creation.

The 1970s

The defeat of the Labour Party in the 1970 General Election did not significantly alter the declining role of sponsored MPs within the top leadership of the PLP. Even in the 1971–72 session of Parliament, when the number of sponsored MPs on the Parliamentary Committee jumped to five out of fifteen because of the resignations of Harold Lever and George Thompson over the Common Market issue, the proportion of trade unionists was still less than their nearly forty per cent share of the PLP as a whole. But this underrepresentation was due to the change in the type of MP being sponsored by the unions. The more traditional types were older and had been in the House for a long time. MPs such as Charles Pannell, Alan Beaney, and Fred Lee were nearing the end of their careers in the House of Commons. Work on the committee was something that could be left to younger men who had more to gain.

The newer 'professional representatives' who were elected in the 1960s and 70s were younger, with expectations of things to come. Their committee candidacies were a promise of the future. For example, in the 1973 committee elections there were thirty-three candidates for the twelve positions other than leader, deputy leader, and chief whip. Only two sponsored MPs reached the top twelve, but twelve of the next twenty-one were trade unionists.[70] Many of them, such as William Rodgers, Stanley Orme, Eric Varley, and Eric Heffer, could expect to move higher in the future. And only one failed to receive an appointment in the 1974 Labour government. In any event, the sponsored MPs' underrepresentation went unnoticed because of the changing and increasingly heterogeneous composition of the Trade Union Group.

Shifting our attention from the elected Parliamentary Committee to the appointed Shadow Cabinet or frontbench spokesmen between 1970 and 1974, we can see further evidence of the sponsored MPs' lack of representation. In 1970–71 they held only one primary position (Fred Peart was minister for parliamentary affairs) and thirteen secondary positions. By the 1972–73 session this had changed, with the trade unionists increasing their share of primary spokesmen to three (Fred Peart for defence, Reginald Prentice for employment, and John Silkin for health and social security) and fourteen secondary positions.[71] The sponsored MPs might have had additional representation if individuals such as Richard Marsh had not left the House of Commons, and if Peter Shore had been willing to accept such responsibilities at the start of the 1970 Parliament.[72]

The three major departments of concern to the unions are Employment, Environment (which includes transport and local government), and Trade and Industry (which includes fuel and power and steel). Sponsored MPs did not constitute the majority of primary spokesmen for these areas, but they did provide the bulk of the secondary spokesmen. And, as we have already indicated, both individually and collectively they played a major part in the PLP's opposition to the Tory Industrial Relations Bill.

The relative success of the Labour Party in the two elections of 1974 provided another opportunity for Harold Wilson to form a government and show his appreciation of the parliamentary stature of the sponsored MPs. As shown in Table IV–2, the sponsored MPs did better in the initial appointments in the 1974 government than they had in the 1964–70 period. Within the Cabinet their earlier decline had been partially checked with six sponsored MPs included in the twenty-one Cabinet positions. But only two of the six were heads of departments that had traditionally been of major concern to the unions – Eric Varley, a former miner, was at Energy; and Peter Shore, formerly head of the party's Research Department and sponsored by the TGWU, was at Trade. While Fred Peart received the almost traditional GMWU post at Agriculture, Fisheries, and Food, the remaining trade unionists served in less traditional posts: Roy Mason, a miner, at Defence; Reginald Prentice, sponsored by the TGWU, at Education and Science; and CAWU's newly sponsored Shirley Williams at the Prices and Consumer post.

Below the Cabinet the sponsored MPs did quite well with a larger share of the positions (even if we exclude the Whips' office) than they had had between 1964 and 1970. While trade unionists were found in a variety of ministries, their traditional concerns were evident with two miners (Varley and Eadie) at Energy, six trade unionists among the nine MPs at the Environment ministry; two of the four Employment positions and two out of five in Anthony Wedgwood Benn's Industry department. The dominant material concerns of the trade unionists seemed little affected by the changes in their background, and the minor changes in the government during the summer of 1974 and following the October General Election did little to change this picture.

But numbers are only part of the picture. None of the trade unionists in the 1974 Labour government could be termed a major union figure. No one of them could claim the authority to speak to or for the union movement in the country the way that Ernest Bevin or even Frank Cousins might have tried. Union leaders such as Jack Jones or Hugh Scanlon made it quite clear that they were the movement's spokesmen, and negotiations to solve the United Kingdom's pressing economic problems would have to be carried on directly, not through some former trade unionists now serving in the House of Commons.

The rejection of normal party politics indicated by this development is compounded by the changing social background of the Labour Party's leadership. The disappearance of traditional working class figures from the top ranks of the party will pose a major problem in the 1970s and 80s when it will be more and more difficult for the party to pretend to resemble the social groups from which it draws its support.[73] And if this is true, for how long will the party be able to retain its working class support? The rise of the Celtic fringe and the resurgence of the Liberals in the two general elections of 1974 are not likely to bring hope to the hearts of Labour strategists.

The resignation of Harold Wilson in early 1976 had little direct impact on the trade unionists as a group. No sponsored MP was a candidate, and the Group split its vote in much the same as the balance of the PLP. The only notable feature of the contest was the division between MPs sponsored by the TGWU and the AEF who were more likely to support Michael Foot and those sponsored by the GMWU and the NUM who supported James Callaghan.[74] This merely reflected the ideological positions of these unions. In the reorganisation of the Government that followed Callaghan's victory, the relative position of the sponsored MPs was not altered significantly.

Whips, 1945–1975

Throughout the history of the PLP the Whips' office has been viewed as the special preserve of the sponsored MPs, because it was the one position where they could do little harm to the party and yet still feel they had an important function to perform. The chief whip is frequently a trade unionist. William Whiteley, sponsored by the NUM, held the position from 1942 until 1955 and was thought to have done a good job by both Herbert Morrison and Hugh Dalton, even if he failed to retire soon enough.[75] The chief whip's post was again occupied by a sponsored MP in 1966, when John Silkin of the TGWU was appointed to the position by Prime Minister Wilson. Silkin received much criticism from more traditional figures within the PLP, such as Emanuel Shinwell, who were upset by his unwillingness to take a strong line against rebels and by his support for the late Richard Crossman's relaxed style as leader of the House of Commons. It was partly in response to this criticism that Wilson appointed Robert Mellish, also sponsored by the TGWU, to the position in 1969. It was hoped that Mellish would take a stronger line on discipline within the PLP, but his actions during the controversy over 'In Place of Strife' indicated that the chief whip is something more than an agent of the party leader.

Between 1945 and 1966 half the whips were sponsored MPs,[76] and the proportion has increased since then. In the 1945–51 Labour government most of the assistant whips were miners, but not since then has the NUM been able to monopolise these positions to the same extent. In the 1964–70 Labour government the Whips' office actually increased its proportion of sponsored MPs serving there, the only group of offices where that happened (see Table IV–2). This increase continued in the 1974 government when almost all of the whips (eleven out of thirteen) were trade unionists.

For most MPs appointed to a position as a whip, the experience of nearly three-quarters of a century indicates that it is not a road to advancement, and aspiring Labour politicians seeking to move up the greasy pole of office are advised to start elsewhere. [77] Assistant whips may gain an appointment in the Royal Household when their party is in power, but they cannot realistically expect much else. Even the chief whip's position seems to be the prerogative of those who were first elected to it when the party was in Opposition, or who have been appointed to it by a Labour prime minister after achieving some success elsewhere. Should the Labour Party hold office more frequently in the future than it has in the past, the chief whip's position will become much more the gift of the prime minister.

Evaluation

In the years since World War II the role of sponsored MPs in the PLP has varied, but a number of generalisations can be made. They have constituted one major segment of the PLP which has had to be listened to with respect on those subjects attracting its interest and attention. It was Wilson's failure to do so which led to the debâcle over 'In Place of Strife'. While the Trade Union Group has occasionally provided a focus for efforts to influence the PLP, on topics other than industrial relations and the status of the trade unions the Group is usually as divided as other parts of the party.

Some individual sponsored MPs, including Ernest Bevin, Aneurin Bevan, James Griffiths, Alfred Robens, George Brown, and Ray Gunter, have played very important parts in the leadership of the PLP. But sponsored MPs have generally been underrepresented in most of the leading bodies of the PLP. Their showing might have been poorer if there had not been a widespread recognition of the importance of having some trade unionists in the leadership, as a constant reminder to Labour Party supporters that it is the workers' party. Frank Cousins was recruited to serve in this function in the Labour government of 1964, but his resignation in 1966 seems to have convinced Harold Wilson that such representation was no longer necessary and he did little to check the disappearance of the traditional working class representative in the latter years of the government. The lack of additional trade unionists in the party leadership is partly due to the traditional sponsored MPs' lack of the particular skills needed for positions of parliamentary leadership.

With the changing social background of British politics in the years since 1945, the pattern of union sponsorship will continue to change. The House of Commons will see fewer of the traditional sponsored MPs, who possess only an elementary education and are sponsored by a union strong in heavy industry. In their place will be found more of the professional representatives drawn from sections of the population who have obtained a higher education with a minimal experience in the mines or on the shop floor.

As their importance as a distinctive group within the PLP decreases, the representation of sponsored MPs within the party leadership will decline, but so also will the leadership's ability to feel and understand what their supporters want. In addition, the newer sponsored MPs will cease to be the solid core of the PLP, ready to do battle with any opponents of the parliamentary leadership. The sponsored MPs' ideological orientations will increasingly reflect the general divisions found within the PLP as a whole. Since the traditional sponsored MPs were usually men of the right, this means that there will be a leftward shift in the PLP.

Chapter V

The Impact of Background on Parliamentary Behaviour

The Trade Union Group and the participation of sponsored MPs in PLP leadership and in Labour governments since 1945 are only one aspect of the contemporary picture. In trying to explain the relatively poor showing of sponsored MPs in the PLP leadership, an important factor is the pattern of their participation in the day-to-day activities of the House of Commons.

Debate and the Question Hour

First we shall analyse the sponsored MPs' specialisations during Debate and the Question Hour.[1] For Debate we shall note when certain subjects come up on the floor of the House, who takes part in those Debates, and what they say. MPs having some special tie with organisations interested in an area of public policy are traditionally expected to make their 'interest' public in the course of Debate, and we shall frequently find such declarations of interest in the Debates.[2]

Analysis of the Question Hour is more difficult because of the number of questions involved. There were over 14,600 oral and written questions directed at thirty different departments or committees during the 1962–63 session of Parliament alone. Using data obtained from the office of the Clerk of the House of Commons and from Hansard, we have compared the proportion of those questions directed by sponsored MPs and non-sponsored MPs.[3]

Other writers have suggested that trade unionists are most in-

106

terested in industrial affairs and least concerned with foreign policy and defence.[4] Following these suggestions, we have used these three topics to gage the pattern of sponsored MPs' participation in Debate and the Question Hour.

Defence Policy

The lack of participation by the sponsored MPs in general debates on defence policy is immediately apparent from looking at Hansard. An example is seen in the Opposition censure motion in December 1960, attacking Harold Macmillan's Conservative government for not sufficiently encouraging multilateral disarmament. Despite the bitter split within the Labour Party and within the PLP on the question of unilaterialism *versus* multilateralism, only one sponsored MP, George Brown, the shadow minister of defence, took part in the Debate.[5] Another example occurred in 1963, when Brown and John Burns Hynd were the only sponsored MPs among thirteen Labour participants in the debate on the Conservative government's 'Statement on Nuclear Defence Systems'.[6]

If we analyse the questions that sponsored MPs asked the military departments, their inactivity is less obvious, as shown in Table V–1. These results would be more clearcut if it were not for the activity of one sponsored MP, Roy Mason. During the course of the 1962–63 session, Mason engaged in a campaign to reveal the existence of a British 'military-industrial complex' consisting of retired civil servants or military officers with positions in industry. He contributed almost one-third of the Admiralty's questions, three-fifths of the questions directed to the Air Ministry, nine-tenths of those directed at the Defence Ministry and half of those directed to the War Office,[7] which helps to explain the mixed and ambiguous results shown in Table V–1. Having assembled the data, Mason used them for a series of oral questions directed to the prime minister about regulations to prevent any conflict of interest.[8]

Foreign Affairs

A more distinct pattern emerges if we shift our attention to participation in foreign affairs debates. As with defence, most of the union MPs did not take part. When they did, they were apologetic and willing to acknowledge their real or imagined limitations in the international sphere. The infrequency of their participation was acknowledged in 1961 by Ellis Smith:

It is many years since I took part in a foreign affairs debate. I
do so now because I am becoming increasingly uneasy at the
trend of events in foreign affairs and at the relative agreement
that exists in the House. I represent those great industrial areas
which, in the main, keep our exports going. I have taken part in
two world wars. I have studied history. I know that thousands
of the best of our sons, most of whom were as good as any of us
are, lie in graves all over the world. I know how easy it could
have been for some of us to have been among them at 18 or 19
years of age, yet here we stand, having enjoyed life, with
strength and power to use our intelligence and physique.
Therefore, the time has arrived when working class representatives in the House should assert themselves and take part in
debates of this character.[9]

Despite Smith's demand, there was little response from his fellow
trade unionists. A faint echo was heard a year later when Cyril
Bence, speaking in support of American action during the 1962
Cuban missile crisis, began by saying: 'I ought to apologize to the
House on this occasion because this is the first time in eleven years
that I have had the audacity to address it on foreign affairs. I have
never done so before because I have always found the subject very
difficult.'[10]

The only trade unionists to show a significant interest in foreign
affairs were George Brown, Fred Mulley, and John Burns Hynd, the
same three MPs who were prominent in defence debates.

Table V–1 shows the pattern of questions directed by sponsored
and non-sponsored MPs at the four departments concerned with
foreign policy. The figures indicate a definite difference between the
two groups of MPs, with the trade unionists only a third to a half as
active as other MPs.

Generally, whether we look at Debate or Questions, the same
pattern emerges: trade union MPs devote a smaller amount of their
energy to foreign policy and defence topics than do other MPs. In the
Question Hour the sponsored MPs were more active for only two of
the eight departments concerned with these topics, and that was partly due to the unusual activity of one MP.

Industrial Affairs

While the trade unionists did not generally participate in Debate and

TABLE V – 1

ORAL AND WRITTEN QUESTIONS DIRECTED AT SELECTED GOVERNMENT
DEPARTMENTS IN THE 1962 – 1963 SESSION OF THE HOUSE OF COMMONS BY
UNION- SPONSORED AND OTHER MPs

	GROUP OF MPs			
SELECTED DEPARTMENTS	ALL MPs NOT MEMBERS OF THE GOVERNMENT, OFFICERS OF THE HOUSE OF COMMONS, OR SPONSORED BY A UNION *(N – 464)*		UNION-SPONSORED MPs *(N – 87)*	
	No.	%	No.	%
Admiralty	431	3.4	31	1.5
Air	140	1.1	48	2.3
Defence	206	1.6	50	2.4
War Office	316	2.5	45	2.2
Subtotal for Military Departments	1,093	8.6	174	8.4
Colonies	463	3.7	41	2.0
Commonwealth	123	1.0	2	0.1
Lord Privy Seal (for Foreign Office)	810	6.5	48	2.3
Technical Cooperation	111	0.9	10	0.5
Subtotal for Foreign Affairs Departments	1,507	12.1	101	4.9
Aviation	245	2.0	59	2.8
Labour	651	5.2	257	12.3
Post Office	371	3.0	149	7.1
Fuel and Power	217	1.7	75	3.6
Science	363	2.5	117	5.6
Transport	1,071	8.6	192	9.2
Subtotal for Industrial Departments	2,918	23.0	849	40.6
Subtotal for all other Departments	7,005	56.3	960	46.1
Total	12,523	100.0	2,084	100.0

Sources: The figures for the union-sponsored MPs are derived from *Parl. Deb*. 1962–63. The
figures for 'All MPs . . .' are based on data provided by the office of the Clerk of the House of

Commons *minus* the figures for union-sponsored MPs. Only in 1969 was the expectation that an MP should 'declare his interest' extended to the Question Hour (see *Parl. Deb.* 1968–69, Vol. 779, col. 1148 [11 March 1969] and cols. 1562–64 [March 13 1969]).

during the Question Hour when foreign affairs and defence topics were before the House, they were active on most industrial topics. It is widely recognised, for instance, that the chairman of the Trade Union Group has a right to be called on during debates on industrial relations.[11] More specifically, for most of the departments concerned with industry, including Aviation, Labour, Fuel and Power, Transport, and the Post Office, the sponsored MPs were the Chief Opposition spokesmen in the 1959–64 Parliament. In addition, they provided the bulk of Labour's backbench speakers in debates on these topics.[12] In the Debate on the Payment of Wages Bill in 1960, for example, Albert V. Hilton (NUAW) stated: 'I represent agricultural workers, the lowest paid workers in the country. It is on their behalf that I would like to say a few words.'[13] As with most trade unionists, Hilton had grave reservations about the government's proposal to allow workers to be paid by cheque.

White collar employees received special recognition in the 1959–60 session, in the form of Richard Marsh's (NUPE) Private Member's Bill on working conditions in offices. Speaking in support of it, Fred Mulley (CAWU) called attention to his union's particular interest in the proposal.[14] Some of the younger white-collar-union sponsored MPs beginning to appear in the House of Commons in the 1950s were particularly interested in Marsh's bill and resisted the Conservative government's half-hearted opposition on the second reading. They were also active in opposing the government's Offices, Shops, and Railway Premises Bill in the 1962–63 session.[15]

The sponsored MPs also provided the sharpest criticism of Selwyn-Lloyd's 'pay pause' in 1961–62, demanding that it should be accompanied by an equally effective ban or limitation on profits.[16] The attempt by the government to enforce the 'pause' led to especially hard feeling among nurses and others in the public service, including the nationalised industries, which was reflected in a very bitter denunciation of the policy by Percy Collick (ASLEF).[17]

The domination of Labour's contribution to industrial debates by trade union spokesmen was paralleled by a similar concentration of effort in the Question Hour, as shown in Table V–1. Compared with other MPs, the sponsored MPs asked all six industrial departments a higher proportion of written and oral questions. The difference is most apparent in dealing with the Ministry of Labour and the Post Office, but the differences involving the other four departments point in the same direction.

Specialised Committees

The tendency to focus their attention on industrial topics can also be seen in the part played by sponsored MPs in the select committees of the House of Commons between 1959 and 1964. The only committee to attract many such MPs was the Committee on Nationalised Industries, which had been set up at their urging to enable the House of Commons to undertake closer supervision of the nationalised industries, such as coal and transport. Austin Albu, William Blyton, Ernest A. Fitch, and Tom Steele were members of the committee for all five sessions, while Tom Fraser, Jeremy Bray, and Ernest Popplewell served for one or more sessions. Sponsored MPs constituted less than one-sixth of the membership of the House of Commons, but they made up over a third of the membership of this committee.[18]

The Miners

The trade union MPs concentrate on industrial affairs, but there is still further specialisation among them. The MPs sponsored by the NUM offer the clearest case of this. Traditionally the miners have been the largest group of MPs sponsored by a single union, and as a group in the House of Commons they play a role in regulating the participation of their members in debates. They do this through an informal rota of mining MPs, two or three chosen from the group to make the first attempt to participate in debates affecting the coal industry.[19] Other members of the group, unless required to do otherwise by their position in the PLP, will not try to take part until these speakers have done so. The system is designed to ensure, not that the best speakers always have the first opportunity to express their views,[20] but that *all* miners' MPs will be able to take part in mining debates. To ensure that the views expressed are relevant and useful to the debate, the selected MPs are first briefed by officers of the NUM.

How effective is the rota system? Despite some complaints most of the NUM MPs seem to feel that it introduces a desirable element of egalitarianism into the group, for through the rota most NUM spon sored MPs do participate in coal debates over a period of time. For example, in the 1945–50 Parliament, when the Labour government nationalised the coal industry, there was a general pattern of mining MPs deferring to one another so that all might have some opportunity to speak. [21] A few miners did not speak in the various coal debates, including members of the government as well as older MPs, such as W. M. Watson (Dunfermline Burgh) and Sir C. Edwards (Bedwelty). But most of the mining MPs did have an opportunity to speak. Only two spoke more than three times and the normal pattern was twice during the Parliament. It is significant that while the mining MPs spoke out during the debates over nationalisation of the coal industry, they played no major role in the process of nationalisation, which was accomplished through consultation among the government, the NUM, and the mine owners. [22] The same pattern of debate can be seen in the 1959–64 Parliament, when there were six general debates affecting the coal industry. [23] Ten of the thirty-two MPs sponsored by the NUM failed to speak in these debates. Of the remaining twenty-two only one without front bench responsibility spoke more than twice, and fourteen spoke only once. Analysis of the ten silent MPs reveals that two died early in the Parliament and two others had front bench responsibilities for ministries other than fuel and power.

The rota was also at work in the 1971–72 session of Parliament, which witnessed the first national strike on the coal industry since 1926. Of the twenty NUM-sponsored MPs in the House, sixteen took part in the five coal industry debates (including several concerned with the strike in January and February 1972), with thirteen of the miners speaking before there was one repeat. [24] The only MP to speak more than twice was Alex Eadie, the chairman of the miners' group of MPs. Of the four who did not take part in these debates one, Eric Ogden, did not represent a mining constituency; a second, E. A. Fitch, was a former whip and member of the chairman's panel; and a third, Allen Beaney, was due to retire in 1974.

The mining MPs' speeches are the dominant ones on the Labour side of the House. This can be seen by looking at the debates on the frequent coal industry bills. The bill introduced by the Conservatives in 1959–60, for example, would have allowed the National Coal Board to borrow additional money to aid its modernisation efforts. On the bill's second reading the miners supplied five of the seven Labour speakers. On the committee stage the miners could supply only three out of nine Labour Spokesmen, but they recovered and had five out of seven on the report stage. [25] In the debate over another coal industry bill in 1962–63 all of the Labour speakers, including the shadow minister of power Tom Fraser and the assistant shadow minister Will Blyton, were sponsored by the NUM. [26] Again during the 1971–72 session the miners provided sixteen out of thirty-one Labour speakers (and they made thirty-one of the approximately forty-four speeches) in debate affecting the coal industry.

The particular concern of the miners can also be seen in the division lobbies. For example, when Gerald Nabarro, a Conservative MP, sought to weaken the 1960 Coal Industry Bill by diminishing the Coal Board's borrowing power, two miners (Thomas J. Brown and Robert E. Woof) chose to go into the government's lobby to help defeat Nabarro's proposal, even though the PLP officially abstained on the vote. [27]

Simply trying to control who takes part in debate is one aspect of action on the floor of the House. The NUM also finds that it occasionally has important points which must be made in the House because of a breakdown in the consultative process or the failure of the government to accept its point of view in behind-the-scenes talks. For example, Will Blyton, acting for the NUM, threatened to introduce over 500 amendments in committee to correct what the union felt were errors in the 1952 Mines and Quarries Bill. On the committee the miners dominated the Labour side and were able to persuade the government to accept many of their proposals. [28]

In keeping with the normal practice of the House of Commons, the miners never make any secret of their union ties when participating in these debates. For example, William Stones began a speech on the 1960 Coal Industry Bill by saying, 'I should, perhaps, declare my interest in speaking in this debate as a fully paid up member of the Mineworkers' Union.' [29] Likewise the party's elder statesman, James Griffiths, when speaking on the 1962 Coal Industry Bill, said: 'I declare my interest in this matter. I am a member of the National Union of Mineworkers.' [30] And a decade later, Michael McGuire could declare his interest in a debate on the 1972 Consolidated Fund Bill by saying, 'When I was in the industry – and I and many of my hon. Friends around me are fully paid-up members of the union . . .'. [31]

During the 1972 miners' strike both Alex Eadie, the chairman of the miners' group of MPs in the House of Commons, and the group's

secretary G. E. Davies made numerous references to their position
and their association with the executive of the NUM. For example, in
an adjournment debate on 18 January, Davies began:

> I want first to declare an interest. I am an ex-miner and a
> member of the National Union of Mineworkers. As an ex-of-
> ficio member of the National Executive of that union I have
> been privileged – though it has not been much of a pleasure –
> to sit through and listen to the discussions with the Coal Board
> which have taken place about this [wage] claim. [32]

And later in the same debate Alex Eadie stated:

> I think that I have a right to speak in the debate because I have
> heard honourable gentlemen opposite speculate to some extent
> on the negotiations [between the Coal Board and the NUM]. I
> am an *ex-officio* member of the National Executive of the
> National Union of Mineworkers by virtue of the fact that this
> year I am Chairman of the Miners' Parliamentary Group.
> Indeed, I took part in the negotiations. I have heard honourable
> Members talk about the intent of the miners and their leaders
> to reach a settlement. At our last meeting in London we sat for
> six hours endeavouring to reach a settlement. [33]

Time and time again the miners' MPs make reference to their own
experience in the mines. When he first spoke in the House in 1959,
Tom Swain had been away from the coal mine for only nine weeks. [34]
In opposing the 1959 move by Gerald Nabarro to reduce the Coal
Board's borrowing power, Thomas J. Brown could describe from personal experience the problems the industry faced as it ran out of good
coal deposits. [35] And in 1972 Alex Eadie, first elected to the House in
1966, could refer to his experiences as a working miner in the early
1960s. [36]

The MPs are always quick to take note of any threat to the coal industry, and they seek 'to insist that no pit closures to cut back
production should take place until, or unless, alternative employment
whether within the industry or in another industry is available to fully accommodate the displaced men.' [37] Thus they are concerned to
protect their industry from other power sources, such as oil, natural
gas, or atomic energy. For example, in the early 1960s the NUM MPs
helped to persuade the government to make the Longannet Power
station a coal-burning one, thus providing jobs for 10,000 miners.

For this the NUM could be very grateful.[38] Again, in 1971, the MPs called attention to the economic threat that the importation of coal posed for the industry.[39]

The longterm decline of the coal industry reached a crisis in 1967. Continued pit closures led the miners' MPs to demand action in the House of Commons, but their effectiveness was limited by their 'chronic shortage of first-rate debating talent'.[40] However, they did have a role to play. Public pressure was applied through a meeting of the full NUM executive committee and all the sponsored MPs in June 1967. While not expecting real help from the politicians, the NUM viewed the meeting as a means of keeping the rank and file membership of the union satisfied while other actions to solve the crisis were being explored.[41] This use of the MPs for publicity purposes could also be seen during the 1972 strike when they were encouraged to join picket lines established by the union.[42]

The major result of the 1967 confrontation was a promise by the government to halt pit closures for a year: a promise that had minimal effect on the industry. When the chairman of the Coal Board, Lord Robens (a former USDAW-sponsored MP), announced that employment in the industry was expected to decline to only 65,000 by 1980, the NUM even began to question its traditional allegiance to the Labour Party, although it took no action about it.[43] As second result of the 1967 dispute, the minister of power Richard Marsh (sponsored by NUPE) was replaced by Roy Mason, a miner, in early 1968. Mason tried to help the industry, but even he was prepared to allow the construction of more atomic power stations rather than the coal-burning ones demanded by the miners.[44] In any event the defeat of the Labour Party in 1970 meant that Mason had little opportunity to do much to help. In fact, the industry has suffered an almost continual decline in manpower since 1947,[45] and neither party has seemed willing to halt the longterm decline of the industry. The heritage of industrial bitterness which characterises industrial relations in mining communities accompanied by this decline laid the basis for the 1972 and 1974 miners' strikes. The impact of the 1974 strike alongside the rapid increase in mideast oil prices since 1973 provided the background for the settlement of miners payclaims in 1975 outside of the Social Contract and a marginal increase in the workforce. But with the promise of a rapid increase in the flow of British North Sea oil about 1980, one can only predict that the prospects facing the miners will grow dimmer.

It is generally felt that sponsored MPs are inactive when labour disputes are debated in the House of Commons, though the miners' MPs' reactions to the 1972 strike gave ample evidence that this is not always the case. Then they initiated two adjournment debates on aspects of the strike; they reported to the House on some of the negotiations that were taking place between the Coal Board and the NUM; and one of the MPs, Eric Varley, provided the key that helped to secure government intervention in the dispute when he announced that the NUM was prepared to meet with responsible ministers if they were invited to do so.[46] Despite this activity, however, an examination of their role in the House of Commons reveals that they are Labour MPs first and miners' MPs second.[47] The union is prepared on occasion to use the MPs to raise points, ask questions, or provide general publicity, but it does not see them as its main weapon against the decline of the industry. On that subject the NUM will speak for itself.

The pattern of specialisation shown in Debate is repeated in the activity of sponsored MPs during the Question Hour. The miners' MPs in particular are more active in asking questions of the minister of fuel and power than are all other sponsored MPs (see Table V–2). During the 1972 miners' strike, for example, out of forty-nine oral and written questions asked about the strike in January and February, the miners contributed almost fifty per cent of these questions and asked sixty per cent of the supplementary ones.[48] The MPs were less likely to call attention to their union affiliation in this context, but it was not always ignored. For example, when Tom Swain was talking about a Private Notice Question on 3 February, he stated: 'I am speaking as . . . a representative of the miners' group'.[49]

The miners offer one of the clearest cases of particular interests being represented in the House of Commons,[50] but they are hardly typical of the sponsored MPs as a whole. The congruence between their personal experience as miners (they still provide the core of the traditional cloth cap figures in the House), their organisational affiliation to the NUM, and the dominant position of mining in most of their constituencies is unusual. It is this last factor, of course, which most differentiates the miners from other sponsored MPs. And because of the overlapping of experience, affiliation, and constituency, there are attempts to counteract the view that mining MPs are specialists. According to one NUM official; for example, 'All Miners'

TABLE V – 2

DIRECTED AT THE MINISTRIES OF FUEL AND POWER
AND OF TRANSPORT

Oral and written questions in the 1962–1963 session of the House of Commons

	MPs sponsored by the NUM (N–30)		MPs sponsored by the 3 rail unions (N–14)		All T.U. sponsored MPs (N–87)		All other MPs* (N–464)	
Department	No.	%	No.	%	No.	%	No.	%
Fuel and Power	40	4.5			75	3.6	217	1.7
Transport			38	14.1	192	9.2	1,071	8.6
All other	(inc. transport) 849	95.5	(inc. fuel/power) 231	85.9	1,817	87.2	11,235	89.7
Totals	889	100	269	100	2,084	100	12,523	100

* Excluding Members of the Government and Officers of the House

sponsored MPs are, as you will probably be aware, members of a Miners' Political Group in Parliament seeking to improve the conditions of miners in particular, but always, of course, fully conscious of the fact that all classes of persons in the constituency must be catered for.' [51] The fact that an NUM-sponsored MP such as Eric Ogden, who represents a non-mining constituency, seldom takes part in mining debates supports the official's position. If the decline of the industry continues as it has in the last fifteen years, we can expect the mining MPs to be far less specialised in the future.

The Railwaymen

The railway industry illustrates another kind of specialisation, for the constituencies represented by these union-sponsored MPs are not always predominantly railway constituencies. The railwaymen lend themselves to the type of analysis which we have been using in this part of the study because of the industrial nature of their unions and the existence, until the late 1960's, of a government department which had primary responsibility for the industry covered by the unions.

The NUR provides information to the railway MPs when requested, but contact seems to be very much weaker than between the miners and the NUM. The NUR is also less willing to take the initiative in calling on its MPs.[52] In the TSSA there is closer contact, with MPs usually holding major jobs within the union such as those of president and treasurer. In addition, one other TSSA MP is responsible for maintaining contact between the MPs and the union.

In the 1945 General Election some twenty-three Labour MPs were elected with the sponsorship of one of the three railway unions, the NUR, ASLEF, or TSSA. Only two held office in the government and neither was associated with the Ministry of Transport. The MPs sponsored by the three railway unions played no part in the drafting of legislation to nationalise the railways, though they were involved in its passage through the House of Commons. They sat on the standing committee and were able to secure some minor changes in those sections of the bill involving working conditions.[53]

The fourteen railway MPs in 1959–64 did not dominate railway debates as much as the miners did mining debates.[54] Unlike the miners, the railwaymen did not have a regular rota to determine who would try to participate in debates, but some of them did try to avoid speaking if another railwayman had already done so.[55] Some railway representatives, such as William T. Proctor and Henry Hynd, failed to take part in any of the railway debates between 1959 and 1964, and, lacking anything like the miners' rota, they were not likely to be given an opportunity. Still, the railway MPs dominate the PLP's transport group,[56] and they are as prepared as the miners to speak out in defence of their unions and industry.[57] The unions thank the MPs when they have assisted the union in some way, as they did in the case of the 1962 Transport Act.[58]

Evidence of the weaker ties between railway MPs and their unions is suggested by the relative infrequency with which they declared their interest in transport debates. Occasionally they did so, but more often their interest was declared for them.[59] For example, during the debate on the Ministry of Transport's estimates in 1964, D. Webster, a Conservative, attacked the NUR. In the exchange that followed with Leslie Spriggs, it was the Conservative spokesman who called attention to the fact that Spriggs was sponsored by the NUR.[60]

Yet another example of both specialisation and interest representation in the House arose out of the Labour government's decision in January 1975 to end official British support for the Channel Tunnel. In the special emergency debate that followed this announcement, two of the eight Labour MPs were sponsored by railway unions, and both were critical of the government's action because of its adverse effect on the development of a rail link with the European continent. The second of these two MPs, Mr. Peter Shape, began his contribution by saying: 'I declare my interest as a member of the National Union of Railwaymen and Secretary of the All-Party Committee on the Channel Tunnel'.[61] In the division that followed the debate, six of the nine railway MPs voted against the government, two (including Mr. Walter Johnson, an assistant whip) did not take part in the vote, and only one, Mr. T. M. Mcmillan from a Scottish constituency, supported the decision to abandon the Tunnel.[62]

Far more than the miners, the railwaymen were willing to claim that they were not primarily concerned with railway matters. Speaking to the NUR annual conference in 1960, John B. Hynd could proclaim: 'I am quite sure that the Conference of this union would not say that we were merely concerned with railway matters in Parliament but would recognise our contribution in the wider field of political activity.'[63] The railwaymen do not, of course, experience the congruence of industrial union, and constituency expectations that is found among the miners.

Furthermore, transportation includes more than the railways. Conflict between the railwaymen and road haulers was pointed out by Ray Gunter (president of TSSA) when he argued:

The great road interest should face the primary need of withdrawal in certain areas and in certain respects from long–distance freight-carrying. I understand the anguish which they suffer. I blame no one for this. I understand what it means when my own men are made redundant. They hate to see what is their own disappear. It is a hard experience when they are no longer necessary. They want to hold what they have. The long–distance road haulage interests will also suffer, and in the interests of the nation they, too, will have to be more forthcoming.[64]

This competition with the road haulers makes it less necessary for us to try to distinguish between railway questions and other parliamentary questions directed at the Ministry of Transport, although it introduces an element of possible distortion not found when analysing the miners. Keeping this in mind, we have in Table V–2 examined the questions asked by those MPs sponsored by the three railway unions. While less specialised in Debate than the miners, the railwaymen are more specialised in the Question Hour.[65]

Other Sponsored MPs

Patterns of specialisation and union orientation shown by the sponsored MPs as a whole, and by the miners and railwaymen in particular, have their parallel among Members sponsored by other unions, even if this is more difficult to identify with precision. The lack of congruence between union organisation and industry, or the fact that an industrial union such as the NUAW has only one or two sponsored MPs, makes it difficult to identify significant patterns of specialisation, but it is still worth devoting some attention to the MPs sponsored by other unions. One important group, the TGWU-sponsored MPs, are frequently the object of lobbying by TGWU members from all over the country. Members of the union come to London and meet with the sponsored MPs to present their grievances. The MPs use this information to ask questions, to initiate debate on the floor of the House of Commons, or to make private inquiries of the relevant ministry.

The TGWU group met with regional union officials in 1960 to discuss the problem of unemployment in the motor industry. The initial outcome of the lobbying was indicated in the union's journal: 'We were all agreed that immediate Parliamentary action was necessary by questions and debate, and your Group will take all possible steps within the Parliamentary Labour Party to ensure that the interests of our Members and the general prosperity of the motor industry are kept constantly before Parliament.'[66]

The TGWU group was concerned with the following topics in the 1959–64 Parliament: unemployment, transport legislation, fishing industry, fuel oil policy, and improved harbour facilities in various parts of the country.[67] The range of topics shows the TGWU is a general union that recruits members everywhere, even though it is particularly strong in the non-railway side of transport.

This specialisation has parallels among other sponsored MPs. One example is William R. Williams, sponsored by the UPW, who served as shadow postmaster general from 1960 until his death in 1963.

Again early in 1960, the Ministry of Agriculture issued new regulations concerning the maximum weight that farm employees could be required to lift without assistance. This was heavier than the equivalent for other industries, and Albert V. Hilton (NUAW) moved a Prayer in the House to have the measure annulled. In his remarks during Debate, Hilton said: 'For a number of years, farm workers have been pressing through my union, the National Union of Agricultural Workers, for legislation on this matter so that a maximum weight might be introduced and they might not be expected to lift or carry anything above that weight, thus bringing them into line with workers in other industries.' [68]

Hilton's remarks were supported by Reginald Prentice of the TGWU, which also organised a number of farmworkers, and by Edwin G. Gooch, the president of the NUAW. The union had been consulted during the preparation of the regulation, but the government agreed to give further attention to the union's views and Hilton's Prayer was withdrawn. [69]

The NUAW also uses its sponsored MPs to obtain information from the government through Questions, which can be used both in the preparation of the union's wage demands [70] and as a means of making direct representations to various government agencies. For example, in September 1960 these MPs led a deputation to see the minister of housing and local government on the question of inadequate housing for farmworkers. [71] Hilton also defended the NUAW in 1961 against charges that its wage demands were contributing to inflation. [72]

After Labour's return to power in 1964, one of the measures introduced to try to help solve the country's economic problems was a selective employment tax, to encourage more people to work in industries producing for export. Unions representing people in the distributive trades were opposed to the tax, and when Richard E. Winterbottom of USDAW spoke in the House against the tax, his speech was publicised by the union. [73] Another example occurred in 1966 when Roland Moyle, sponsored by NUPE, asked the minister of health what steps were being taken to implement recent proposals on the training of ambulance staffs. [74] The minister's reply, though ambiguous, indicated that the proposals would not be put into effect immediately. NUPE, which organised the ambulance staffs, was unhappy with the minister's position and urged prompter action on the proposals. [75] References to similar action by sponsored MPs in areas of concern to their unions can be seen in a number of union journals.[76]

Despite this, unions clearly prefer to use consultation rather than risk the uncertainties of working through their sponsored MPs to achieve union goals. Even on basic issues such as nationalisation they prefer to deal directly with the government. This was true with regard to nationalisation of the railways and the coal mines. It was also true in the first nationalisation of the steel industry, despite the fact that an MP sponsored by the steel workers had drawn up a practical plan for nationalisation.[77]

Specialisation and Interest Representation

The pattern of specialisation or interest representation shown by sponsored MPs in the years since 1945 had its parallels in the sectarianism of earlier union-sponsored MPs. For example, George Barnes wrote of the pre-World War I period: 'Fred Richards could hold forth with great gusto on the technicalities of boat making and Alex. Wilkie was never better pleased than when dilating on the grievances of dockyard shipwrights'.[78] And the formation of early Labour governments had to take account of the various industrial groupings which supported the party.[79]

Trade union MPs specialise by relying on their experience before entering the House of Commons, and in this they resemble other groups, such as company directors, farmers, or teachers, found in the House. But their specialisation does not mean that trade union MPs participate in all matters pertaining to economic and industrial affairs. In fact they often avoid one topic in this area, i.e. industrial disputes and strikes, for fear of further disturbing troubled waters.

Despite this last point (or perhaps because of it), the organisational affiliation of the trade union MPs gives emphasis to their specialisation and lays them open to the charge of neglecting the public interest. Their failure to take an active interest in military and defence policy and in foreign affairs adds credence to this charge. By publicly flaunting their rejection of the nineteenth century liberal or radical concepts of representation – concepts which emphasise the independence of the MP from outside commitments and are still among the more common definitions of the role of the MP[80] – the trade unionists offend the defenders of these traditional myths of representation. But they fit readily with the collectivist theories that are becoming more important in the latter part of the twentieth century, and they help to ensure that the British working classes have parliamentary representatives with personal experience as workers. Whether the new trade union MPs who come from the professions or are sponsored by the white collar and general unions will continue to fill this role is an open question.

Legislative Behaviour and Personal Background

The specialisation among the sponsored MPs discussed above is related to their traditional background in industry. However, this industrial background and union support are only one aspect of an entire set of experiences and characteristics which these MPs bring to the House of Commons.

Parliamentary Performance

Our quantitative analysis of legislative behaviour is concerned with three different types of activity: Questions, including Oral, Supplementary, and Written Questions; standing committee participation, including both the number of summonses and the number of meetings attended; and Debate. For each of these activities an index measures the rate of an MP's participation. These indices were constructed for all sponsored MPs who served through the entire 1959–64 Parliament (N = 87) and for all MPs included in a sample (N = 226) drawn from other Members of the 1959–64 Parliament. [81] Ninety non-union sponsored Labour MPs and 136 Conservative backbenchers were included in the sample. The differences in rates of participation in the various types of parliamentary activity for the three groups of MPs are shown in Table V–3. The data must be interpreted with some caution, however, because of the nature of the populations on which they are based. Members of the government were deliberately excluded, and the Conservative figures, describing only the activities of backbenchers, are included for information only. The analysis will focus on the two groups of Labour MPs.

Examination of Table V–3 shows a clear difference in the indices of legislative behaviour for the two groups of Labour MPs. In every case the non-sponsored Labour MPs are more active. In the case of Debate, Oral Questions, and Supplementary Questions, they are almost twice as active as the trade union Members. But even on standing committees the sponsored MPs are less active than their non--sponsored colleagues.

TABLE V–3

LEGISLATIVE BEHAVIOUR (by Group Means)

		GROUPS		
		OPPOSITION		GOVERNMENT
MEAN INDI-CES OF BEHAVIOUR PER GROUP MEMBER	TYPES OF LEGISLA-TIVE BEHAVIOUR	Trade Unionists (N – 87)	Other Labour MPs (N – 90)	Conservative Backbench MPs (N – 136)
Number of questions per member of each group (based on totals for three sessions of Parliament)	Oral questions	41.5	86.7	69.1
	Supplementary questions	33.8	85.5	65.4
	Written questions	16.5	28.9	24.1
Rate of standing committee participation per member of each group (based on total for five sessions of Parliament)	Mean number of standing committee sessions that an MP was summoned to	53.9	69.6	63.5
	Mean number of standing committee sessions that an MP attended	38.0	51.8	46.4
Mean length of index entry per member of each group (based on total for four sessions of Parliament)	Debate	160.3	314.7	249.8

This inactivity is a purely quantitative matter, which need not be equated with ineffectiveness or unimportance.

Many MPs are content with the role of a national auxiliary, quietly supporting the party line in each division, or undertaking an unglamourous junior ministerial post. These MPs provide ballast; their inactivity and lack of initiative contributes to the stability and predictability of parliamentary life. By the same token, when the trade union MPs in the Labour Party or the 'knights of the shires' in the Conservative Party begin to express disquiet, party leaders are alerted to the seriousness of a political situation. [82]

Whether the remarks of a previously quiet and loyal backbencher ever lead to a shift in party policy or strategy cannot readily be discovered.

Social Background of Political Decision Makers

The lower rates of activity by the sponsored MPs are not easily explained. For our purposes, preliminary analysis indicated that age and education might be significantly related to the differences in behaviour. Clearly the sponsored MPs are older than the other two groups of MPs. Their mean age in 1959 was 57.2, while that of the non-sponsored Labour MPs was 52.9 and of the Conservatives 47.7. This difference in mean age is due to the fact that 43% of the sponsored MPs were 60 years of age or older, but no more than 25% of either of the other groups were that old. At the other end of the age spectrum, only 2% of the sponsored MPs were under the age of 40, but 10% of each of the other groups were that young.

In addition, as already indicated, the educational background of the trade unionists distinguishes them from other MPs. One-third of the trade unionists still had only an elementary school background in 1959 and only 10% had attended university. The Other Labour group had only 1% with an elementary school background and 62% having attended university. The Conservative Backbenchers had no one with only an elementary school background and 49% had attended university.

There are certain a priori reasons for assuming that the differences in age and education would be crucial in explaining the behavioural variations, but there is very limited empirical evidence to support this reasoning. [83] In order to test the validity of the hypothesis that some or all of the differences in behaviour might be explained by the differences in background, we determined the correlation between each of these variables and each type of behaviour.

Age. The correlations of age and parliamentary behaviour are shown in Table V–4. Age is significantly related statistically to behaviour for the trade union MPs, though the correlations are so low as to be of questionable political importance. For the other Labour MPs it is only significant for Written Questions and Debate, and the correlation for Debate is negative, indicating that participation increases with age rather than decreases. Among the Conservative backbenchers there is a statistically significant relationship only between age and standing-committee activity.

That the pattern of correlations among sponsored MPs is more consistent than among the other two groups may be partly explained by the age distribution within each group. As already shown, the sponsored MPs include few Members under forty and a much larger proportion of Members over the age of sixty. The younger Members are more active and the older ones less so. The lack of a sizeable number of MPs over the age of sixty in the other two groups conceals the relationship if it exists there.

Education. The correlation coefficients between education and legislative behaviour are shown in Table V–5, but they provide a less satisfactory explanation of behaviour. Only three of the correlation coefficients reach a statistically significant level. Even more confusing is the frequent occurrence of negative correlation. We had assumed that activity would increase with education, but the figures indicate the opposite in a number of cases. Even among the union-sponsored MPs, there is one (statistically insignificant) negative correlation.

The lack of significant correlations between education and behaviour may be due to the arbitrary system of categorising education, which attempted to take account of both quantitative and qualitative factors, or it may be due to the lack of MPs with only an elementary education among the two groups of non-sponsored Members. As with the few non-sponsored MPs over the age of sixty, the latter explanation seems more plausible because it is the trade union MPs with only an elementary education who tend to be least active in the House of Commons.

TABLE V – 4

CORRELATION OF LEGISLATIVE BEHAVIOUR AND PERSONAL BACKGROUND
(by Group)

	Type of Legislative Behaviour	Correlation with age			Correlations with Education		
		Opposition		Government	Opposition		Government
		Union Sponsored MPs N – 87	Other Labour MPs N – 90	Conservative Backbench MPs N – 137	Union-Sponsored MPs N – 86*	Other Labour MPs N – 89*	Conservative Backbench MPs N – 135*
Questions	Oral	−.242	−.063	.066	.189	−.064	−.052
	Supplementary	−.343	.049	.047	.251	.053	−.062
	Written	−.297	−.206	−.066	.183	−.158	.066
Standing Committees	Summonses	−.291	−.143	−.266	−.039	−.156	−.146
	Attendance	−.274	−.072	−.259	.034	−.174	−.119
	Debate	−.304	.215	−.015	.108	−.008	.043
Coefficient of correlation must equal the following values for each N to be statistically significant at the 5% level		.212	.174	.141	.212	.174	.141

* MPs in each group whose educational achievements are unknown
have been excluded from this analysis.

The combined impact of age and education for the sponsored MPs' legislative behaviour is indicated in Table V–5. Among older sponsored MPs, higher education is related only to increased activity in standing committee summonses and Debate. Among the younger sponsored MPs, an increase in formal education is more often related to an increase in formal activity. This is most apparent in Oral Questions, standing committee summonses, and Debate. This relationship is reduced or non-existent for the other three types of behaviour. However, older sponsored MPs with only an elementary education are found most often in the least active category.

TABLE V – 5

RELATIONS AMONG AGE, EDUCATION, AND BEHAVIOUR
OF UNION-SPONSORED MPs*

UNION-SPONSORED MEMBERS
(N – 86)

TYPES OF LEGISLATIVE BEHAVIOUR	BEHAVIOUR INDEX	Education			
		Low		High	
		Age		Age	
		Younger	Older	Younger	Older
Oral	Low	8	12	17	20
Questions	High	6	3	18	2
Supplementary	Low	5	13	16	19
Questions	High	9	2	19	3
Written	Low	11	13	25	19
Questions	High	3	2	10	3
Standing Committee	Low	5	14	14	14
Summonses	High	9	1	21	8
Attendance Standing	Low	8	13	19	19
Committee	High	6	2	16	3
Debate	Low	10	11	11	13
	High	4	4	24	9

Education is defined as follows: *Low* – elementary, *High* – all categories (excluding one unknown).
Age is defined as follows: *Young* – Members aged 59 or below. *Old* – Members aged 60 or above.
Behaviour indices are defined as follows:
1. Oral and Supplementary questions: *Low* – 39 questions or less. *High* – 40 questions or above.
2. Written questions: *Low* – 19 questions and below. *High* – 20 questions or above.
3. Standing committee summonses and attendances: *Low* – 39 summonses or attendance and below. *High* – 40 summonses or attendance and above.
4. Debate: *Low* – 99 or below. *High* – 100 and above.

On the whole, Table V–5 supports the conclusion that age, rather than education, determines variations in the legislative activity of trade-union sponsored MPs. Education, however, does reinforce the impact of age.

Age and Leadership

The evidence presented so far regarding the impact of age or education on quantitative measures of parliamentary activity is ambiguous. The evidence that age is an important variable is far from convincing. Another type of activity which might be examined is leadership within the PLP, the Labour Party, or Labour governments. The data presented in Table V–6 show the success of sponsored MPs in attaining leadership positions in relation to their age at their first election to the House of Commons. For all four groups, those who were under forty-one when first elected have greater success than those who were forty-one or above.[84] Sponsored MPs elected in 1970 or later are not included in Table V–6, but there is no reason to expect that they will follow a different pattern once they have sufficient opportunity to gain office. While they did not do well in the minority government appointed following the February 1974 Election, they will soon have their chance.

The reasons why age should be so important in determining parliamentary activity and leadership within the Labour Party are not completely clear. Part of the explanation lies in the physical condition of the MPs. Advancing age increases the problems of adjustment, especially for the trade unionists, who find themselves in a very unfamiliar situation and are more subject to heart disease because of the resulting stress and strain.[85] The trade union MPs also start their parliamentary careers at an older age (their mean age was six years above that of their non-sponsored Labour colleagues in 1959 while their mean seniority was roughly the same); they are less able to adapt to the patterns of behaviour expected of an MP, and they have less time in which to do so. In addition, having had long associations with their unions before entering the House of Commons, the sponsored Members find it more difficult to respond to some of their other clienteles. This was reflected in Aneurin Bevan's comments: 'If the new Member gets there too late in life he is already trailing a pretty considerable past of his own, making him heavy footed and cautious'[86] and it is supported by one whip's suggestion that MPs entering the House after the age of fifty are seldom able to make a full

TABLE V – 6

RELATION BETWEEN AGE AT FIRST ELECTION AND OFFICE
HOLDING OF SPONSORED MPs WHO SERVED BETWEEN
1945 AND 1970

AGE WHEN FIRST ELECTED	BEFORE 1945			1945–1954			1955–1963			1964–1969		
	Yes	No	Total	Yes	No	Total	Yes	No	Total	Yes	No	Total
Under 41	11	3	14	17	4	21	9	1	10	8	7	15
41 and above	30	17	47	23	55	78	9	20	29	9	34	43
Unknown	1	5	6	7	–	7	–	–	–	–	–	–
Total	42	25	67	47	59	106	18	21	39	17	41	58
	$X^2 - 7.11$ df $- 2$ P 0.05			$X^2 - 27.36$ df $- 2$ P 0.001			$X^2 - 10.46$ df $- 1$ P 0.001			$X^2 - 14.2$ df $- 1$ P 0.001		

Sources: D. Butler and J. Freeman (eds.), *British Political Facts, 1900 – 1967*, pp. 16 – 106; F. M. G. Willson, 'Some Career Patterns in British Politics: Whips in the House of Commons, 1906 – 1966', *Parliamentary Affairs*, XXIV, No. 1 (Winter 1970 – 1971), pp. 41 – 2; *Dodd's Parliamentary Companion*, 1966 – 70; Labour Party Annual Conference, *Reports*, 1970 – 73; and *The Times Guide to the House of Commons*, 1970 and 1974.

Note: Only sponsored MPs who served in the House of Commons between the general elections of 1945 and 1970 are included in the above figures. Sponsored MPs whose service terminated before the 1945 election, or who were first elected at the 1970 General Election or later, are not included.

MPs are credited with office holding if they served at any time in at least one of the following: PLP Parliamentary Committee and/or its predecessors before World War II; Shadow Cabinet (since 1955); member of the World War II coalition; member of the Labour governments between 1945 and 1951 and between 1964 and 1970; as a whip or as a peer. The above figures also reflect appointment to any of these positions between 1970 and 1974 (including the minority Labour Government formed after the February 1974 General Election).

contribution to the work of the party. Indeed, the party leaders would prefer a method for ensuring that such men are not adopted as candidates.[87] In the past many politicians have indicated that the early 40s were the last possible time to start a parliamentary career if one hoped for success in it.[88]

The presence of the newer sponsored MPs who began to appear in the 1960s, with increased formal education and an earlier starting age in their political careers, indicates that the first century of trade union parliamentary representation is also last in which the ordinary rank and file union members can expect to see a sizeable contingent of people like themselves in the House of Commons. And to the degree that an organisation's support is conditional on the recipient's being typical or representative of its followers, the Labour Party may well anticipate problems in maintaining support from the unions in the future. 'They will make their political views heard all right, but it will only be through the Labour Party if the Labour Party adapts itself to representing them and people like them in contemporary terms'.[89]

Part III:
The Nature of the Ties Between MPs and Their Unions

Chapter VI

Communication and Conflict

Channels of Communication between Sponsored MPs and their Unions

In the public context, the main justification for the sponsorship of MPs is that this is the only way the unions can ensure adequate political protection for their interests. If this is the actual reason for sponsorship, strong channels of two-way communication between the sponsored MPs and their unions should exist, so that the Member can be kept informed of what his union is doing and what help might be given in Parliament, and the union can be kept informed of the political climate in the House of Commons in order to plan its programme accordingly.

Another reason for maintaining adequate channels of communication between the unions and MPs is that, in the opinion of the House of Commons, the sponsored Members are considered authorities on their unions:

Sponsored MPs tend to regard themselves as the official representatives of their unions in Parliament and are certainly regarded by the House of Commons as a whole as being in a position to speak with authority on matters affecting their unions. Certainly any sponsored Member whose union was involved in a Parliamentary Debate would be given a considerable priority by the Speaker while the Whips would always consider the argument that his union was involved in a very powerful reason for the inclusion of a sponsored Member.[1]

If the sponsored MPs are to fulfill this expectation, they must renew their knowledge of the union from time to time or they are likely to find their specialist knowledge sadly outdated.

Headquarters Communication

Thus, from the point of view of the unions, the Members, and the House of Commons, it is a reasonable assumption that strong channels of communication exist between the sponsored MPs and their unions. To test this assumption, an investigation will be made of existing channels. The contemporary situation is quite different from that of the nineteenth century, when the first union leaders were elected to the House of Commons. Then the links among the unions, their MPs, and the House of Commons were personal ones, because the MPs were simultaneously leaders of the unions.

Almost without exception, the channels of communication created since World War I flow between MPs and their unions' national headquarters (and, in the case of the miners, the various regional headquarters). The union leaders, for both administrative and political reasons, seek to ensure that all contact between the unions and sponsored MPs takes place through the unions' headquarters. The Engineers' union, for example, issued instructions from headquarters that all official attempts by local branches of the union to contact the AEF MPs must go through regular union channels. [2] Given the varied political sympathies of members of the AEF, it is not surprising that there have been reports of unhappiness over this regulation. [3] The centralisation, or attempted centralisation, of contact with the sponsored MPs gives union leadership the power to influence the material sent to the MPs by rank and file trade unionists, but such control will not necessarily be exercised arbitrarily. Headquarters may simply function as messengers. For example, in 1960 the head office of the NUM 'passed on' to its sponsored MPs a resolution from the Midlands area of the union which supported unilateral nuclear disarmament. Nationally, of course, the NUM was backing the multilateralists.

The centralization of links between MPs and unions is reflected in the general inactivity of MPs in the local affairs of their sponsoring unions. Continued stress on the distinctions between the political and industrial wings of the labour movement has occasional exceptions, as when Charles Howell, then an MP, served between 1959 and 1964 as the secretary of his local NUR branch.

Most unions retain some formal contact between their national executive committees and their sponsored Members. In a number of unions regular joint meetings between the executive committee and the MPs are held, for the mutual exchange of views.[4] Because of the large number of miners, their meetings have usually been attended by the chairman and secretary of the miners' group of MPs together with the NUM's national executive committee. In the NUR there are periodic meetings between the MPs and the political subcommittee of the union's executive. In addition, until 1959, the Member who served as secretary of the NUR group of MPs was given an office and other assistance at the NUR headquarters. This has been discontinued in more recent years, partly because the MP has since been given a small payment, although he continues to call at the NUR headquarters once a week for political discussions with members of the union's staff.[5] In the TGWU, the MPs meet regularly with the union's political officer, who serves as secretary to the group. Attempts to establish a similar practice in the NUGMW have not been very effective.

A second device for informing MPs of their union's position is to supply them with copies of executive documents.[6] This procedure does not necessarily lead to two-way communication.

A third device used by a number of unions is the inclusion of MPs on the union executive committee, not because of their status as MPs, but because of their union position.[7] The parallel between this and the position of the early trade union MPs is obvious. In the case of ASTMS one of their MPs, Russell Kerr, is a member of the executive committee, though it is not clear whether his membership derives from his status as an MP or from some other position within the union.[8] The inclusion of MPs in union executive committees to improve communication has varied results. In the case of TSSA, for example, while Ray Gunter was both an MP and president of the union he was able to play an active part in both the union and in the PLP. But when the late Ellis Smith was simultaneously president of the Patternmakers union and an MP, he seldom attended the union's executive committee meetings.

In addition to these formal channels, there are informal contacts, resulting from personal friendships between MPs and union leaders; and of course union leaders can always ring up the MPs to ask them to raise points in the House.

Most unions make a special effort to inform MPs of their views on

matters of particular concern to the unions, and for this the unions'
staffs will prepare a brief for the MPs to use. The NUM does this
regularly for debates on the mining industry, and most other unions
do it occasionally. But it is not a universal practice. The MP of the
Woodworkers' union, for instance, had to take the initiative to find
out if the union had any particular views on the Factory Act passed
by Parliament in 1960–61.[9] Since unions are often involved through
consultation in the drafting of legislation, direct resort to their sponsored MPs is usually a sign of failure to achieve the desired goals in
these behind-the-scenes consultations. Sometimes contacts between
Members and unions are used to try to prevent the MPs from
speaking on questions, especially industrial disputes, which might
embarrass the unions. [10]

Some unions, attempting to keep informed about the activity of individual sponsored MPs, require them to file periodic reports. [11] In
the case of USDAW a brief version is published in the annual report
of the union. For the miners, an annual group report is included in
the NUM's conference record.

Rank and File Communication

Most of the communication between unions and their sponsored MPs
is channelled through union headquarters. Two types of direct formal contact between sponsored MPs and the unions' rank and file
membership are made by the MPs' participating in union conferences
and contributing to the union journal.

Most of the sponsoring unions provide for the attendance of one or
more of their MPs at the union's conference. In some unions the MPs
are only visitors, taking no active part in the official proceedings of
the conference;[12] but the practice of having one MP address the
conference or submit a printed report is more usual,[13] in which case
the MP may be questioned on his report.[14] In the Shopworkers'
union (USDAW) the MPs, because they are sponsored, are permitted
to take part in debate on the floor of the conference, creating a certain amount of informal communication between the sponsored
members and the USDAW conference delegates. Even where unions
do not provide for discussion or comment on the parliamentary
reports to their conferences, there are occasional lapses. For example,
at the NUM conference in 1964 a member of the executive committee
intervened to praise the efforts of the MPs in the campaign against
smokeless fuels. Other attempts to comment on the report were

prevented by the conference chairman because 'the Parliamentary Group Report is here for information purposes and is not subject to the normal Conference procedures'.[15] While MPs' reports to union conferences are described as reports of their parliamentary activity, even the most casual inspection reveals that they are usually nothing more than general remarks on the overall political situation for the past year, with little reference to what the union's sponsored MPs have done. Finally, it should be pointed out that some unions make no regular provision for their MPs to present a report to the conference, take part in its proceedings, or even attend as visitors.[16]

Articles by sponsored MPs in union journals are usually a monthly version of the conference reports, seldom departing from general statements and generally emphasising the need for continued association between the Labour Party and the trade unions. Only occasionally will they become specific and elicit any sort of response from union members. Among unions with several sponsored MPs there is a clear tendency to rotate the contributions, so that all will obtain some exposure in the union journal. The MP's report is part of the journal's political section, and there is some feeling that the journals could increase their general political coverage.[17] But it may be questioned whether this would result in any large-scale increase in the amount of political information disseminated to the ordinary rank and file union members, given that only about eighteen per cent of the union members trouble to read their journals at all.[18]

The one-way nature of these links between sponsored MPs and union rank and file is increased by the poor internal communication within unions. For many union members their connection with the union begins and ends at the place of work, where the shop steward is the single most important figure.[19] But in many unions the shop stewards are not integrated into the official union organisation and are unable to transmit workers' grievances to the union and thus to the sponsored MPs.[20] Thus the union leaders' attempts to regulate and control all contact between MPs and rank and file union members become even more effective.

Communication with the TUC

Until recently the only institutional linkage between the sponsored MPs and the TUC was the custom by which the assistant secretary of the TUC attended occasional meetings of the Trade Union Group.[21] This has become less common since the 1960s, and one leading TUC official recently indicated that he viewed the Trade Union Group no differently from any number of other groups on both sides of the House of Commons: he was prepared to attend meetings when invited, but saw no reason for making special efforts to keep in touch with that particular group.[22] The weakness of the links between the sponsored MPs and the TUC is due to the fact that the MPs are sponsored by individual unions and not by the TUC. For this reason there has always been a problem of coordination between the MPs and the TUC, which dates back to the early part of the twentieth century and was reduced only when a TUC leader such as Walter Citrine made a special effort.[23] With the growth of direct government consultation there was no longer as much need for the TUC leadership to make this effort.

Communication Between MPs and their Unions: an Evaluation

How effective are the channels of communication between the unions and their MPs? In a survey of the views of the trade-union sponsored MPs, fifty-nine of the seventy-one responding said that they were 'not satisfied with the influence of Trade Union Members of Parliament within the Unions'.[24] Ten of the remaining twelve were either sponsored by USDAW or serving on the NEC of the Labour Party. The data suggest that the Shopworkers' practice, of supplying their sponsored MPs with all executive committee documents and allowing them to participate in the debates of the union conferences, fosters the Members' satisfaction with their role in the union movement.

Some union leaders are also dissatisfied with the existing state of communications, but they seem disinclined to act, because of the changing rationale of trade-union sponsorship of MPs. While lip service is still given to the traditional justification of utility, in the years since World War II a number of union officials have begun to acknowledge that assistance to the Labour Party, tradition, and prestige may be the actual reasons for the continuation of sponsorship.

Another major reason for this failure of communication is the joint recognition that the MPs might become a dangerous rival source of leadership within the unions.[25] Union leaders avoid such a threat to their own position by keeping the channels of communication centralised and relatively inefficient.

Martin Harrison, a leading student of relations between the unions and the Labour Party, has suggested: 'Few trade union Members of

Parliament can hope to give rank and file members any impression that they are doing a useful job. Moreover, many have only a vicarious knowledge of the decisions their own union is taking. Even within their own unions many of them tend to become unknown, vaguely superannuated figures'. [26]

This view was wistfully echoed by one of the sponsored MPs: 'Finally, on the question of what AEU [AEF] Members of Parliament really do. I attended a branch meeting the other night to speak on this subject and after an interesting evening I came away convinced that the majority of the members do not realize the importance of a strong parliamentary representation to our members'. [27]

The implications of this poor state of communications between sponsored MPs and their supporting unions in the mid-twentieth century are not completely clear. One point, however, seems obvious: the unions' expectation of an earlier period, that their Members would follow general union policy, has become less credible in an era when the MPs are no longer in intimate contact with the unions and cannot always keep informed about their unions' activities. But this also means that MPs today are more susceptible to pressure from union leaders.

The 'Kept Men'

It is not considered acceptable for a Member of the British Parliament to act as the paid political agent of some outside interest. No salary or other form of financial assistance from an outside body must be paid in exchange for specific parliamentary acts. When the MP takes part in debate, asks a question, or votes on matters of interest to the outside organisation, he has traditionally been expected to 'declare his interest'. [28] More generally, his primary responsibility is in theory to further the interests of his constituency and the nation.

Since the first trade union MPs were elected to the House of Commons in 1874, they have received various forms of assistance from their sponsoring unions. In the early years this was an absolute necessity, since there was no state payment of MPs until 1911. Union assistance has taken two primary forms, money and/or clerical aid. The financial assistance has sometimes included direct payments to the sponsored Member, as well as the financial support of his CLP and electoral expenses under the terms of the Hastings Agreement. In the 1959–64 Parliament, the direct financial assistance amounted to as much as £250 per year (for former officers of the NUGMW), but most unions paid less that that. The NUM and USDAW gave £200 to their MPs. ASLEF gave £150 to former officers serving in the House. BISAKTA, the Postoffice Workers and the NUR gave £100 to their MPs, and three other unions, the NGA, NUPE, and CAWU each gave £50.

Rather than making payments directly to its sponsored MPs, the AEF used to provide its sponsored Members with three fulltime secretaries. Following the salary increase for MPs after the 1964 election, the union reduced its assistance to the group to £100 per month, despite protests from the MPs. Thereafter the AEF group had to take the initiative in finding its own secretaries. [29]

Financial assistance may be used by unions (or other organisations) as a device for ensuring that MPs speak and act in agreement with them. And it is precisely on these grounds that such payments to MPs have been criticised by various authorities. The report of the Select Committee on Members' Interests (Declarations) in 1969 concluded: 'That it is contrary to the usage and derogatory to the dignity of this House that a Member should bring forward by speech or question, or advocate in this House or among his fellow Members any bill, motion, matter or cause for a fee, payment, retainer or reward, direct or indirect, which he has received, is receiving or expects to receive'. [30] So long as payments to an MP do not involve this expectation, they are accepted as a legitimate form of activity. The unions' occasional attempts to insist that sponsored MPs owe them some sort of responsibility raises questions about the limits actually imposed by existing conventions regarding outside payments. But usually union leaders accept the norms of parliamentary independence and act as buffers between the sponsored MPs and the union rank and file members.

Financial assistance to sponsored Members sometimes creates a paradox. This occurred in the early 1950s in the dispute within the Labour Party over German rearmament. A few unions, such as USDAW, require that their sponsored Members be subject to the whip of the PLP, and during the same rearmament dispute one of the Shopworkers' sponsored Members, Ernest Fernyhough, lost the whip because of his opposition to party policy. The union was forced to halt its aid to Fernyhough, even though it also opposed the party position. [31] When Fernyhough regained the whip of the PLP, his payments were resumed.

The same requirement caused serious problems for E. J. Milne in 1974. Milne had been a sharp critic of the Labour Party organization in the Northeast and the alleged corruption that infected the organisation. His local CLP finally refused to readopt him prior to the first election in 1974. Nonetheless, Milne stood for election as an Independent Labour candidate and was triumphant. But he lost the seat in the second election of 1974. USDAW sponsored MPs who lose their seats in the House of Commons are guaranteed a position with the union, but Milne's status as an independent MP for six months in 1974 not only lost him his pension rights but also the opportunity to return to work for the union. [32]

Union–MP Conflict

Writing in *The Observer* in 1968, Nora Beloff stated categorically: 'In the past nothing short of death or electoral defeat has ever deprived an MP of his union's support.' [33] Replying to a Tory inspired 1975 Commons debate on the rule of law, Alexander W. Lyon, M.P. (Minister of State at the Home Office) stated:

> The hon. Gentleman went further and said that Members of Parliament who are sponsored by trade unions must be under the influence of their trade unions. During the period in which Members of Parliament have been sponsored by trade unions that charge has been made more than once, and it has never been proved. Indeed, the independence of many of my colleagues who have been sponsored by trade unions now and in the past shows that they have never been told to vote or act in the House in a way which was inconsistent with their conscience. [34]

Both Beloff and Lyons are wrong! There have been a number of cases in which unions have refused support because of their MPs' failure to follow union policy. There have been threats of such action in other cases. We shall outline some of the prominent examples in the following pages, to point up the problems resulting from the role confusion of sponsored MPs. [35]

The first way in which unions can show political bias is by certifying someone as a possible parliamentary nominee. As we saw earlier, it was fear of this sort of bias that inspired opposition to a change in certification procedures within the UPW (see p 58 above). The second occasion for possible bias is in the actual nomination of someone before a CLP adoption meeting. As already indicated, a leftward drift in some of the major unions, such as the TGWU and the AEF, combined with the changing backgrounds of newer sponsored MPs, which are producing greater support for the left wing of the PLP, suggest that finding a friendly, winnable constituency is only one consideration in this decision about whom to nominate. Since most students of candidate selection in Britain feel that ideological considerations generally play little part in the actual adoption decisions of CLPs,[36] this means that the political views of the unions, as shown by the type of individuals they nominate for adoption, are seldom examined in any detail outside the unions themselves.

Once they are elected, union rules are seldom specific about the duties expected of the sponsored MPs, apart from the occasional requirement that they be subject to the Labour Party whip. And leaving the rulebooks aside, the unions are unable to define clearly what they expect MPs to do.[37] Traditionally they have insisted that MPs be veteran union members, but this practice continues to be followed more in form than in substance. Despite this lack of formal direction, trade unions have been prepared to take disciplinary action against MPs who disagree with them. This was first apparent in the nineteenth century, when the TUC removed Charles Fenwick from his position as secretary to the Parliamentary Committee because of his failure to support the eight hour day. This was only an indication of what unions might do, since Fenwick was acting in agreement with his own union, the Northumberland miners, in opposing the TUC.

Richard Bell and the Railway Servants

Several union – MP conflicts occurred between 1900 and 1910, the first involving Richard Bell and the Railway Servants' union (the predecessor of the NUR). Bell was the general secretary of the union from 1897 until 1910, and in 1899 he was chosen as a prospective candidate for Parliament by the Derby Trades Council. Following his adoption, the Labour Representation Committee (LRC) was created and Bell stood for election under its name. In the 1900 election Bell's expenses were paid by the Railway Servants from the union's general fund, and after the election he was paid a parliamentary salary of £200 a year from the same fund. But as soon as he took his seat, Bell began to move away from Keir Hardie, the other LRC MP, towards the Liberal Party.

Bell attracted little criticism of his attempts to further the interests of the members of his union. 'In many respects Richard Bell proved to be an admirable MP. He was extremely conscientious and hard working and never hesitated to intervene to secure the redress of grievances. In the ten weeks ending January 21, 1902, he made no less than forty-one representations to Ministers concerning the excessive hours of work of railwaymen.'[38] Still, Bell's flirtation with and eventual embrace of the Liberal Party caused difficulties with his union. In 1904 the Railway Servants agreed to continue supporting him despite his refusal to sign the constitution of the LRC. In the election of 1906, standing without the endorsement of the LRC but with the support of his union, he was re-elected. At the same time he was joined in the House of Commons by two other members of the Railway Servants' union, Walter Hudson and George Wardle, who were members of the Labour Party. From the beginning there was conflict between Bell and his two fellow unionists.[39]

In conjunction with W. E. Harvey, a Liberal MP, Bell made a behind-the-scenes move to secure additional inspectors to enforce the Railway Act of 1893, and this was one source of disagreement between Bell and his co-unionists. Hudson and Wardle introduced a measure calling for limitation on the hours of work of railwaymen while Bell was working on his project. Rather than disrupt his own scheme, Bell opposed their proposal, and when it came up for a vote he 'was one of the tellers in the Government lobby while Messrs. Wardle and Hudson were tellers in the other lobby counting up the Labour members' votes'.[40] Unfortunately Bell's position was at variance with the union's while Hudson and Wardle's was not.

Because of the continuing disagreement over politics between Bell and his union, the Railway Servants' executive committee considered and narrowly defeated a motion in 1909 calling for Bell's resignation as an MP and for the retention of his services only in the industrial sphere.[41] Nonetheless Bell withdrew from both the union and parliamentary politics in 1910, when the president of the Board of Trade, Winston Churchill, appointed him superintendent of Employment Exchanges. His additional problems with the Derby Labour Party are suggested by the ease with which the Railway Servants secured the Derby Labour candidature for J. H. Thomas.[42]

The Lib-Lab Miners

A number of cases of union–MP conflict arose out of the decision of
the MFGB to affiliate to the Labour Party in 1909. Most of the
miners' MPs followed the union and joined the Labour Party in the
House of Commons. Those who did not were 'compelled' to change
or to face the loss of their union salaries. The Welsh miner 'Mabon'
made the change, even though it made no difference in his political
beliefs.[43] But three of the old Lib-Labs, Thomas Burt, John Wilson,
and Charles Fenwick, refused to sign the Labour Party constitution
and thereby lost their union salaries.[44] Despite this, their high
personal standing in their constituencies meant that no Labour candidates opposed them in 1910.[45]

In the early 1920s J. G. Hancock, another Lib-Lab, was denied the
Labour whip because of his membership of the Liberal Party. No
longer a member of the PLP, Hancock 'lost the £100 a year
Parliamentary allowance (plus election expenses) which Labour
miners' MPs drew from the MFGB Political Fund'.[46] The MFGB
(the predecessor of the NUM) was the most decentralised British
trade union, with its regional organisations choosing candidates
while financial control was exercised from the centre. Hancock had
considerable local support and was able to continue to serve in
Parliament until 1922, despite the opposition of MFGB headquarters.

The Nottingham Miners

The Nottingham miners were involved in a dispute with George
Spencer, one of their MPs and former leader, as a result of the
General Strike of 1926. During the struggle that followed the strike,
Spencer left the MFGB and the Labour Party to organise his own
'nonpolitical' union to secure the best possible terms from the mine
owners to end the discord in Nottinghamshire. Disowned by the
MFGB, Spencer was then denied the Labour Party whip for what
The Times termed his 'industrial' rather than 'political activity'.[47]
With neither MFGB nor Labour Party support, and committed to his
'nonpolitical' union, he did not stand for re-election in 1929. Eight
years later Spencer rejoined the MFGB, but did not seek a new
parliamentary career.

J. H. Thomas and the National Union of Railwaymen

Conflict between an MP and his sponsoring union also arose out of the political crisis of 1931 and the formation of the national Government by J. Ramsay MacDonald. J. H. Thomas, a leader of the NUR and MP since 1910, had been Lord Privy Seal in the Labour government and now followed MacDonald into the new government. Thomas' activities during the twenties had not endeared him to all of his colleagues; they were particularly distrustful of his snobbishness, and their attitude seemed justified when he joined MacDonald in the National Government. The NUR took the first step by terminating his leave of absence as political general secretary. He was then asked to resign either his union position or his position in the National Government. Thomas refused to resign from the government, but he did offer his resignation from the union position. The NUR accepted his resignation, dropped him from its list of sponsored candidates, and stopped his annual union salary of £250.[48] Thomas retained considerable local support in Derby, including that of the local branch of the NUR,[49] and in 1931 he was re-elected while all the NUR-sponsored candidates joined many other Labour candidates in defeat.

Union–MP Conflict in Other Unions

Another union–Member conflict involving the miners arose at the end of the World War I coalition when Stephen Walsh, parliamentary secretary to the Local Government Board, agreed to resign only after pressure from the Lancashire and Cheshire miners who were supporting him.[50] And an example of union pressures which did not result in the loss of support arose from the 1931 crisis. Sir Robert Young, a former general secretary of the Engineers' union, had served as chairman of Ways and Means of the House of Commons under the second Labour government. After the 1931 crisis, Young wrote to his local CLP, to the Labour Party NEC, and to his union for advice on what his course of action should be. Quite clearly he was willing to allow these bodies to define his role in the crisis. When the union advised him to resign as chairman of Ways and Means, he did so without argument, despite his being criticised in the House of Commons for having allowed an extra-parliamentary organisation to determine his conduct.[51]

With the split between the ILP and the Labour Party in the early

1930s, at least one union caused an MP to change his position, and here the two chief trade unionists involved were David Kirkwood and George Buchanan. Kirkwood rejoined the Labour Party almost immediately following its split with the ILP; however, Buchanan resisted until the late 1930s, when, faced with the loss of his £4 a week union allowance as well as the possibility of being confronted with a regular Labour candidate, he too rejoined the party.[52] Buchanan went on to become minister of pensions in the third Labour government.

Loss or the threat of loss of union support has not ceased in the years since World War II. We have already referred to the temporary loss of USDAW support for E. Fernyhough during the Bevanite defence dispute. In 1959 Roy Mason received a letter from the NUM censuring him for his published criticism of union attempts to silence MPs on industrial disputes.[53]

In the TGWU there were recurrent demands at union conferences that George Brown should be dropped from the list of TGWU-sponsored MPs, because of actions which some union members had not liked. For example, Brown received assistance from Cecil King and the Mirror group of newspapers while the Labour Party was in opposition during the 1950s. The Mirror group had opposed the 1958 busmen's strike, and Brown's association with the newspapers was an especially sore point.[54] Despite additional conflict growing out of the defence dispute in 1961–62 and an attempt by the Labour government to impose an incomes policy, Brown seemed secure. But action by the TGWU conferences in 1967 and 1969 finally caused Brown and three other TGWU MPs to lose their sponsored status just before the 1970 General Election;[55] and the TGWU's general policy was reaffirmed in 1974.

Still another case involved the NUR. Unlike most other unions, the NUR does not decide whom it will sponsor until the individual has been adopted by a CLP. The union uses the Labour Party's List B rather than its List A of potential parliamentary candidates; it is the individual's responsibility to get his name onto that list. Stan Mills, a member of the NUR, had been on List B and a parliamentary candidate for Dorking in 1959. In 1961 the NEC dropped Mills from List B because of his support for the Campaign for Nuclear Disarmament, and the NUR leadership refused to intervene to persuade the party to reverse its decision. After the fight over unilateralism had passed its height, the party restored Mills' name to List B.[56] In a similar situation involving DATA during the defence dispute, the union dropped R. L. Howarth from its panel of possible parliamentary nominees because of his failure to support the unilateralists. [57]

Political bias also influenced the AEF during the 1950s and 60s when, under the right wing leadership of Sir William Carron, it refused to support the parliamentary candidacy of Ernie Roberts, a left wing member of the union. [58] Mills, Howarth, and Roberts were not MPs, but the same sort of action could be taken against sitting MPs. In 1966, for example, Charles Pannell was denied renomination for his parliamentary seat by his Communist-dominated local branch of the AEF. The union's national leadership was forced to step in to ensure that Pannell could continue in the House of Commons, and he changed his area of membership within the AEF to avoid similar problems in the future. [59]

The most notable example of longterm union–MP conflict in recent years was that of Aneurin Bevan and the Miners' union. Bevan's clear loyalty to his constituents in Ebbw Vale, [60] gave him a base from which it was impossible to dislodge him. Bevan was able to take advantage of this, combined with judicious retreats at the proper moments, to avoid pushing the Miners' union to a showdown. His first brush with the union came as a result of his support for Sir Oswald Mosley's 'New Party' in 1931. Bevan was to speak to a meeting of the Mosley group, but the morning before his speech the MFGB announced that he would be dropped from their list of sponsored candidates if he spoke. 'Nye never appeared and no apology was received. His bluff had been called.' [61]

But Bevan was not always so easily cowed. In 1938, with an assurance from the South Wales miners that they would back him against a regular Labour candidate, he braved expulsion from the party over the issue of a popular front with the Communists. [62] The local autonomy in the miners' union clearly worked to Bevan's adtantage.

Another conflict arose in 1942 when Herbert Morrison, home secretary in the coalition Cabinet, warned *The Daily Mirror* about an indiscreet political cartoon which the paper had published. After criticising Morrison's actions in the House of Commons, Bevan was threatened by a member of the TUC General Council, who indicated that 'the General Council was seriously considering whether it was worthwhile spending money on MPs who spoke as Bevan had spoken'. [63] Bevan immediately replied that this threat could be a breach of the privileges of parliament. The matter was dropped, but not forgotten.

In 1944 yet another conflict arose between Bevan and the unions outside Parliament. Bevan was attacking the minister of labour, Ernest Bevin, for regulations issued in response to strikes during the war (the famous Regulation IAA). The general council of the TUC was still unhappy with Bevan because of the earlier incident.

> Mr. Ebby Edwards, at that time chairman of the General Council, was instructed to write to Mr. Ebby Edwards, secretary of the Mineworkers' Federaton, urging fresh disciplinary action. When Bevan heard of this move he telephoned Ebby Edwards to ask him whether the Miners' Federation wanted a privilege case raised in the House of Commons. If they did not, they would be well advised to drop any talk of sanctions against him. The advice was taken. [64]

Bevan's willingness to invoke parliamentary privilege will be discussed below.

The most recent example of union—MP conflict came during the dispute over Britain's decision to enter the Common Market. [65] When the Heath government finally put the matter to a vote in the House of Commons on 28 October 1971, both parties suffered major defections from their ranks, with thirty-nine Tories voting against their own government and sixty-nine Labour MPs (including Roy Jenkins, then deputy leader) voting with the government. As shown in Table VI–1, the union-sponsored MPs were less likely to rebel against the Three Line Whip laid down by the Labour Party than were the non-sponsored MPs.

Given the traditional loyalty of the sponsored MPs, this is not surprising, until we note which MPs were loyal and which took part in the revolt. All the sponsored MPs in the Tribune Group supported the PLP leadership, while stalwarts of the right wing, such as Charles Pannell, Roy Gunter, Tom Bradley, and William Rodgers, were found among the rebels. It was the older trade unionists, like Pannell and Gunter, who felt compelled to vote against the more leftwing position of the PLP leadership, while the younger MPs were more likely to support it. [66] And the number of rebels might have been larger if considerable pressure had not been put on the sponsored MPs by unions opposing entry. For example, at a TGWU conference in July 1971 an executive officer urged the union to

TABLE VI – 1

SPONSORED MPs AND THE COMMON MARKET VOTE

Member's Position	Sponsored MPs	Non-sponsored Labour MPs	All Labour MPs
Supported Government	14	55	69
Abstained	10	10	20
Supported Labour Party	87	111	198
Totals	111	176	287
	$df - 2$	$X^2 - 13.8$	P 0.01

Sources: *The Political Companion*, No. 9 (October – December 1971), pp. 76 – 85; The Labour Party Annual Conference, *Report* (1970), pp. 289 – 312, Appendix 3.

withdraw support from any of its MPs who voted against the party in support of Britain's entry into the Common Market. [67] This view was not accepted by the union conference, although the threat was allowed to remain open when another officer declared that the party outweighed the unions, that a candidate once elected was responsible to his constituents and could disagree with the union, but that the union would take it into account at the time of the next nomination. And a resolution adopted by the TGWU conference specifically stated that the union, when deciding whom to sponsor, whould 'take account of applicants' political views and previous stewardship'. [68] How this might have been applied to the one Common Market rebel sponsored by the TGWU, Maurice Foley, is uncertain, since he resigned his seat in early 1973 to take a position with the European Economic Community.

The only reported action after the Common Market vote involved the AEF in 1971 when three of its MPs voted in favour of entry in opposition to the position of the union. A resolution presented to April 1972 national committee meeting of the AEF would have resulted in their losing union support. The resolution was defeated by a vote of thirty-four to eighteen and Austin Albu, Charles Pannell and B. T. Ford were able to relax again. [69]

But the union action contributed to the retirement of Albu and Pannell in the first General Election of 1974.

The Common Market referendum of 5 June, 1975 also caused

problems for some sponsored MPs. With most unions opposing a Yes vote and about half of the MPs supporting it, the conflict is not surprising. What is noticeable is the speed with which it happened. Less than a month after the referendum, the Yorkshire area council of the NUM voted to censure its sponsored MPs who had supported a Yes vote and to set down guidelines to which the MPs must adhere in the future.[70] While the miners claimed that the EEC issue was closed, it was clear that the union was claiming extraordinary authority over the MPs. The union's action was referred to the Commons Select Committee on Privileges two days later,[71] and the Committee reported in October that the union's efforts did constitute a serious contempt of the privileges of Parliament.[72] But the Committee went on to recommend no further action against the union because the national leadership of the NUM had repudiated the action of the Yorkshire region.

The five MPs supported by the Yorkshire miners, Roy Mason, Edwin Wainwright, Alfred Roberts, Joseph Harper and Alec Woodall, continued under conflicting pressures. Meetings within their respective CLPs demonstrated support for the MPs by rank and file Party members and by union representatives from the NUR, NUPE and USDAW who reaffirmed the concept that MPs represented constituents other than miners. But the London Co-operative Society went on record to support the action of the Yorkshire miners council.[73] And while there was considerable outcry over the union-MP conflict which derived from the EEC referendum, less noticed was a proposal to impose a retirement age on MPs sponsored by the Yorkshire miners, as the Durham and the Derbyshire miners had done previously, with the suggestion that political difference was a contributing factor to this action.[74] Roberts and Wainwright were sixty-seven in 1975, and Harper was sixty-one. Only Mason at fifty-one and Woodall at fifty-seven could view the imposition of a reasonable retirement age with any equinimity.

But the general threat remained, and in recent years has been particularly identified with the policy of the TGWU. The resolutions adopted by TGWU conferences in the late 1960s and early 1970s, made it clear that the union was concerned with the positions taken by its sponsored MPs. This led to some of the conflict (to be discussed later) involving the dispute over the prices and incomes policy. It also provided the background for a number of other individual disputes. In 1972, for example, Peter Doig told the Transport workers to drop their support for him because of union criticism of Doig's opposition to some aspects of miners' picketing during the 1972 miners' strike. Doig clearly resented the attempts by the union to pressure him. [75] A more ambiguous situation developed in 1973 when the Transport House branch of the TGWU urged that Reg Prentice be dropped from the union's list of MPs because of his position on compliance with the Conservative Industrial Relations Act. [76]

Nothing came of this action, but it was remembered in 1975 when Prentice criticised the unions for "Welshing" on the Social Contract. Despite his own radical actions as Secretary of State for Education, Prentice seemed out of touch with union militants in the TGWU and with Party rank and file activists. Prentice's alienation from his CLP led to its decision on 23 July to drop Prentice as its potential candidate for the next General Election. With the union also considering dropping Prentice from its list of sponsored candidates, [77] his future as a Labour MP seemed limited indeed.

While Prentice's problem stemmed primarily from local activists in his CLP, the theory of representation that underlay it was analogous to the position held by union militants who demanded MP responsibility to the supporting union. As made clear by Frank Allaun and others in correspondence in *The Times*, it was the organisation that the MP should answer to, not the party in general, the entire constituency of the country at large. [78]

Still another example of reported union pressure occurred in January 1975 when Hugh McCartney, sponsored by the TGWU, joined with two other Labour and three Conservative MPs for a tour of the Republic of South Africa. McCartney's participation in the tour upset the left wing of the PLP and the Whips' Office. More importantly, it led Alex Kitson, the Scottish leader of the Transport workers, to announce that he would question McCartney about his overseas visit and 'caution' him about such activity if his answers were not satisfactory. [79]

All of these cases merely reaffirm what sponsored MPs already know. They run the risk of losing their sponsored status at any time because of conflict with their unions, and this is especially true if the conflict put the MP at odds with the Labour Party as well. 'The belief that rebels cannot be sponsored by a union is still prevalent among Labour MPs, and Victor Yates maintained that this was the reason he did not become a sponsored candidate until before the 1964 general election'. [80]

Parliamentary Privilege

MPs are protected from outside pressure by a number of factors: party discipline allows them to substitute one set of group pressures for another. Strong local support will allow an MP to ignore political parties, but few have that degree of support. The most important legal defence of their independent position is found in what is known as parliamentary privilege. Basically, the privileges of Parliament are the historic rights claimed by Parliament, which allow it to function free from external pressure. Violations of these privileges may be punished by Parliament without recourse to ordinary courts, and the House of Commons maintains a regular select committee to investigate alleged violations.

The idea that privilege protects a sponsored MP from union attempts to coerce him is widely accepted among the trade unionists in the House of Commons, [81] even if they resented attempts by some MPs, such as Aneurin Bevan, to use it for the protection of minority points of view. [82] Many union leaders outside Parliament have considerable respect for parliamentary privileges. In late 1975, for example, when the General Secretary of the NUR threatened to stop support for the union's MPs if they did not oppose cuts in the railway industry, he was persuaded to withdraw his remarks simply by raising the question of a violation of privilege. [83] Union leaders also find privilege a useful concept in resisting effort by their rank and file members to coerce MPs.

The actual degree of protection afforded by privilege, as opposed to the myth of such protection, is controversial. A decision by the USDAW to cease its support of W. A. Robinson in 1944 led to an investigation by the parliamentary Select Committee on Privilege, which concluded that no violation had in fact taken place. But the report went on to say: 'A statement that such support would be withdrawn unless certain action was taken in Parliament in relation to the business of the House might come within the principles laid down in the precedents as a breach of privilege. It depends on the circumstances'. [84]

The second leading case involved W. J. Brown and the Civil Service Clerical Association. Brown entered into a contractual relationship with the association in 1942 to represent its views in Parliament. When the association terminated the contract in 1946, Brown raised the question of privilege. But again the report of the select committee concluded that no violation of privilege had occurred and then went on to state: 'Not every action by an outside body which may influence the conduct of a Member of Parliament as such could now be regarded as a breach of privilege, even if it were calculated and intended to bring pressure on the Member to take or to refrain from taking a particular course'. [85] In fact, in neither the Brown nor the Robinson case was anyone or any group cited for a violation of parliamentary privilege. The actions of the House since 1947 have confirmed this pattern. When Frank Cousins was virtually ordered by the TGWU to lead the fight against the Prices and Incomes Bill in 1966 and then to resign from Parliament, the Speaker rejected the contention that this was a breach of privilege. [86]

The claim of privilege was raised again in 1971, when the TGWU conference heard a speech attacking its sponsored MPs and threatening them with loss of support if they voted in favour of entry into the Common Market. When the question of referring this to the select committee was discussed in the House of Commons, a number of sponsored MPs urged that the matter be dropped for fear of what the committee might conclude. As one TGWU MP expressed it:

> The question of sponsorship by trade unions is purely a voluntary arrangement and any honourable Member, if he feels intimidated in any way, is entitled to withdraw at any time from that sponsorship. Nevertheless sponsorship is a long and honoured tradition in the House of Commons.
>
> As a Member sponsored by the TGWU, I have had no pressure put upon me at any time on any issue before the House. In pursuing this matter, the House is getting into an *all-too-fragile* atmosphere. The matter should be dropped without further debate [87] [emphasis added]

Nonetheless, the TGWU's actions were referred to the Select Committee on Privileges, whose interim report merely reaffirmed the action of the House in the Robinson case without asserting that this 1971 action was a breach of privilege. [88]

One thing is clear in all these cases. Union pressure may be a breach of privilege if the circumstances are right. But such circumstances will probably be rare and hard to find. On the other hand, it is equally clear that as long as the MPs and the union leaders believe that privilege protects the MPs from union pressure, both are likely to act in accordance with that view.

The decision of the Privileges Committee in October 1975 that the action of the Yorkshire Miners did, in fact, constitute a serious contempt of the Privileges of Parliament was of no help in clarifying the matter. The Committee's refusal to recommend further action because the national leadership of the NUM had repudiated the action of the Yorkshire region's action meant that its findings in the case may have no real significance. On the other hand, it is true that this was the first case where the Committee did make a positive finding in the face of union action and it may form the basis for more serious action in the future. And it clearly reinforced the belief of both union leaders and MPs that union action might constitute a breach of privilege. As long as the leaders and MPs believe that, they are likely to behave in such a way to avoid the matter in the future.

Evaluation

Union–MP relations in the mid-twentieth century can be viewed in a number of different ways. For the most part existing channels of communication are relatively weak and inefficient, insofar as they are meant to enable the unions to make regular use of the MPs in the House of Commons. Neither the MPs nor the unions are seriously interested in keeping the channels open.

Some unions continue the practice of an earlier era by providing token financial assistance for MPs, and they are prepared to withdraw support because of political differences. In some cases, such as that of Richard Bell, this can mean retirement from the House of Commons. In most cases, however, neither the threat of union action nor the action itself is sufficient to force out the MP. But the idea that the sponsored MPs are responsible to their sponsoring union is of continuing importance, even if unions are less likely to take action against MPs than they were fifty years ago.

The MPs' major protection from union pressure seems to be a strong local base. If the MP retains the confidence of his local electorate and constituency party, neither union retiremet rules nor political pressures can remove him from his seat. [89] The chief legal protection of the MPs' independence – parliamentary privilege – seems to be of questionable value in the light of the Robinson and Brown cases. However, the *myth* that privilege provides protection discourages union pressure and gives the MP the courage and strength to resist such pressure.

To further illustrate the topic of union–MP relations, the following chapters will present two case studies of recent political disputes within the Labour Party. The issues involved in these disputes were: the question of multilateral *vs.* unilateral disarmament in 1960–61; and the Labour government's prices and incomes policy in 1964–69. The topics for the case studies were chosen for three reasons. First, both were characterised by a high degree of conflict between the position espoused by the Labour Party and that of many trade unions. Thus they illustrate the effect of conflicting pressures on a sponsored MP. Second, they covered two diverse areas, which our earlier analysis of floor action in the House of Commons suggested might produce different patterns of union–MP relations. Third, both disputes took place in the last fifteen years and any conclusions which might be derived from them would have greater relevance for the 1970s and 1980s than case studies drawn from an earlier era.

Chapter VII
Union–MP Relations and the Defence Dispute of 1960–1961[1]

A study of the defence dispute within the Labour Party in 1960–61 throws further light on the relations between sponsored MPs and their unions; but it has one major drawback. The defence dispute was not an industrial conflict. Despite the deep commitment of a few trade unionists, there were many who felt that the issue was secondary to the principal economic functions of the unions. When trade unionists were asked what they felt to be the most urgent problem facing the TUC in 1959, only thirteen per cent mentioned the H-Bomb (and this was the only noneconomic or nonindustrial issue mentioned). By 1964, this had shrunk to four per cent.[2]

The only two unions to poll their rank and file members on the subject were the Typographical Association (TA) and the National Association of Operative Plasters. Both supported the multilateralists, with a majority of three to one in the TA.[3] With so many union members backing the multilateralist position, an MP's refusal to follow the 1960 party conference in supporting the unilateralists may have had less impact than might otherwise have happened.

The Issue of an Independent Deterrent

The basic issue involved in the dispute was whether Britain should retain its 'independent deterrent' and try to secure multilateral disarmament by all nations having nuclear weapons, or whether to disarm and thus set a moral example for the rest of the world to follow.

Within the labour movement these alternatives formed the basis for discussion. Even the 'Foreign Policy and Defence' statement issued by the Party NEC in July of 1960 acknowledged that Britain's 'independent deterrent' was in fact not independent. The statement further urged that the United Kingdom should work for world disarmament and abandon its own nuclear weapons. Britain's contribution to the western alliance should be in the form of conventional military might, while the United States would provide the nuclear weapons.[4] This statement might have been acceptable to the supporters of unilateral disarmament, except that it would not have eliminated the use of British bases by nuclear-armed American planes and ships.

The unilateralists, on the other hand, wanted Britain to abandon her own nuclear weapons, to cease testing and manufacturing them, and to stop allowing British soil to be used as a base for American nuclear weapons. Some unilateralists were genuine pacifists who opposed all war on religious or moral grounds; some were nuclear pacifists who feared what might happen to Britain in the event of nuclear war, especially if Britain were to provoke attack by maintaining her own nuclear weapons system; some were anti-American, resenting the success of rampant American capitalism and the way in which the United States had supplanted the United Kingdom as a major world power; still others were Little Englanders who wished to retreat from Britain's overseas commitments and concentrate their attention on the British Isles. There were also some who were not utterly antagonistic to the Soviet Union. Finally there was an element of the British anti-German sentiment which had been so important in the battle over German rearmament in the early 1950s. If Britain were to keep the Bomb, it would be only a matter of time before Germany would also demand it. This anti-German feeling played a part in the subsidiary issue of the training of German troops in Wales.

Organised in the Campaign for Nuclear Disarmament (CND), and in other groups such as the Committee of One Hundred headed by Bertrand Russell, the unilateralists were an important force in British politics throughout the middle and late 1950s and early 1960s. Their annual Easter March from Aldermaston to London sometimes included thousands of demonstrators. But as Kingsley Martin stated: 'Unless they work through the Labour movement, nuclear disarmers are simply marching about to satisfy their own conscience and expressing their sense of the sin and horror of nuclear war'.[5] The Labour Party's status in Opposition and the pacifist tradition of some of its supporters suggested that converting the party to the unilateralist position would not be all that difficult.

The Unions and the 1960 Party Conference

The major obstacles to any such takeover of the Labour Party were the trade unions, the traditional opponents of the party's pacifist elements. When Frank Cousins came to power in the TGWU in 1956, a possibility emerged that he might be willing to join the unilateralists. Cousins was far more radical than either Arthur Deakin or Ernest Bevin, his predecessors as general secretary of the TGWU. In 1959 the TGWU conference voted to support the unilateralists, and the support of unilateralists in other unions was indicated when the most conservative of Britain's six largest unions, the NUGMW, temporarily joined the unilateralist camp.[6]

Many union conferences in 1960 approved resolutions favouring some sort of unilateral disarmament. The AEF, USDAW, and the NUR joined with the TGWU in supporting unilateral disarmament. The NUGMW did not repeat its action of 1959, but only one other of the six largest unions, the NUM, joined it in opposing the unilateralists. The crisis was reached on Wednesday, 5 October 1960, at the conclusion of a long debate over the party leadership's statement on foreign policy and defence, when the Party conference defeated the leadership and in place of its statement adopted a unilateralist resolution moved by the AEF, which advocated not only Britain's abandonment of her own nuclear capability, but also a refusal to allow American nuclear weapons to be based in Britain.[7] A particular annoyance was the American submarine base at Holy Loch in Scotland.

The action was not unexpected, and in the course of the debate Hugh Gaitskell, the leader of the PLP, inaugurated the next stage of the dispute when he said:

> I say this to you: we may lose the vote today and the result may deal this Party a grave blow. It may not be possible to prevent it, but I think there are many of us who will not accept that this blow need be mortal, who will fight and fight and fight again to save the Party we love. We will fight and fight and fight again to bring back sanity and honesty and dignity so

that our Party with its great past may retain its glory and its greatness. [8]

Gaitskell's open defiance of the conference decisions marked the opening of a struggle concerning the sources of legitimate authority within the party,[9] and the MPs soon found that they must support one side or the other.

Of the nineteen unions sponsoring MPs in the 1959–64 Parliament, eight of them, sponsoring forty-one MPs, supported the unilateral resolution passed by the 1960 party conference. Eleven unions, sponsoring fifty MPs, opposed the unilateralists. This division of the unions according to their position at the 1960 conference is something of an oversimplification for most of them had serious internal differences on the question. Even within the TGWU there was a significant element which opposed Cousins and the unilateralists. It had been a TGWU resolution (theoretically not opposing NATO) which had led to the confused results at the 1960 TUC. [10] The miners supported the multilateralist position over the objections of several of their regional branches. Had the unilateralists in the Yorkshire Miners' Association been able to capture control of that organisation, they might have been able to ally with the Communist-controlled Scottish and South Wales miners to defeat the multilateralists from Durham, the West Midlands, and Nottinghamshire. As it was, the multilateralists barely managed to retain control of the Yorkshire Miners' Association. [11]

The three remaining major unions supporting the unilateralists were also deeply divided. The AEF's unilateralism was the result of Communist infiltration of the union's power structure, aided by the union's cumbersome, indirect electoral system. The fact that the union's president, Sir William Carron, was opposed to the unilateralists could not alter the situation. USDAW supported the unilateralists for several reasons. This union has strong links with the Co-operative societies, and just ten days before the union's conference in 1960 the Co-operative Party had come out for unilateralism, undoubtedly influencing some of the delegates to the Shopworkers' meeting. USDAW also had strong links with the old radical ILP tradition. Finally, some of USDAW's support for the unilateralists resulted from the 1959 split in the Labour Party over Hugh Gaitskell's attempt to change *clause four* of the party constitution dealing with nationalisation.[12] The NUR also joined the unilateralists, but its decision at the 1960 NUR annual general meeting (AGM) had been made by a one-vote margin, because some of the delegates to the AGM had not realised the implication of their votes. [13] How strong their commitment to unilateralism would be on the basis of one vote was a moot point.

The internal divisions of the unions were further aggravated when the leaders of three of the unilateralist unions – Alan Birch (general secretary, USDAW), Sir William Carron (president, AEF), and Sidney Green (general secretary, NUR) – joined with seventeen other union leaders to announce their personal support for Gaitskell and the multilateralist position. [14] Thus, while the voting at the party conference apparently clearly defined the unions' positions, a host of confusing and conflicting forces lurked in the background.

With Gaitskell's speech to the 1960 party conference, the multilateralists began to try and use the internal divisions of the unions as the basis for a campaign to convert the unions to the official defence policy. The organisation used by the multilateralists, the Campaign for Democratic Socialism (CDS), hoped to generate enough rank and file pressure to persuade the unions to change their position before the 1961 party conference, in order to heal the divison within the party. [15]

Gaitskell and the PLP: Support, Opposition, and Revolt

The unilateralists may have won at the party conference, but they still had to secure the compliance of the PLP. Gaitskell's open defiance of the conference had earned the criticism of some who, while not being unilateralists, felt that he was needlessly splitting the party. In an almost unprecedented move, Gaitskell's opponents offered Harold Wilson as an alternative candidate for the leadership of the PLP in the 1960–61 parliamentary session. But Labour MPs demonstrated their support for Gaitskell by giving him a two-to-one margin over Wilson. [16] In late November 1960, support for Gaitskell was further demonstrated during the election of twelve members of the PLP's Parliamentary Committee, when three of Gaitskell's supporters, Michael Stewart, Ray Gunter, and Douglas Houghton, were added and the number of votes for Wilson and Fred Lee (an ally of Wilson's) was sharply reduced. Wilson had received the highest number of votes in the election to the Parliamentary Committee in 1959, but in 1960 he ranked ninth out of twelve (although by 1961 he had regained first place). A bloc of some seventy 'loyal' trade unionists, who had circulated a list of 'twelve recommended names' before the election, was partly responsible for the changes in the Parliamentary Committee in 1960.[17] Charles Pannell, the secretary of the Trade Union Group, confirmed press reports of support for Gaitskell among the sponsored MPs in his report on the Group's activities for 1959–60:

> We come together again at a moment of crisis. The Party Conference, by a small majority, finds itself at variance with the overwhelming majority of the Parliamentary Party and the decision of the Trade Union Congress.
>
> Our tradition in the past has been to assert that we are not a pressure group and so we have concentrated our energies on industrial matters. In the new and strained situation of today, while still wishing to maintain the principle that there shall not be parties within the Party, nevertheless we as the trustees of those who founded this Party and for whom it primarily exists, must now consider whether we should widen the scope of our discussions so that with colleagues of like mind we may ensure the effective electoral continuance of our Movement.[18]

Pannell was suggesting a role which the Group has generally ceased to play in the years since World War II.

Division 22

There was still very little public information on how individual MPs stood in the controversy. The degree to which Gaitskell's defiance of the party conference had affected the PLP became public knowledge on 13 December 1960, when the Opposition introduced a motion in the House of Commons which was critical of the government's defence policies without accepting the unilateralist position. When the House divided on this motion, the Opposition mustered only 163 votes.[19] This was the high point of unilateralism in the PLP, for ninety-two Labour MPs failed to vote in spite of a Three Line Whip.[20] The twenty-three sponsored MPs among them accounted for only a quarter of the nonvoters, while in the PLP as a whole sponsored MPs comprised over a third of all Members.

The ninety-two MPs who failed to vote in Division 22 were not all unilateralists. One report has divided them into three groups. The first includes about twenty Members who had been prevented from voting by illness or other nonpolitical reasons; some of these men were paired with Conservatives and no particular significance can be ascribed to their absence. Another twenty members had quarrelled with Gaitskell's open defiance of the party conference. This left only about fifty-two hard-core unilateralists. [21]

An alternative way to classify the MPs is based partly on the press reports following Division 22. The seventy-two MPs reported to have remained in their seats during the Division included eight sponsored MPs.[22] There were, of course, an additional fifteen sponsored MPs and five other Labour MPs who failed to take part in the vote. The complete list of twenty-three non-voting sponsored MPs will be used in the remainder of our analysis because the Members who failed to vote without publicly abstaining included a number whose sympathies would probably have been with the abstainers. They may have been absent from the division because of illness or for other reasons that prevented them from making public their views.

Union-MP Agreement

Having determined the positions of MPs in this dispute, a different question can then be asked: to what extent did the MPs agree with the views of their unions? Using categories developed by Philip Williams and Keith Hindell based on the unions' votes at the 1960 and 1961 Labour Party conferences, the unions can be classified as multilateral in both years (MM); unilateral in 1960 and multilateral in 1961 (UM); or unilateral in both years (UU). [23] MPs agreed with the MM unions by obeying the Three Line Whip in Division 22. They agreed with UM unions if they failed to vote in the division since these unions were still officially unilateralist in December 1960. Agreement with the UU unions has also been defined as not voting in Division 22. As shown in Table VII–1, the sponsored MPs did not show a significant amount of agreement with their sponsoring unions.

More detailed analysis of those MPs sponsored by the NUM based on the position taken by regional organizations at the 1960 NUM conference further supports this conclusion. [24] For a majority of the MPs sponsored by the miners' union, as well as for a majority of all sponsored MPs, the expectation of party loyalty took precedence over expectations of loyalty to the sponsoring group.

TABLE VII – 1

SPONSORED MPs AGREEMENT OR DISAGREEMENT
WITH SPONSORING UNIONS

Union Position	Agree with Union	Disagree with Union	Total
MM	39	11	50
UM	9	17	26
UU	3	12	15
Total	51	40	91

$$(X^2 - 22.17; P \ 0.05; df - 2)$$

Role Confusion and Potential Influence

The lack of any significant correlation between the positions of the unions and of their sponsored MPs might suggest a failure of the unions to control their parliamentary representatives, but it does not prove that the unions actually attempted to influence the MPs. Evidence of attempted or potential influence must be found elsewhere. One fertile source are the union records and reports in 1960, 1961, and 1962, which reveal a number of attempts to hold sponsored MPs responsible to the unions for their actions. Of the nineteen unions sponsoring successful candidates at the time of the 1959 General Election, eight are known to have shown some dissatisfaction with the conduct of their MPs during 1960, 1961, or 1962. These eight unions sponsored seventy-six of the ninety-one sponsored Members remaining in the House of Commons on 13 December 1960.[25]

In no case did the criticism of the MPs secure official union support. Beyond this, the precise strength of the critics is difficult to determine. The issue came to a vote, for which we have results at only one union conference. Elsewhere, criticism was restricted to the public utterances of delegates in conference debate, or to resolutions which were proposed but failed for one reason or another to be considered at the conferences, or to resolutions which were defeated without any indication of the strength of their support. The potential policy influence of MPs resulted from the actions of a minority whose strength remains unknown.

Criticism at Union Conferences

In three instances the potential influence of MPs was restricted to very brief outbursts during debate at union conferences. Roy Mason, sponsored by the NUM, had taken the initiative of having a number of pamphlets printed which attacked the unilateralists, particularly those opposed to the training of German troops in Wales and to the presence of the American Polaris base at Holy Loch. Mason was attacked for distributing these pamphlets by R. Beamish, a delegate from South Wales, who was moving the unilateralist resolution at the 1961 NUM conference. [26]

In USDAW the criticism occurred in 1962, when, with reference to the defence dispute, one delegate asked: 'My branch wishes to know whether it has been necessary during the year to take action against any of our Parliamentary representatives for failure to support Union policy in the House, and whether it is or not, will the Executive Council advise us as to what form such action would take.' [27] In reply, the union's president Walter Padley, himself a sponsored MP, suggested the attitude of the union leaders toward such criticism: 'The answer to that is that no action has been taken. The conduct of our Members of Parliament is governed by the rules relating to the Parliamentary Representation Scheme, which are at the end of the Rule Book. You will notice that Members of Parliament are subject to the Whips of the Parliamentary Labour Party'. [28] Padley, of course, had been one of the Members who failed to vote in Divison 22.

The constitutional theory underlying criticism made of sponsored MPs was made explicit in the remarks of a delegate to the 1961 UPW conference. The delegate's speech was reported as follows:

> The 1960 decision of the Labour Party Conference at Scarborough reflected the views of the lay membership of the Party. Since its inception the Party had accepted that the annual Conference was its sovereign body. That was precisely the view which they, in the UPW, took. Therefore, who were they to say

that the Labour Party should do otherwise? He hoped they would not. The Executive Committee of the Labour Party and the Parliamentary Labour Party, had, however, said otherwise and they had sought to reverse the Annual Conference decision. But who were they to presume to take it upon themselves to reverse the democratic decision of the Labour Party's annual conference? What right had they to do so? They had no right. To draw an analogy, it was as if the EC of the UPW completely reversed a decision taken at the Annual Conference during that very week. *The only difference was that whereas the UPW membership elected the EC, the lay membership of the Labour Party did not elect the Parliamentary Labour Party.* [29] [emphasis added]

That MPs might have some responsibility to the people who elected them, i.e., to their constituents, or to any other clientele, such as the party, was ignored. There is no clearer expression of the radical, anti-parliamentary tradition upon which the unions based their attempts to make sponsored MPs responsible to them.

PLP Compliance with Party Conference Decisions

In addition to this criticism in debate at the NUM, USDAW, and UPW conferences, resolutions calling for compliance by the PLP with the decisions of the party conference were introduced at other union meetings. A resolution of this sort, proposed at the AEF conference in 1961, failed to be discussed; and there is no way to determine the precise amount of support it might have been able to secure. [30]

Two staunch multilateralist unions were also confronted with attacks on the independence of the Parliamentary Party. In the NUGMW a resolution calling for PLP compliance with party conference decisions was soundly defeated. [31] The union leaders had learned their lesson in 1959 and were not prepared to allow the unilateralists any new gains. The other union confronted with a resolution calling for priority for the party conference decisions was TSSA, the railway clerks' union. An amendment to the TSSA resolution would have required members of TSSA's parliamentary panel to accept this conference domination. [32] Both the amendment and the resolution were defeated. For neither of these unions could one estimate the amount of support for such attacks on the independence of MPs.

Compliance with Union Conference Decisions

The Miners. In keeping with its decentralised organisation and with the fact that, at the national level, the NUM was supporting the multilateralists, criticism aimed at the parliamentary representatives came from the Derbyshire Miners' Association, which sponsored two MPs: Thomas Swain and Harold Neal. In Division 22, Swain lived up to his leftwing reputation by publicly abstaining, while Neal followed the leadership of the PLP. In response to this, as well as to Neal's failure to oppose the Holy Loch Polaris base, the Derbyshire Area Council adopted the following resolution: 'That this Branch of the NUM Derbyshire Area protests against our representative in the Miners' Parliamentary Group in failing to support the protests against the installation of the Polaris base, when it was raised in the recent debate at Westminster'.[33] The resolution was approved by the area council on 28 December 1960, by a vote of thirty-one to eleven. When questioned by the press about the resolution, the area secretary said: 'This was a direct protest against Mr. Neal's action. He observed the official Labour Party line. He should have followed our dictate'.[34] Obviously the Derbyshire miners had no doubts about the responsibilities of their MPs.

The Railwaymen. The NUR supported the unilateralists in 1960 by a bare one-vote margin at its own conference. At the NUR's annual general meeting in 1961 one resolution attacked the union's sponsored MPs' failure to comply with the party conference decision, while another attacked the MPs for their failure to obey the decisions of the NUR's conference. (In the crucial Division 22, only one of the union's five sponsored MPs had abstained.)

The first resolution, calling for compliance with party conference decisions by the unions' MPs, stated:

> That the Annual General Meeting reaffirms the policy on defence supported and agreed at the 1960 Labour Party Conference, and instructs the National Executive Committee to use its every resource in furtherance of that policy with organizations to whom we are affiliated. Further that an instruction be issued to all members of our Parliamentary Panel

to abide by and support decisions agreed at the National Conference of the Labour Party and Trades Union Congress. [35]

The degree of support for this resolution is unknown, since it was not acted upon at the union's conference. [36]

The second and much stronger NUR resolution was aimed even more specifically at the union's sponsored MPs. The text of the resolution read as follows:

> That this Annual General Meeting notes that some of the NUR Parliamentary Group have publicly dissociated themselves from the policy of the Union (on disarmament) as laid down by the 1960 AGM.
>
> This meeting decides that any member of this Union's Parliamentary Panel who opposes Union policy (as decided by Annual General Meetings) shall be required to resign from this Parliamentary Panel with the loss of the privileges this Union gives in financial support. [37]

This resolution expresses an even more restricted view of the source of legitimate authority within the labour movement than did the resolutions of other unions. NUR adoption of it would have severely curtailed the union's ability to continue sponsoring parliamentary candidates within the Labour Party.

During the debate on the resolution, some of the delegates urged the MPs to follow union policy in exchange for continued financial support. But other delegates indicated that the MPs did not receive enough support from the union to justify this claim. [38]

The strongest speech against the resolution was made by the union's general secretary S. F. Greene, who raised three points. First, he felt that any action by the union could easily result in a breach of parliamentary privilege, and he made special reference to the Brown case. Secondly, the NUR rules required sponsored MPs to obey the whip of the PLP and made no reference to agreement with union policy. Thirdly, he called attention to other instances of conflict between the union and sponsored MPs in which action had not been taken against the Member. [39]

The resolution was defeated by a margin of fifty-four to twenty-two. [40] In this instance union criticism of sponsored MPs secured the support of twenty-nine per cent of the delegates, in spite of the opposition of the union's own leadership. This vote is practically the only quantifiable indication of the strength of the anti–parliamentary tradition within the labour movement, and thus provides little basis for conclusions relative to the strength of the tradition in the remainder of the movement. However, it is relevant to note that the professional staff of the NUR underestimated the actual vote in favour of the criticism, until confronted with the record of the union's annual general meeting for 1961. [41]

The NUR witnessed additional attacks on its sponsored MPs in 1961. Ernest Popplewell minced no words in his speech to the NUR meeting:

> It is as one of your representatives that I am here, who, having secured the confidence of a constituency party, have been elected to Parliament, and am pleased to be one of the small band which reflects the opinions of the Union *so far as it is possible to do so* in this much wider and national field.

Popplewell went on to say,

> Members of Parliament belonging to the NUR have been in considerable difficulties. The constitutional position is that we have four masters and it is natural that we cannot obey all four masters. We do our utmost by close contact and co-operation with Head Office to ensure that all actions taken by our organisation are followed up *as far as it is possible to do so* [emphasis added]. [42]

In the unusual Question Period following his speech, Popplewell was forced to defend Gaitskell's position from hostile attacks by delegates. [43]

The Transport Workers. Criticism and attacks on sponsored MPs went further in the NUR than in any other union in the defence dispute. The TGWU, however, saw a different form of conflict with its MPs. Frank Cousins was the major leader within the union movement on the unilateralist side, and his union was one of the two which continued to support the unilateralists between the 1960 and 1961 party conferences. Most of the MPs sponsored by the TGWU took the multilateralist position. Eleven of the fourteen TGWU MPs supported Gaitskell in Division 22. George Brown, one of the union's Members, was deputy leader of the Labour Party, chairman of the Trade Union Group, and a firm supporter of Gaitskell throughout the dispute.

In the TGWU the dispute between the union and its MPs took on a more muted tone because of Frank Cousins. MPs' opposition to the unilateralist position (especially that of Brown and Reg Prentice) was noted in the report of the 1960 party conference, published in the union journal.[44] The union's annual report for 1960 handled the situation as follows:

> The Executive Officers have attended meetings of the (Parliamentary) Group on several occasions to discuss Union Policy. Particularly important occasions were the various meetings to consider the Foreign Policy and the Defence issue, and also immediately after the General Election to discuss lines of approach in the new Parliament.[45]

The refusal of the MPs to alter their attitudes on the defence issue, together with the pressure from the union, led to what one Member described as rather 'tense and strained' relations between the two at the height of the dispute.[46]

At the 1961 TGWU conference there were some three hundred resolutions dealing with the defence issue, foreign policy, the parliamentary group, and union procedure – all stemming from the defence dispute – offered for consideration. The resolutions on the defence issue were combined into two composite resolutions: one supporting the unilateralist position and affirming the decision of the 1959 TGWU conference, and one supporting the multilateralist position. The composite unilateralist resolution was approved by the conference, while the other resolution was not even voted upon.[47]

The resolutions concerning the status of the union's sponsored MPs were not considered by the TGWU conference. Cousins avoided floor action by making an executive statement on the subject, which tried to make it clear that:

> The Union had never tried to impose its views upon the Members of the Union's Parliamentary Group and to make it conditional that they should accept these as a parliamentary instruction. If the line was taken of insisting that Members of the Group should adhere to Union policy decisions it would be questionable whether the Union could lay itself open to a charge of trying to usurp parliamentary functions by seeking to apply policies which might be in direct conflict with the views of their constituents whose interests it was their first duty to

represent in matters brought before the House of Commons. Such action could be regarded as a breach of privilege and whilst, obviously, the Union expected the Members concerned to conform in a broad general way of taking note of Union policies determined from time to time, conference would readily recognise the difficulty of making this a continuing obligation upon them.[48]

Cousins' statement disposed of a number of resolutions, some of which actually called for an end to the sponsorship of Members who did not follow union policy,[49] and the union was thus prevented from taking any formal action against its sponsored MPs at that time.

The potential influence of the unions on their sponsored MPs has been described. There seems to have been a clear inability or unwillingness on the part of the unions to force their will on their MPs. In addition, it is obvious that the union leaders were unwilling to allow anything that might appear as coercion or punishment of the MPs' actions in the House of Commons. What would happen if the union leaders were unwilling to defend their MPs is another question.

Attempts by Sponsored MPs to Influence Unions

Another form of potential influence is an MP's attempt to influence his union. One example are the activities of Roy Mason, for which he was criticised at the 1961 NUM conference. In the AEF, the sponsored MPs made use of their traditional joint meeting with the union's Labour Party conference delegation to try, unsuccessfully, to persuade it not to support the unilateralists in 1960.[50] The sponsored Members also wrote several articles in the union's journal to argue against the unilateralists,[51] and they may have aided in the conversion of the Engineers from the unilateralist to the multilateralist position between the 1960 and 1961 party conferences.

The TGWU also came in for its share of attention. In 1957 it had been the intervention of one of its MPs, Robert Mellish, which kept the TGWU Labour Party delegation from joining the unilateralists.[52] In 1961 George Brown took an active part in trying to change the union's position. He made a strong attempt to speak to the TGWU conference, but was unsuccessful because of a union rule which barred union officers on leave of absence from the union from speaking to the conference.[53] In conjunction with the CDS, Brown

organised a rally for the TGWU delegates on the eve of their conference. 'The meeting was poorly attended and was picketed by militant busmen who distributed leaflets telling Brother Brown, in un-
fraternal and unparliamentary language: "If Mr. Brown will mind
his own bloody business we promise to mind our own bloody
business".'[54] The busmen had still not forgotten 1958.

MPs were active in at least two other unions. In the NUR an ineffective meeting was held between the political subcommittee of the
union's executive committee and the NUR-sponsored MPs before the
1960 party conference.[55] In the National Union of Textile Garment
Workers, the MP, M. Cliffe, persuaded the union's conference in
1961 to reverse its 1960 decision, despite the wishes of the union's
general secretary.[56]

While the peculiar nature of the subject involved in this dispute tends
to limit the degree to which it can be used as a basis for broader
generalisations, we have suggested that there are members of the
trade union movement who still regard their sponsored MPs as paid
agents of the unions. That this view is generally rejected by both the
MPs and the union leaders is also fairly clear. We say 'generally',
because of the rather ambiguous personal statements of both groups.
As one Member has expressed it,

> My Union is quite in order, at their annual conference, in
> making a decision, on a majority vote, in order to try to in-
> fluence the main body of the Labour Party and Trades Union
> Congress . . .: But because my Union – of which I am not an of-
> ficial – never regarded me as a delegate and has never given me
> one single instruction on how to vote in the fifteen years I have
> been in Parliament and would deem to do so now, I should take
> the same line as Mr. George Brown, one of my Union
> colleagues – he is the shadow Defence Minister. I share his
> views regarding the position (on the H-Bomb) and I shall re-
> main a loyal supporter of Mr. Gaitskell.[57]

This statement would seem to be a fair summary of the position of
most, if not all, the union-sponsored MPs. But the same men frequently state that they are sent to Parliament by their unions to
further their unions' interests. Only under pressure are they prepared
to exchange the union's interests for those of their constituents, their
party, or the nation as a whole.[58]

Trade union officials are equally ambiguous, as indicated in the statements of NUR officials. The same confusion was expressed by the Northumberland area secretary of the NUM, when he wrote: 'All Miners' sponsored MPs are, as you will probably be aware, members of a Miners' Political Group in Parliament seeking to improve the condition of miners in particular, but always, of course, fully conscious of the fact that all classes of persons in the Constituency must be catered for'.[59]

In part this ambiguity is related to the transition occurring within the sponsorship system, as it moves from the era in which sponsored MPs were active (or retired) trade unionists, rewarded with a seat in the best club in Europe where they could express their union's views, into an era, starting in the late 1950s, when the MPs are the younger, better educated technicians whose ties with the unions are marginal. The ambiguity in the role expected of trade-union sponsored MPs may decrease if unions come to recognise how important are the expectations of party loyalty regarding the legislative behaviour of sponsored Members, and if they also realize that they have alternative ways of influencing public policy through consultation. The next chapter will examine the problems of the sponsored MP's role confusion when he is confronted with a dispute over policy which is of more immediate concern to the trade union movement.

Chapter VIII
The Struggle over Prices and Incomes Policy, 1964–1970

The evidence of the defence dispute suggests that the parliamentary voting of sponsored MPs is not subject to control by their sponsoring unions. At the same time, it is clear that a minority within the British trade union movement view their sponsored MPs as delegates, responsible to the unions for their actions.

In order to examine union–MP relations further, a second case study, involving prices and incomes policy, has been made with special attention given to the measures undertaken by the Labour government in 1966 and 1967. The basic goal of this policy was to reduce domestic inflation and make British goods more competitive in overseas markets. The means chosen included restrictions on wage and price increases, and, eventually, devaluation of sterling. [1]

Unlike the defence question, an incomes policy touches on one of the fundamental reasons for the existence of trade unions, the improvement of the workers' standard of living. The Labour Party, the creation of the trade unions, shares this feeling. As one commentator expressed it, 'The soul of the party is involved as it is not involved over Vietnam'. [2] Public opinion polls have given much the same result. Only at the height of the defence dispute did the question of the Bomb take precedence over the question of wage increases. Nevertheless the unions' greater interest in economic questions is not without its own ambiguities. 'Unions are as jealous of their freedom in wage bargaining as they are eager to see planning in the rest of the economy'. [3] This view would help to weaken or confuse the more extreme opposition to incomes policy.

A second difference between the struggle over an incomes policy and the defence dispute involves the status of the Labour Party. During the defence dispute the party was in Opposition, and actual implementation of its policy was not going to take place until some future and uncertain date. But the incomes policy struggle, which took place when the Labour Party was in power, raised the question of government action at that moment. Leaving aside the question of union interest, incomes policy was clearly a far more urgent matter.

A third difference between the two disputes lies in the relationship between the PLP and the annual party conference. These two parts of the party had been in disagreement which attracted attention in the defence dispute, but the Labour government and the PLP managed to retain the reluctant support of the party conference throughout the struggle over an incomes policy. Government opponents were thus deprived of one important argument when trying to attack those MPs who supported the government.

Incomes Policy

The Labour government's policy on prices and incomes changed between 1964 and 1970 from one of voluntary restraint to one of required restraint. The early efforts by George Brown's Department of Economic Affairs to develop some kind of incomes policy without legislation were abandoned early in 1966, and the continuing economic problems which the voluntary incomes policy failed to solve led Brown to draft legislation that would impose tighter controls. Criticism by Stanley Orme and other sponsored MPs led to a series of meetings between Brown and the sponsored MPs, both before and after the 1966 General Election, but the trade unionists remained unhappy. Their dissatisfaction was symbolised by Frank Cousins' resignation from the government on 3 July, the day before the Bill was published.[4]

The Prices and Incomes Bill included three parts. The first created a statutory base for the Prices and Incomes Board (PIB) and allowed the PIB to compel witnesses to give evidence.[5] Part Two authorised the government to require early warning of price and wage increases and to delay some increases until the PIB had reported. Businesses or unions could be prosecuted for failure to obey orders to delay such increases. The third part exempted corporations from some restrictive practices legislation when they were implementing recommendations of the PIB.

When the Prices and Incomes Bill was introduced in the House of Commons on 14 July, fifty-three Labour MPs signed an Early Day Motion protesting '. . . that the present Prices and Incomes Bill containing penal legislation against trade unions should be rejected'. [6] While there were to be further rebellions within the PLP over the incomes policy during the next four years, none would be as large as this one. [7]

The continued decline of the British economy led the Wilson government to announce on 20 July an additional section to the bill which would authorise the government to forbid all price and wage increases for six months and to restrain them severely for another six months. For the next three and a half years the Labour government experimented with various forms of wage and price restraints, but the basic outline of its policy was established with the passage of the 1966 Prices and Incomes Act. Afterwards there were numerous meetings between members of the Cabinet and sponsored MPs, and between Cabinet members and business and union leaders outside Parliament, but these had only a marginal impact on the general policy.

Initially the incomes policy failed to solve Britain's economic problems and the Labour government was forced to supplement it by announcing a devaluation of sterling by 14.3 per cent on 18 November 1967. Devaluation and the incomes policy took a long time to work, but the British balance of trade eventually began to show a surplus in late 1969.

Union–MP Agreement

Details of the latter development of the incomes policy need not concern us here. Its initial form during the first half of 1966 provides the basis for determining agreement or disagreement between the sponsored MPs and their unions. Sponsored MPs made their position clear when the bill was introduced on 14 July 1966 and twenty-three signed the motion protesting it. These MPs comprised forty-four per cent of the signatories to the motion, a somewhat higher proportion than one might have expected from other studies of revolts within the PLP. Table VIII–1 lists these rebel sponsored MPs. It may be of some significance that the bulk of these sponsored rebels had entered

TABLE VIII – 1

SPONSORED MPs SIGNING THE EARLY
DAY MOTION OF 14 JULY 1966

Name	Union	Year of entry	Age in 1966	Educational level
Atkinson, N.	AEF	1964	43	Secondary
Beaney, A.	NUM	1959	61	Secondary
Booth, A.	DATA	1966	38	Secondary
Cousins, F.	TGWU	1965	62	Elementary
Davies, S. O.	NUM	1934	80	University
Ellis, J.	TGWU	1966	36	Secondary
Fletcher, E. J.	CAWU	1964	55	Secondary
Fletcher, R. L.	TGWU	1964	45	University
Heffer, E.	ASW	1964	44	Elementary
Hobden, D.	UPW	1964	46	Elementary
Horner, J.	FBU	1964	55	Secondary
Hughes, R.	TGWU	1966	41	Secondary
Kelley, R.	NUM	1959	62	Elementary
Kerr, R.	ASTMS	1966	45	University
Lee, J. M. H.	TGWU	1966	39	University
Orme, S.	AEF	1964	43	Secondary
Park, T.	TGWU	1964	39	University
Perry, G. H.	NUR	1966	46	Secondary
Probert, A.	TGWU	1954	57	Secondary
Swain, T.	NUM	1959	55	Secondary
Varley, E.	NUM	1964	34	Secondary
Walker, H.	AEF	1964	39	Secondary
Woof, R. E.	NUM	1956	55	Secondary

Sources: The MPs' names are taken from the House of Commons *Order Paper* (1966–1967), p. 2302 (14 July 1966).

The sponsoring unions are based on the Labour Party Annual Conference *Report* (1966), Appendix VI.

The year of entry, age in 1966, and educational level are taken from *The Times House of Commons* (1966).

Parliament in 1964 or 1966 and were either middle class MPs or representatives of the technical and white collar unions. Allowing for exceptions such as Thomas Swain and Stephen O. Davies, the traditional working class element was absent among the rebels.

The positions of the sponsoring unions on the incomes policy are more difficult to determine. The best available source for data on their attitudes is the 1966 TUC, where the composite TGWU resolution opposed any wage standstill while the general council's report accepted it.

The use of the 1966 TUC to identity union positions when determining agreement or disagreement between unions and their sponsored MPs is open to methodological question, because unions do not always affiliate to the Labour Party on the same membership base as they affiliate to the TUC, due to 'contracting out' by some members and decisions by union leaders to under- or over-affiliate. In some unions this numerical difference may be considerable. The TUC data were used here for three reasons: the nature of the substantive issue was less likely to produce disagreement between a union's delegations to the TUC and to the Labour party conferences; in those cases where data were available on the stand taken by a particular union at the party conference there was no disagreement with its TUC position; and comparable data were not available on the positions of all unions at the 1966 party conference.

The 1966 TUC supported the incomes policy by a small margin, and this lack of enthusiasm was reflected in public opinion polls which showed a majority for the policy but a healthy minority opposed to it. Even fifty-one per cent of the members of the TGWU included in the poll supported the policy, despite the position of their union.[8]

Using the reported position of individual unions at the 1966 Trades Union Congress and the positions of the MPs as shown in the July 14th EDM, we can then analyse agreement between the unions and their backbench MPs in Table VIII–2.

Unions and MPs agreed when the unions supported the government's policy and the MPs did not sign the 14 July motion, and also when the unions opposed the government's policy and the MPs signed the 14 July motion. Unions and MPs disagreed when unions supported the government's policy and the MPs signed the 14 July motion or when the unions opposed the policy and the MPs did not sign the motion. Although an incomes policy more closely affects the *raison d'etre* of trade unions than do foreign policy and defence, it still creates no special basis of agreement between unions and their MPs. Expectations of loyalty to the Labour Party are more important even for the sponsored MPs.

TABLE VIII – 2
AGREEMENT BETWEEN UNIONS AND BACKBENCH SPONSORED
MPs ON PRICES AND INCOMES POLICY*

Position	MPs Agree with Union	MPs Disagree with Union	Total
Unions supporting Government	50	12	62
Unions opposing Government	11	26	37
Total	61	38	99

$(X^2 - 99.5; df - 1; P \ 0.05)$

* For a detailed breakdown of the position taken by each union in relation to the position of its backbench MPs, see W. D. Muller, 'Union-MP Conflict: An Overview,' *Parliamentary Affairs*, XXVI, No. 3 (Summer, 1973), p. 348, Table 2.

Union Expectations regarding MPs' Behaviour

The lack of systematic agreement between the unions and their sponsored MPs is not by itself enough to show that there was no attempt at influence. In fact there were a number of instances where unions tried or were perceived to be trying to influence the MPs' positions on incomes policy. This union pressure even extended to non-sponsored Labour MPs and led to the resignations of David Ennals from ASTMS in 1966 and of Willie Howie from DATA in 1968.[9] In early 1967 *The Economist* warned that some sponsored MPs were worried about future union support if they continued to support the policy, [10] and one sponsored MP justified his opposition to the incomes policy in 1968 on the grounds that his union also opposed it. [11] Clearly pressure was being applied in some unions to influence their MPs. The major sources of evidence for this assertion are union journals, the official records of union conferences, and the comments of union officials.

Union Leaders and MPs

DATA. Many union officials, unhappy about the incomes policy despite the action of the 1966 TUC, did not hesitate to make their feelings known to the sponsored MPs. For example, in 1966, DATA held a special meeting of the union's executive committee, its two sponsored MPs, and the other members of its panel of potential parliamentary candidates. One MP agreed with the union in opposing the incomes policy and one did not, but no formal decision was made; the MPs were officially left to follow the course they felt best.[12]

When the Labour government persisted with its incomes policy, the DATA executive committe adopted a resolution in 1968 which urged the union 'to review the sponsorship of M.P.s who consistently support policies which are in opposition to the interests of DATA members and contrary to D.A.T.A. policy'.[13] It was this action which led to Mr. Howie's resignation from the union, but it appeared to have no impact on DATA's two sponsored MPs, who were both re-elected in 1970 with union sponsorship.

The Miners. Nationally the NUM supported the government's incomes policy, but some regional units did not. For example, serious official displeasure was expressed by the Scottish area executive of the miners' union when they asked their three sponsored MPs to justify their support of the policy with special reference to the problems of wage increases for several hundred miners.[14] Three months later, in November 1966, the Scottish area of the NUM called a public meeting to question the MPs on the issue.[15] There is no evidence that the union efforts produced any change in the MPs' positions, although Tom Fraser, an ex-minister, resigned in the summer of 1967 to take a position with a regional Scottish electrical board.

These official actions of DATA and the Scottish miners were directed at MPs who supported the incomes policy. A more serious example of this in the TGWU will be discussed below. There are no verified examples of official union pressure on MPs who opposed the incomes policy.[16]

Rank and File Discontent

Threats or attacks on the MPs, however, could be indirect. In one obvious method of attack, the withdrawal of financial support, union rank and file members expressed their feelings by means of a general tendency to 'contract out' of the political levy, thus leaving their unions' political fund with smaller resources to support the Labour Party in general or their sponsored MPs in particular.[17] For the most

part union leaders opposed 'contracting out', and instead urged their
members to continue to support the party. For example, John Bondfield, joint general secretary of the National Graphical Association
(NGA), wrote:

> Disenchantment with the Wilson Government is now so
> widespread among trade unionists that public discussion of it
> cannot be much longer delayed.
>
> This is certainly true of the NGA. Far too many members are
> deciding the matter individually by 'contracting out' of our
> Political Fund. Indeed, if the rate of withdrawals is not stemm-
> ed soon we shall be compelled to reduce our political com-
> mitments because the money will no longer be there to meet
> them. . . . I earnestly appeal to members who have withdrawn
> their support from the Political Fund to reconsider their deci-
> sion and to those who have signified their intention to
> withdraw support to hold their hand for the moment. [18]

The question of affiliation of entire unions or parts of unions to
the Labour Party was of equal importance. Even if rank and file
members continued to pay the political levy, it was possible for the
union leaders to reduce the number of members they affiliated to the
party or even to disaffiliate completely. But these were drastic
courses of action and unlikely to find many supporters. Only one union, the National Society of Pottery Workers, was prepared to disaffiliate from the party. [19] The figures for total union affiliation
between 1966 and 1969 varied very little. The figures for 1967 are
10,000 higher than for 1966, but the number of trade unionists affiliated through their unions in 1968 had fallen by almost 200,000.
Half of this was regained in 1969. [20]

One of the stronger cases for continued support of the party was
made by Sidney Hill of NUPE. Speaking to his union's annual conference in 1967, Hill paid tribute to the work of NUPE's sponsored
MPs, 'who had handled cases from all over the country on behalf of
NUPE members, submitting them to the appropriate Ministers and
getting them considered. And their help had been invaluable in connection with the reference to the Prices and Incomes Board.' He continued:

> If we disaffiliated from the Party we would have no sponsored
> MPs to go to for help, and, as has been said by a previous

speaker, neither should we have the opportunity of putting forward NUPE members for local Councils'. [21]

Refusal to pay the political levy and the threat of disaffiliation, of course, are fairly general attacks on union–party ties and are not specifically intended for the sponsored MPs. In several unions the MPs became the specific objects of attack by groups or individuals within the unions.

DATA. In DATA, the attack resulted originally from an article in *The DATA Journal* by one MP, Ted Bishop, which discussed the distribution of wealth and income in the United Kingdom and credited the Labour government with trying to rectify some of the existing inequalities. One of the devices used for this purpose, the incomes policy, he mentioned almost as an afterthought. [22] This weak defence of the incomes policy elicited two letters from Len Formby in the following months which took issue with Bishop's position. In the first letter he called on Bishop to oppose the incomes policy. [23] Replying in the January issue of the journal, Bishop attacked Formby's ignorance of the work he had done on behalf of DATA. [24] Not to be outdone, Formby again wrote to call attention to the opposition of other DATA MPs to the government's policy, and to defend his original letter in the face of Bishop's counterattack. Formby claimed the government's narrow victory at the 1966 TUC indicated rank and file disagreement with the policy and was contributing to the organisation of numerous trade union defence committees for the purpose of protesting against the government's policy. [25] In a sequel to this exchange, Bishop wrote an article for the April issue of the *Journal* in which he outlined the responsibilities and the proper role of an MP. 'MPs are not delegates: indeed their special relationship to their constituencies, their trade union or other sponsoring body makes that impossible, particularly if there is conflict in the outlook of such organizations and with their party nationally'. [26] He had shifted the basis of his own defence and left out any reference to specific policies, such as prices and incomes.

The Shopworkers. Rank and file criticism of USDAW's sponsored MPs appeared in the union journal and in discussion at the 1967 union conference. Debate in the journal, *The New Dawn*, took the form of three letters in October and November 1966. The first contained an attack on union leaders who claimed that sponsored MPs could not be subject to pressure from the union because they represented geographical constituencies. [27] The author felt that the USDAW MPs should have opposed the incomes policy. An area organiser of the union replied in the next issue of the journal that union pressure on MPs was illegal, and that the MPs actually expressed the views of USDAW members in the House of Commons. There was no specific mention of the incomes policy. [28] The third letter again called attention to the disagreement between many of the USDAW MPs and their union (which opposed the incomes policy), and it praised those Labour MPs who supported the union by opposing the government. [29] That there were no further letters indicates that concern with the MPs' position was not widespread.

The 1967 USDAW conference was also the scene of an attack on the MPs for not supporting the union's position in the incomes dispute. The criticism was met by the general secretary, who apologised for it and reiterated that the MPs had constituency responsibilities. [30] When the conference debated the incomes policy, the government's position was defended by two USDAW-sponsored MPs and attacked by a non-sponsored MP. [31] No action was taken concerning the sponsored MPs.

Other Unions. Three other unions showed minor signs of disagreement with MPs' support of the incomes policy. In NGA this took the form of a single letter in the union's journal calling attention to the failure of their two sponsored MPs to oppose the incomes policy. [32] In the AEF and TSSA, attempts to secure conference support for efforts to involve their sponsored MPs in the fight against the incomes policy failed to be considered. [33]

The Transport and General Workers' Union

There can be no question that it was this union which carried its opposition to the Labour government's incomes policy furthest, and that it did the most to impress on its sponsored MPs that they were responsible to the TGWU. The background of the TGWU's actions needs to be clarified.

Frank Cousins, who had been general secretary of the union since 1956, entered the Labour Cabinet in October 1964 as minister of technology. He had a leave of absence from his union position, but he returned to the TGWU following his resignation from the Cabinet in July 1966. Cousins objected both to the principle of the incomes policy and to its application to his union. In 1966 he objected when a wage claim by TGWU busmen was referred to the PIB by George Brown, and the TGWU announced its refusal to cooperate with the PIB in future.[34] Cousins resigned from the Cabinet on 3 July 1966 because of the Prices and Incomes Bill. Following his resignation, he held at least two meetings with the other twenty-six MPs of his union in an effort to persuade them to follow his lead and oppose the bill.

At the first of these meetings he seemed to be having some success until '. . . an elderly and normally taciturn member of the group, sixty-three-year-old George Jeger, broke in to say that in Parliament the first loyalty was to the party, not to the union. The meeting ended without taking tactical decisions'.[35] The second meeting with the TGWU MPs was on 12 July 1966, followed immediately by a meeting of the entire Trade Union Group.[36] Cousins spoke to both and had some success in persuading the TGWU MPs to sign the Early Day Motion of 14 July.

The TGWU instructed Cousins to remain in the House of Commons following his resignation from the Cabinet and to oppose the Prices and Incomes Bill. While in Parliament he was to turn over part of his parliamentary salary to the union. Some MPs, feeling this constituted a contractual relationship between Cousins and the TGWU, unsuccessfully claimed that it was a breach of privilege.[37] In any event, Cousins was clearly willing to place loyalty to the union above loyalty to either party or constituency. When, in early 1967, the TGWU asked him to resign his parliamentary seat and his CLP requested him to remain in the House of Commons, he chose to resign and return to the union on a fulltime basis.[38]

The TGWU remained the most active opponent of the incomes policy. At its biennial conference in July 1967 the union was confronted with a variety of resolutions relating to the sponsored MPs, to relations with the Labour Party in general, and to the prices and incomes policy.[39] The conference decided to continue TGWU opposition to the incomes policy. But no action was taken on proposals for disaffiliation from the Labour Party, because Cousins' policy statement opposing them kept the relevant resolutions from coming to a vote.

The conference unanimously adopted a resolution on the union's parliamentary panel, which read:

That this Conference calls upon the General Executive
Council to reconstitute the Parliamentary Panel at the end of
the present Parliament. Existing members of the Union's
Parliamentary Panel should be permitted to apply for enrol-
ment on a newly constituted Panel, together with new
applicants in the usual way.[40]

This resolution contained no explicit reference to the behaviour of
the existing TGWU-sponsored MPs, but the debate accompanying
the resolution's adoption made clear that it was specifically aimed at
the MPs and their attitude toward the incomes policy. One delegate
expressed the view: 'You can't expect us to buy dog licences for dogs
that bite us'.[41] Another speaker said that 'Mr. Brown not only
constituted a danger but was a disease which the union could do
without'.[42]

Cousins was very critical 'of union-backed MPs who found reasons
for not resigning when he did in protest at the Government's policy,
and who failed even to raise their voice in a way which might have
influenced the Government to take a different course'; but he still
urged some moderation on the conference delegates in order to avoid
the possibility of a breach of parliamentary privilege. This point was
again unsuccessfully raised in the Commons on 17 July.[43]

For their part, the TGWU MPs were of mixed opinion about the
union's action. Malcolm Macpherson, James Bennett, George Jeger,
Renee Short and Margaret McKay were quite specific in rejecting
union attempts to dictate to them. Frank Cousins and Roy Hughes
supported it.[44] Despite the concern shown by the MPs, a Labour
Party official felt that the union had acted in haste to satisfy rank
and file militants. More moderate views would prevail before the next
general election and nothing would happen.[45] But Cousins'
retirement in 1969 and his replacement by Jack Jones, who encouraged the 1969 TGWU conference to readopt the parliamentary
panel resolution, suggested that this view was too optimistic. And in
fact the panel was reconstituted in early 1970 just before the General
Election. In the reconstitution, four sitting MPs, candidates for
re-election to the House of Commons, were dropped.[46]

Despite the discussion at the 1967 TGWU conference, there seemed to be no single factor underlying the failure of the four MPs
(George Brown, Malcolm Macpherson, John Lee, and Tom Oswald)

to be renominated for the new TGWU parliamentary panel. The reasons for Brown's loss of sponsored status are perhaps the clearest. He had been involved since the late 1950s in a longstanding feud with the TGWU growing out of his comments on a number of labour disputes involving the transport workers, his work as a consultant on industrial relations for the Mirror newspaper group (see p. 148 above), his action in opposing the union in the defence dispute in 1960–61, and finally the conflict over incomes policy in the late 1960s. The longterm resentment of TGWU militants finally had some impact in 1970.

The factors underlying the loss of sponsored status for the other three MPs are less clearcut. Along with Brown, two of them, Macpherson and Oswald, had been among the TGWU MPs who had supported the incomes policy and were in conflict with union policy. Macpherson had also opposed the union in the defence dispute. But the remaining MP, John Lee, had been an active opponent of the incomes policy. If policy differences are not a sufficient explanation, what alternatives are there? Two are suggested by the backgrounds of the TGWU MPs in the 1966–70 House of Commons.

The twenty-seven TGWU MPs elected in 1966 included three teachers, two solicitors, a barrister, an economist, and three journalists. Only six MPs might be said to approximate to the traditional 'cloth cap' image of working class representatives, and only one of these, Frank Cousins, had been elected to the House for the first time later than 1961. The demand originally made in the nineteenth century for trade union representation, on the grounds that only workers could hope to understand the problems of workers, was echoed by the general feeling of resentment among TGWU militants against the increasingly white collar and non-working class background of the union's parliamentary panel in the 1960s.[47] Two of the MPs dropped from the panel in 1970, Macpherson and Lee, fall into this non-working class category. Macpherson was a university teacher, while Lee was a barrister.

Yet another factor seems to have played some part in the failure of two of these MPs to retain their sponsored status. Macpherson and Oswald were two of the three oldest MPs on the TGWU panel. Both were sixty-six in 1970, just a year younger than the oldest TGWU MP, George Jeger. The unions had been criticized for many years for allowing the House of Commons to be used as a retirement ground for elderly trade union officials, and the failure of the TGWU to renominate these two men can also be seen as a reaction to this criticism.

In any event, the union did exercise its option and the four incumbents were not included among its sponsored candidates for the 1970 General Election. The decision was not announced until shortly before the election, when the TGWU attempted to soften its impact by making special election grants of £500 to the CLPs that had adopted the four purge victims. But continued financial support for CLPs with sponsored MPs was not forthcoming. The constituency parties would have to find such funds from a new source or else find new candidates acceptable to the union.

How much the union's action affected the result of the election is more difficult to answer. Two of the candidates denied union sponsorship, Brown and Lee were defeated, while Macpherson and Oswald were re-elected to the House of Commons. But the percentage swing against each of the four candidates was not far out of line with the average for their respective regions. It would seem safe to conclude that union action had little impact on the pattern of voting.

Evaluation. Information and opinions were exchanged freely between the unions and their sponsored MPs on the issue of incomes policy. With the exception of the TGWU and DATA, no serious efforts were made to repeat the abortive insistence on responsibility to the unions which had characterised the defence dispute. Because the Labour Party remained essentially united, with both the PLP and the annual conference supporting the prices and incomes policy, opposition within the unions was expressed in terms of that policy. The question of the responsibility of the sponsored MPs was seldom raised.

Most union leaders did not seem to want to raise the question of responsibility, and their actions thus reflected the positions they had taken in the defence dispute. Some even explicitly denounced the TGWU action.[48] Neither they nor their members liked the prices and incomes policy, but their opposition took other forms.

Attempts to Influence Unions

As in the defence dispute, real and potential attempts by unions to influence their MPs were matched by the MPs' attempts to influence their sponsoring unions. The contribution of the USDAW MPs to their union conference in 1967 has already been described. The AEF's MPs met with the union's Labour Party conference delegation in 1965 to argue unsuccessfully for union support of the government's position.[49] And in 1967 Fred Lee bluntly defended the incomes policy in his speech to the AEF's national committee meeting.[50]

Cousins' opponents in the TGWU, including George Brown, were unable to speak to the biennial conference.[51] But both sides publicised their positions in the union journal, *The T & G W Record*. Brown defended the early stages of the incomes policy in an article published in May 1965.[52] In September 1966 Cousins and Jeremy Bray contributed articles to the same issue of *The Record* which took opposite sides in the dispute.[53] In October 1966 Trevor Park bitterly denounced both the policy and the government's method of forcing the bill through the House of Commons.[54] These articles were confined mostly to a discussion of the incomes policy and said little about the MPs' relations with their unions.

Conclusion

The overview of union–MP conflict and the two case studies that we have presented here provide some basis for generalising about the relations between the trade unions and their sponsored MPs. First, it is clear that expectations of party loyalty take precedence over union loyalty for all but a few MPs. Second, MPs are aware of attempts by unions to exact a measure of responsibility in exchange for sponsored status. Third, union attempts to make the MPs answerable to them are usually abortive because union leaders are unwilling to risk the possibility of violating parliamentary privilege. Unions whose leaders do not share this view of privilege as a shield for the MPs are more likely to take action against MPs whose opinions they dislike. The TGWU has been most prominent in these efforts in recent years. Fifth, MPs who find themselves at odds with both their union and the Labour Party are the most likely to be subjected to pressures. Finally there is some evidence to suggest that the new breed of sponsored MPs who began to appear in the 1960s, the 'professional representatives', may be less willing to accept party discipline than were their more traditional predecessors.

Conclusion:

The Start of the Second Century

The second century of formal trade union representation in the House of Commons started in 1974. At this point in time it is clear that the role of union-sponsored MPs is only partly understood by students and commentators on the British political scene. Most observers treat the sponsored MPs simply as a group of second- or third-rate politicians. If there are second thoughts, these MPs are viewed as delegates or agents of the unions that support them. There is seldom any recognition that the sponsored MPs may have a positive role to play in the British political system, or that there have been considerable variations in the characteristics and roles of trade union MPs over the years. A brief summary of our major findings may help to dispel this misunderstanding of the functions of sponsored MPs.

Patterns of Representation

There have been three distinct phases in the changing pattern of union representation in Parliament. Originally the unions sent their top leaders to the House of Commons, and this practice gradually ended in the decades after World War I. In the second phase, lasting from World War I until the 1950s, the unions were usually represented by lower-ranking officials or even by rank and file trade unionists. Frequently these officials were retired to the House of Commons when they no longer had an opportunity for continued advancement within their unions.

190

The third phase began in the late 1950s, when the unions started sending a new breed of 'professional representatives' who were likely to be younger and better educated than their predecessors. And it was not unusual for them to have only the weakest industrial links with their sponsoring unions. This pattern, which will continue in the second century of union parliamentary representation, represents a significant break with the unions' original desire for working class representation by workers themselves.

The unions' changes regarding their sponsored MPs' legislative activity are also very clear. Originally they sent their leaders to the House of Commons to present the working class or union point of view to the representatives of other groups in British society. In these early years of representation the unions were prepared to bring pressure on the MPs to ensure that they agreed with union policy and spoke for it in the House of Commons. Failure to do so could and did lead to unions efforts to unseat MPs. The problems this posed for the MPs were sometimes acute, as they were frequently confronted by conflicting sets of expectations from their unions, their constituents, their class, the House of Commons, and the Liberal Party. The replacement of the Liberal Party by the Labour Party in the twentieth century did not significantly alter the situation. The resulting role confusion did not make the trade union MPs' position any easier.

Expectations of party loyalty take precedence over other considerations. Our examination of conflicts between MPs and their unions, including case studies of the defence dispute and the struggle over prices and incomes policy, makes it clear that only a small minority within the union movement regard the MPs as union delegates. But the action of the TGWU in the late 1960s and early 1970s shows that even a minority can still secure union action if the union leadership is willing to co-operate. Despite the TGWU's action, the unions are usually more concerned to see that their MPs remain in the good graces of the Labour Party, and this is reinforced by the idea, held by many MPs and union leaders, that union threats would be a violation of parliamentary privilege. There is practical support for the freedom from union pressures, since loss of sponsorship need not mean the end of an MP's personal support, the union will be hard put to block an MP's renomination and election.

Changes in recruitment patterns and in union expectations of sponsored MPs' behaviour are associated with changes in the way union leaders justify the practice of union parliamentary representation. Interest representation played a major role in the original desire of the unions to gain seats in Parliament, but this was supplemented by a number of other factors. Seats in the 'best club in Europe' were one way in which the working classes in a deferential society could honour their leaders while at the same time gaining recognition for their own importance in that society. By the second half of the twentieth century, sponsorship has increasingly appeared to be just one more way that a union can aid the Labour Party while gaining extra prestige for itself.

The leftward shift among some of the major unions in the late 1960s and early 1970s does not contradict the idea that sponsoring MPs is a device to aid the Labour Party. The one new aspect raised by this development has been the question of which faction within the party would benefit most from the unions' help. If the right wing was the main beneficiary during the 1940s and 1950s, it seemed that the left wing would gain more in the 1970s.

These changes have affected the channels of communication between MPs and unions. The early personal links represented by union leaders sitting in the House of Commons have given way to more institutional ties, which are less effective in keeping either the MPs or the union leaders informed about what the others are doing. Sponsored MPs are not happy about this development, but the situation will become worse in the future if the professional representatives continue to increase in number. Union leaders are less concerned about the ineffectiveness of the ties, because of their own consultative status with government and their fear that the MPs may become their rivals for influence and authority within the unions.

There are two main explanations for these changing patterns of representation in the House of Commons. The first is based on the changing social, economic, and political scene in Britain. With the expansion of educational opportunities in the twentieth century, the gradual decline of heavy industry, such as mining, and the increasing importance of industries based on distribution and services, union MPs are recruited from a different occupational and social base. As a result, there has been a gradual decline over the last three or four decades in the miners' representation, with a corresponding increase in the representation of general and white collar unions.

Changes in union parliamentary representation have also evolved out of the Labour Party's adoption in the 1930s of the Hastings Agreement, which forced CLPs to pay more attention to their own financial ability to finance parliamentary candidatures, instead of relying on the good graces of unions or wealthy individuals. Increasing selectivity on the part of the CLPs with respect to the types of nominees they are willing to adopt as candidates forces the unions to pay more attention to the kinds of nominees they are putting forward. This, in turn, has led to pressure within unions to adopt techniques of certification other than the traditional electoral one. The use of certification by examination in the post-World War II era is one sign of this development.

The second basis for an explanation of the changing pattern of union representation is the changing nature of the unions' relations with the British government. In the nineteenth century, when trade unions were generally quite small and weak, the floor of the House of Commons may well have been one of the few places where trade unionists could make the views of the working classes known to the government and other groups in British society. But as the unions gained in strength and many of their demands were accepted by the government and the rest of British society, they were increasingly drawn into a consultative relationship with the administrative agencies of the state, and their need for parliamentary representation declined.

Patterns of Behaviour

Over the years the background of union MPs has led them to be more concerned with matters relating to industry and social welfare than with foreign policy and defence questions. But the fact that they are interested in industrial topics does not mean that the union MPs have always agreed on the positions they should take. With the exception of questions that directly involve the status of trade unions as organisations and their role in collective bargaining, sponsored MPs have seldom been unanimous in their views. From the dispute over the eight hour day in the nineteenth century to the prices and incomes policy in the 1960s, union MPs have been as divided as other sections of the PLP on policy questions. Their background in the trade union movement did give them a general outlook or style of operation, which has had an impact on the PLP as a whole. They have been trained to be loyal to their union organisation, and this loyalty has been carried over to the PLP. They provide a core of support which the leader of the PLP can rely on. And when other MPs are willing to carry party disputes into the press for the whole world to see, the sponsored MPs are made uneasy.

The traditional background of the trade union MPs has earned them the scorn of many of their middle-class colleagues over the years. Two factors in particular have laid them open to these attacks. First, their active membership in unions and their interest in industrial questions in the House of Commons lays them open to charges that they neglect the public interest and violate the Liberal and Radical theories of representation inherited from the nineteenth century. Second, their lower average level of formal education and their older age of entry into Parliament are related to their lower levels of participation in legislative activity. In particular, the relative lack of trade unionists entering the House before their fortieth birthdays, and the large number who remain in the House after the age of sixty, mean that they are among those categories of MPs who are least active on the floor of the House and least prominent in party leadership.

In the first century of union representation in the House of Commons the union MPs consistently relied on other MPs, generally those with middle class background, to assist them in pursuing their goals. This was partly a matter of necessity because the trade unionists have never totalled at the maximum more than one-sixth of the entire House of Commons, and thus they have lacked the numbers to impose their views on the entire House or even the PLP. Moreover, in the pattern of alliance between the two groups of MPs, non-sponsored MPs have normally taken leading positions and the trade unionists have been in secondary positions. This was seen in the prominence of non-union Radical-Liberal MPs in the struggle over the eight hour day in the 1890s, and in the leadership patterns of the Labour Party after it was created in the twentieth century.

Since the 1920s, when the Labour Party achieved the position of 'loyal opposition' or alternative government, the position of leader has been held consistently by non-sponsored MPs with only one brief exception. Examination of Labour cabinets before and after World War II and of the leadership of the PLP in Opposition shows a similarly consistent pattern. Until the creation of the 1974 Labour government, sponsored MPs had been significantly underrepresented on all the leading bodies of the PLP with the exception of the Whips office. Their new representation, which was confirmed following the October 1974 General Election, reflects the changing background of the trade union MPs and may mark the start of a new era – but it will hardly be the era dreamed of by those who began it all by demanding that workers be represented by workers!

No group of politicians can hope to be completely composed of outstanding statesmen and leaders, and the sponsored MPs are no exception. Most British MPs are doomed to a life on the backbenches or, at best, to some very junior position in the government. The sponsored MPs share this fate. But their generally secondary position should not conceal the fact that some of the sponsored MPs have stood with the leading political figures of the last hundred years: Thomas Burt, Henry Broadhurst, Arthur Henderson, J. R. Clynes, J. H. Thomas, Ernest Bevin, Aneurin Bevan, and George Brown are only a few of the more important sponsored MPs.

Summary

We started this study with three objectives. The first was to try and determine whether criticisms of the sponsored MPs have been deserved. The answer must be that they were, because of the sponsored MPs' low level of activity in the House of Commons and their lack of prominence within the leadership of the Labour Party. Both these reasons are related to the age of entry and educational level of the sponsored MPs. The criticism is also partly justified by the sectarianism of trade unionists when they do take part in floor activity.

Second, how have these MPs been influenced by the various groups which they try to serve in the House of Commons? Clearly there has been some change in this area, as class, constituency, and union have all been supplanted by considerations of party loyalty. But the MPs' ambiguity on this point and the attempts of minorities within the unions to try to force them to accept some sort of responsibility to the unions have not eased their position.

Third, the sponsored MPs have for a century provided one ground for claiming that the House of Commons is representative or typical of the British population as a whole, and they have thus helped to maintain continued working class loyalty and support for the institutions of parliamentary democracy. What was important here, as Runciman points out, was not the *actual* distribution of power in British society but the *appearance* that the power of the working class had increased.[1] The sponsored MPs in the House of Commons and in the Cabinet could provide the basis for just such an illusion. Of course they have also given credence to the claim that the Labour Party is the party of the workers.

The Second Century

It is too soon to predict the ultimate outcome of the changes in the types of union-sponsored MPs being recruited, but several tentative generalisations can be offered. The new professional representatives, who are less likely to have the traditional trade unionists' attitude towards party loyalty, will also be less likely to contribute to the future harmony of the party. Second, as the Trade Union Group becomes even more heterogeneous than it is now, it will be less able to appear as an independent faction within the PLP. Third, the new union MPs are not as likely as their predecessors to be interested in or knowledgeable about industrial topics; and therefore the House of Commons, with a lack of thoroughly informed opinion within its own ranks, will find itself even less able to deal with the problems of an industrial society. This will increase the tendency to expand the consultative arrangements which already exist between interest groups and the administrative agencies of the government. Fourth, since the entry age and educational differences between the new sponsored MPs and other MPs are being reduced, we shall witness an end to the relatively lower rate of activity among sponsored MPs and their increasing prominence in party leadership roles. Fifth, if other unions try to imitate the TGWU's action against four of its sponsored MPs in 1970, the entire system of sponsorship will be destroyed. As long as other unions do not follow the TGWU's lead, sponsorship will continue to flourish.

Finally, what are the implications of these changes for the future of the Labour Party in the second century of trade union parliamentary representation? Regardless of their social background, the new professional representatives are less likely to have a working class outlook on life. And with the Labour Party deprived of the one major group of working class figures among its elected representatives, one must question how long it will be able to maintain its image as the party of the workers. As R. W. Johnson has recently written:

The implications of this process are awesome. If present trends continue, within a decade or two working class representation within the Labour Party and thus the political elite, will be virtually terminated. We shall, in that case, be again in the situation which last obtained in the late 19th century when the two major parties, led by homogeneously middle and upper-class elites, vied for the votes of a working class which was itself effectively excluded from political participation or representation at elite level. In a political system where class cleavage is so pronounced at the electoral level, such a development must inevitably threaten the basis of the Labour Party. For the asymmetry which already exists when two vast electoral blocs, sharply distinguished along class lines, vote for party elites who, in effect, pursue much the same consensus policies – this asymmetry can only be heightened and made more precarious if the two elites themselves converge in social type. At 'worst', the result could be the disintegration of the Labour Party to the benefit of the Liberals, Celtic nationalists and others. At the least, it must result in an ever more problematic relationship between the Labour Party and the trade unions, with the unions forced to play an increasingly political, even syndicalist role, at variance with Labour's own. [2]

When we note the general union reaction to the 1971 Industrial Relations Act, the direct industrial action utilised by the AEF in 1974 to protest that act, and the patterns of voting in the two general elections of 1974, Johnson's words take on still greater significance.

There is, of course, a substitute for symbolic representation for the working class. To retain their support, the Labour Party might launch a more aggressive programme aimed at satisfying their material goals. As we pointed out in the Introduction, representation can refer to a method of selection, to a type of person, or to the results of action. [3] Action by the Labour Party could counteract the change in the type of people serving in the House of Commons. Dennis Healey's proposals to make the taxation system more equitable are one such move. Wedgwood Benn's proposals on nationalisation may be another. In any event, the Labour Party will have to work hard to alter the policy impressions created by the mandatory prices and incomes policy of the late 1960s and the abortive reform of industrial relations contained in 'In Place of Strife'. The 1971 Tory Industrial Relations Act and the efforts to repeal it by the Labour government created in 1974 may prove to be a heaven-sent oppor-

tunity for the party to prove once more that it truly is the workers'
party, and to gain time for the development of other policies and
programmes.

Appendices

Appendix I
Trade Union MPs Elected Before 1910

Member	Trade Union Affiliation (if known)
Abraham, W.	Miners (South Wales)
Adamson, W.	Miners (Fife)
Arch, J.	Agricultural Workers
Austin, M.	?
Barnes, G. N.*	Engineers
Bell, R.*	Railway Servants
Bowerman, C. W.*	Compositors
Brace, W.	Miners (South Wales)
Broadhurst, H.	Stonemasons
Burns, J.	Engineers
Burt, T.*	Miners (Northumberland)
Clynes, J. R.	Gasworkers
Crawford, W.*	Miners (Durham/Northumberland)
Crean, E.	Secretary, Irish Trades Association
Cremer, W. R.	Carpenters and Joiners
Crooks, W.	Coopers
Curran, P.	Gas Workers
Duncan, C.*	Engineers/Transport Workers
Edwards, E.*	Miners (North Staffordshire/Midlands)
Fenwick, C.	Miners (Northumberland)
Gill, A. H.	Bolton Spinners
Glover, T.	Miners
Golstone, F. W.	Teachers
Hall, F.	Miners (Yorkshire)
Hancock, J. G.	Miners (Nottinghamshire)
Harvey, W. E.	Miners (Derbyshire)
Haslan, J.	Miners (Derbyshire)
Henderson, A.	Ironfounders
Hodge, J.*	Steel Smelters Association
Howell, G.	Bricklayers
Hudson, W.	Railway Servants
Jenkins, J.	?
Johnson, J.	Miners (Durham)

201

Johnson, W.*	Miners (Warwickshire/Midlands)
Kelly, G. D.*	Lithographic Printers
Leicester, J.	Flint Glass Makers
Macdonald, Alexander	Miners (Scotland)
Macpherson, J. T.	?
Maddison, F.	Railway Servants
Nichols, G.	Agricultural Workers
O'Grady, J.	Cabinet Makers
Parker, J.	?
Parrott, W.	Miners (Yorkshire)
Pickard, B.*	Miners (Yorkshire)
Pointer, J.	Patternmakers
Richards, T.*	Miners (South Wales)
Richards, T. F.	Boot and Shoe Operatives
Richardson, A.	?
Richardson, F.	?
Roberts, G. H.	Typographical Association
Rowlands, J.	Cabmen (?)/Watchcase Makers (?)
Seddon, J. A.	Shop Assistants
Shackleton, D. J.*	Weavers
Smith, A.	Nelson Overlookers
Stanley, A.	Miners (Midland)
Steadman, W. C.*	Barge Builders
Summerbell, T.	?
Sutton, J. E.	?
Taylor, J. W.	Durham Colliery Mechanics
Thomas, J. H.*	Railway Servants
Thorne, W.*	Gas Workers
Twist, H.	?
Vivian, H.	?
Wadsworth, J.	Miners
Walsh, S.	Miners
Ward J.	Navvies
Wardle, G. J.	Railway Servants
Wilkie, A.*	Ship Constructors and Shipwrights
Williams, J.	Miners
Wilson, J.*	Miners (Durham)
Wilson, J. H.*	Sailors and Firemen
Wilson, W. T.	?
Woods, S.	Miners (Lancashire and Cheshire)

* Holder of major union office (see Fig. 1, p.5).

SOURCES: A. W. Humphrey, *A History of Labour Representation*, Appendix III, pp. 192–95.

G. D. H. Cole, *British Working Class Politics, 1832–1914*, Appendix I, pp. 255–301.

H. A. Clegg, A. Fox and A. F. Thompson, *A History of British Trade Unions Since 1889*, Vol. I: *1889–1910, passim.*

Appendix II
Measuring Parliamentary Activity

The Question Hour

The first type of activity to which we devote our attention is the Question Hour and the questions that fill it. The Question Hour is one of the highlights of the parliamentary day.[1] The general importance ascribed to questions is indicated by the fact that they are second only to Debate in the amount of space they occupy in the published *Parliamentary Debates*. In analysing questions it is important to subdivide them into the three different categories used in the House of Commons. These are: (1) oral questions; (2) supplementary questions; and (3) written questions. Slightly different purposes are served by each.

Oral questions are those put down on the agenda of the House of Commons by Private Members in advance of the date on which an answer is expected. Addressed to the relevant minister, who must be prepared to answer them on the appointed day, they may be simple requests for information, complaints about specific acts of the government, or general attacks on the government's policy. Oral questions are more frequently asked by Opposition Members.[2]

Supplementary questions result from the minister's answer to an oral question. The Member asking the original question is customarily permitted to ask one further question following the minister's reply. Other Members, especially the Opposition frontbench, will also be active in seeking to ask Supplementary questions.[3] The minister receives no advance notice of these questions and must be well briefed on the subject if he is to be able to answer them. Frequently, especially when asked by Opposition frontbenchers, the supplementary questions will constitute a major attack on the government's policy.

Of the three categories, written questions probably constitute the least important. There are fewer of them asked, and they receive far less publicity than the other categories of questions. For the most part, they seem to be little more than requests for information. Of course, this does not mean that they might not be used as a basis for attacking the government.

The indices used in measuring quantitative participation in the Question Hour are based on the number of each kind of question asked by each Member. This was frequently determined by an actual count of the Questions as they appear in the pages of Hansard.[4] We determined these totals for the first, second, and fourth sessions of the 1959–64 Parliament. These separate totals were then combined to provide a single total for each question category. The total numbers of each type of question for three sessions are the figures used in the analysis in the second half of Chapter V.

The Question Hour and Specialisation

Examination of specialisation in the Question Hour is tedious, because of the number of questions involved. In the 1962–63 session of the House of Commons, which is the basis of our analysis, there were over 14,600 oral and written questions directed at thirty different departments or committees. We have merely classified oral and written questions according to the minister or department to which they were addressed. We have substituted department for subject area or announced organisational affiliation for reasons of economy, simplicity, and comparability. This procedure may introduce other complications, because all British government departments do not have coherent and consistent jurisdictions, and this will be a major limitation on our conclusions.

The data for the analysis of the Question Hour were obtained from two sources. For the trade union MPs they were compiled by counting the number of oral and written questions they asked, as recorded in Hansard, the printed report of parliamentary debates, and then classifying these questions according to the department to which they were addressed. Comparable data for other MPs are based on figures supplied by the office of the clerk of the House of Commons. These figures represent the total number of written and oral questions put down on the Order Paper (Agenda) of the House to be asked by all MPs. There may be discrepancies between these two sources, because there are occasional questions put down on the Order Paper which do not get asked. This distortion, where it occurs, is of minimal importance.

Our purpose in using this information on the Question Hour is to compare the pattern of questions asked by trade union MPs with that of all other MPs. Thus, when reporting the data in Chapter V, we have subtracted the questions asked by the sponsored Members from the departmental totals for all MPs. The reference to 'other MPs' actually means the MPs who were not members of the government during the session, not officers of the House of Commons, and not sponsored by a trade union. In the 1962–63 session there were 87 sponsored MPs and 464 other MPs who might or did ask questions.

Standing Committees

The second type of legislative activity studied was that in the Standing committees of the House of Commons.[5] Composed of some twenty-five to fifty

Members who consider the details of public bills not discussed by the entire House of Commons, these committees do not normally change the general provisions of a bill, although they may amend it in detail. They are organised as Houses of Commons in miniature but with less party discipline.

In measuring activity on these committees we used two different (but related) indicators. The first is the record of the number of committee meetings to which a Member is 'summoned' or called. The second is the record of the number of committee meetings which the Member actually attended. [6] The total numbers of summonses and attendance for all five sessions of the 1959–64 Parliament were used in these two indices.

The exact relationship between these two indices is not clear. Both are measures of a Member's interest in a subject, since Members are generally summoned to a Standing Committee only when it is considering a Bill of interest to them. The actual attendance figure might indicate a higher interest in the subject, but it might also indicate nothing more than a Member's sense of responsibility in carrying out his parliamentary duties. Despite the very high correlation between these two indices, we included both in the analysis in Chapter V.

Debate

The third type of activity studied is Debate. The House of Commons is, above all else, a debating chamber. It is through debate that the nation is kept informed of the views of the major parties on current political issues. It is through debate that differences within the parties are frequently brought to light. Measuring debate is a difficult problem with no simple solution. For our purposes we have measured the length of the index entry headed 'Debate' under a Member's name in the sessional indexes to the parliamentary debates. [7] By combining these totals for the first four sessions of the 1959–64 Parliament we obtained the figure for Debate used in Chapter V.

Appendix III
Sample Composition

For each type of activity indicated in Appendix II we measured the participation of the individuals included in each of three groups of MPs, and on this we based our analysis in Chapter V. The first group used in this analysis consisted of eighty-seven sponsored MPs. There were originally ninety-three trade unionists elected to the House of Commons in 1959, but six of them died or resigned from Parliament before the summer of 1964. In order to facilitate the analysis, these six were excluded from all calculations. The other two groups are composed of: (1) non-trade union sponsored Labour MPs (referred to as 'other Labour MPs'), and (2) Conservative backbenchers. These two groups were selected in one operation and then divided on the basis of their party affiliation. They were not drawn from the entire House of Commons.

The population from which they were drawn is defined as follows: Beginning with the 630 MPs elected in 1959, we excluded the following groups: (1) 93 union-sponsored Members; (2) 28 MPs who died between 1959 and 1964; (3) 34 Members who resigned from Parliament between 1959 and 1964 (including those who moved up to the House of Lords); (4) 112 MPs who served in the government at some time between 1959 and 1964; and (5) four MPs who were officers of the House of Commons. Allowing for overlapping among these groups, their exclusion left us with a population of 388 MPs.

Using a table of random numbers to determine our starting place, we then drew every fifth MP for inclusion in our comparative samples. This process was repeated three times, giving us a total comparative sample of 230 Members. This sample included 137 Conservative backbenchers, 90 Labour MPs without trade union sponsorship (referred to in the analysis as Other Labour MPs), 2 Liberals and one MP, Alan Brown who changed affiliation from Labour to Conservative. To simplify our analysis, these last three Members were excluded from further consideration, and only the Conservative backbenchers and the Other Labour MPs were used in the second half of Chapter V. Because of the procedures used in determining the population from which they were drawn, it is almost impossible to extend any conclusions based on these groups to the universe of all MPs.

The MPs in each of the three groups were then classified on the basis of age, educational level, constituency majority, and length of service in the House. Preliminary analysis indicated that only age and educational level were sufficiently related to behaviour to be worth reporting.

Notes to the Text

Introduction

The place of publication is London unless otherwise stated.

[1] Great Britain, House of Commons *Debates* (Hereafter cited as *Parl. Deb.*) 5th Series. 1953–54. Vol. 528, col. 75 (27 May 1954). Cf. the comment of the miners' MP, William Brace, in 1911: *Parl. Deb.* 1911. Vol. 21, col. 226 (7 Feb. 1911).

[2] *Parl. Deb.* 1970–71. Vol. 821, col. 1072 (19 July 1971).

[3] S. H. Beer, *British Politics in the Collectivist Age* (New York: Knopf, 1965), pp. 18 ff.

[4] J. D. Stewart, *British Pressure Groups: Their Role in Relation to the House of Commons* (Oxford: Clarendon Press, 1958); P. Self and H. Storing, *The State and the Farmer* (Allen and Unwin, 1962), pp. 42–3; R. A. Manzer, *Teachers and Politics* (Manchester: Manchester University Press, 1970), pp. 18 ff; A. Spoor, *White-Collar Union: 60 Years of NALGO* (Heinemann, 1967), p. 38 *et passim*; H. Eckstein, *Pressure Group Politics* (Allen and Unwin, 1960), pp. 76–8; M. Harrison, *The Trade Unions and the Labour Party Since 1945* (Detroit: Wayne State University Press, 1961), pp. 262–302; S. Blank, *Industry and Government in Britain: The Federation of British Industries in Politics, 1945–1965* (Saxon House/D. C. Heath, 1973), pp. 20, 60; and J. Blondel, *Voters, Parties and Leaders*, revised ed. (Penguin Books, 1969), pp. 205–22.

[5] J. H. Millett, 'The Role of an Interest Group Leader in the House of Commons', *Western Political Quarterly*, IX (1956), pp. 915–26; A. H. Birch, *Representative and Responsible Government* (Allen and Unwin, 1964), p. 113; and Eckstein, *op. cit.*, pp. 76–8.

[6] *Parl. Deb.* 1946–47. Vol. 440, col. 365 (15 July 1947). The debate extends from cols. 284 to 365. A move to have the House disagree with the

208

motion was defeated by a margin of more than 2 to 1.

[7] See K. I. Vijay, 'The Declaration of Interests by M.P.s: An Analysis of the Current Campaign for Reform', *Political Quarterly*, XLIV (1973), pp. 478–86; C. Price, 'MPs and the Open Society', *New Statesman* (21 June 1974), p. 878. The select committee's report is found at: Great Britain, Parliamentary Papers (1969–70), Accounts and Papers No. 57: *Report from the Select Committee on Members' Interests (Declaration)*, H.M.S.O., 1969. (Hereafter cited as *Members' Interests Report*.) See also A. Roth, *The Business Background of Members of Parliament* (Parliamentary Profiles, n.d. [1963]), p. xiv. Other editions of Roth's guide help to keep awareness of the potential problems at a high level.

[8] On consultation see Stewart, *British Pressure Groups*, pp. 3–27; PEP, *Advisory Committees in British Government* (Allen and Unwin, 1960), *passim*; Manzer, *Teachers and Politics*, pp. 11–19. Cf. Michael J. Brenner, 'Functional Representation and Interest Group Theory: Some Notes on British Practice', *Comparative Politics*, II (1969–70), pp. 111–34.

[9] In an earlier era, say during the nineteenth century, when Parliament is thought to have had a somewhat greater role in the making of public policy, legislative spokesmen may have provided the most access to decision making. For example, see Beer, *British Politics*, pp. 38 ff. With the extension of government activity in regulating large segments of modern life, consultation has acquired increased importance in the years since World War I. See Brenner, *op. cit.*, esp. pp. 118–22, 129–30 and M. Edelman, 'Inside Westminster – Where Does Power Lie?' *New Humanist* (June 1972), p. 4.

[10] R. W. Johnson, 'The British Political Elite, 1955–1972', *European Journal of Sociology*, XIV (1973), p. 41; J. Harrod, *Trade Union Foreign Policy* (Garden City, N.Y.: Anchor Doubleday, 1972), p. 69. For a slightly different concept of the stages of trade union representation, see Zygmunt Bauman, *Between Class and Elite*, trans. by Sheila Patterson (Manchester: Manchester University Press, 1972), p. 106. Bauman's book was first published in Polish in 1960, but I did not see it until the present study was virtually completed.

[11] For a survey and analysis of the changing pattern of relations between the trade unions and the British government, see V. L. Allen, *Trade Unions and the Government* (Longmans, Green, 1960), *passim*.

[12] For a thorough discussion of legislative roles, see J. C. Wahlke *et al*, *The Legislative System* (New York: John Wiley and Sons, 1962), *passim*. R. Rose has used the concept of 'role' in some highly suggestive comments about the House of Commons. See his *Politics in England*, 1st ed. (Boston: Little, Brown, 1964), p. 93, Cf. Bauman, pp. 204–9.

[13] Birch, *Government*, pp. 14–17.

[14] L. G. Seligman, 'Elite Recruitment and Political Development', *Journal of Politics*, XXVI (1964), pp. 621–22; R. W. Johnson, 'British Political Elite', p. 69.

[15] B. Taylor (Lord Taylor of Mansfield), *Uphill All the Way: A Miner's Struggle* (Sedgwick and Jackson, 1972), p. xi; Johnson, 'The Political Elite', *New Society* (24 January 1974), pp. 188–91.

[16] For a discussion of the MP's place in the House of Commons, see P. G.

Richards, *The Backbenchers* (Faber, 1972); D. Leonard and V. Herman (eds.), *The Backbencher and Parliament* (Macmillan, 1972); H. Fairlie, 'The Lives of Politicians', *Encounter* (August 1967), p. 22; and J. H. Millett, 'Role of an Interest Group Leader'.

[17] Union-sponsored MPs have been given little systematic analysis despite their many critics. The only two studies that deal with them in anything less than a passing way are: M. Harrison, *Trade Unions*, pp. 262–306; and a recent Fabian pamphlet by J. Ellis and R. W. Johnson, *Members From Unions* (Fabian Society, 1974).

Chapter I

[1] C. F. Brand, 'The Conversion of the British Trade Unions to Political Action', *American Historical Review*, XXX (1925), p. 251.

[2] R. P. Arnot, *South Wales Miners (Glowyr de Cymru): A History of the South Wales Miners' Federation (1890–1914)* (Allen and Unwin, 1967), p. 100. (hereafter cited as Arnot, *South Wales Miners*).

[3] For a comprehensive discussion of the difficulties in identifying the early trade union Members of Parliament, see H. A. Clegg, A. Fox, and A. F. Thompson, *A History of British Trade Unions Since 1889*, Vol I: *1889–1910* (Oxford: Clarendon Press, 1964), pp. 51–52; 283–85. The definition of a trade union MP being used in this study is narrower than that proposed by Clegg and his colleagues. They would include the nature of a legislator's activity as well as the characteristics we have used.

The union-supported MPs who constitute the basis for the following discussion were taken from the lists of early Labour Members found in: G. D. H. Cole, *British Working Class Politics, 1832–1914* (Routledge, 1941), pp. 255–301, Appendix I; and A. W. Humphrey, *A History of Labour Representation* (Constable, 1913), pp. 192–95, Appendix II.

[4] H. Pelling, *A History of British Trade Unionism* (Penguin Books, 1963), p. 127.

[5] R. P. Arnot, *A History of the Miners' Federations of Great Britain*, 3 vols. (Allen and Unwin, 1949–1961), Vol. I, p. 369. (hereafter cited as Arnot, *Miners' Federation*).

[6] Arnot, *South Wales Miners*, p. 380, Appendix II.

[7] R. Gregory, *The Miners and British Politics, 1906–1914* (Oxford University Press, 1968), p. 17.

[8] This view was expressed in A. A. Walton's paper, "The Direct Representation of Labour in Parliament", in Trades Union Congress, *Report* (1869), p. 200. A. K. Russell, *Liberal Landslide: The General Election of 1906* (Newton Abbot, U.K.: David and Charles, 1973), p. 79 (fig. 2) points out that the 1906 LRC candidates' election manifestos mentioned this more than any other issue. Cf. J. E. Williams, *The Derbyshire Miners* (Allen and Unwin, 1962), p. 488; F. Hammrill, "Labour Representation', *Fortnightly Review*, LXI (1894), pp. 553–54.

[9] For example, see D. Lowe, *From Pit to Parliament* (The Labour Publishing Company, 1923), pp. 20–35; T. Burt, *Autobiography*, with supplementary chapters by A. Watson (T. Fisher Unwin, 1924), pp. 234–36,

278; A. Watson, *A Great Labour Leader, Being the Life of the Right Honourable Thomas Burt, M.P.* (Brown, Langham, 1908), p. 156; E. Welbourne, *The Miners' Unions of Northumberland and Durham* (Cambridge: The University Press, 1923), pp. 198–99; P. Bagwell, *The Railwaymen* (Allen and Unwin, 1963), p. 232; H. A. Clegg, *General Union in a Changing Society* (Oxford: Blackwell, 1964), pp. 57–8; W. L. Guttsman, *The British Political Elite* (Macgibbon and Kee, 1963), p. 229; P. Horn, *Joseph Arch (1826–1919): The Farm Workers' Leader* (Kineton, England: The Roundwood Press, 1971), p. 177; Williams, *Derbyshire Miners*, pp. 496, 809; and Gregory, *Miners and British Politics*, pp. 19–20.

[10] W. R. Garside, *The Durham Miners, 1919–1960* (Allen and Unwin, 1971), pp. 326–27.

[11] Watson, *Life of Burt*, p. 145. Cf. Peter Stead, "Working-Class Leadership in South Wales, 1900–1920", *Welsh History Review*, VI (1973), p. 332.

[12] M. I. Cole (ed.), *Beatrice Webb's Diaries, 1912–1924* (Longmans, Green, 1952), p. 74 (entry for 8 December 1916). Mrs Webb could still recognise the significance of the presence of trade unionists among the traditional members of the British elite. See *ibid.*, p. 55 (entry for 20 January 1916). Cf. the reaction of J. Lawson's parents to his first parliamentary speech: 'Father at once expressed his satisfaction that I had been "telling them off", the person who had been "told" being the government'. J. Lawson, *A Man's Life* (Hodder and Stoughton, 1932), p. 264.

[13] For a discussion of the miners' strength in selected constituencies, see Gregory, *op. cit.*, pp. 15–17, 192–201.

[14] H. Pelling, *Origins of the Labour Party, 1880–1900*, 2nd. ed. (Oxford: Clarendon Press, 1965), p. 2; Pelling, *Social Geography of British Elections, 1885–1910* (Macmillan, 1967), p. 97; Bagwell, *Railwaymen*, p. 200; Williams, *op. cit.*, pp. 488–93.

[15] M. Ostrogorski, *Democracy and the Organization of Political Parties*, Vol. 1: *England*, ed. S.M. Lipset (New York: Anchor Doubleday, 1964), p. 281. First published in 1902.

[16] The Earl of Oxford and Asquith (H. H. Asquith), Fifty Years of British Parliament. 2 vols. (Boston: Little, Brown and Company, 1926), II, pp. 182–84; H. W. Lucy, *A Diary of the Home Rule Parliament, 1892–1895* (Cassell, 1896), pp. 385–89.

[17] Lucy, *Home Rule Parliament*, pp. 345–46.

[18] H. Evan, *Sir Randal Cremer* (Boston: Gin and Co. for the International School of Peace, 1910), pp. 332–33. Cf. G. Howell's achievement in securing the printing of an inexpensive edition of the Statutes of the Realm.

[19] T. Burt, in the *Fortnightly Review* (1889), quoted by Watson, *op. cit.*, p. 243. Cf. Burt, *Autobiography*, p. 262.

[20] H. W. Lucy, *Later Peeps at Parliament* (George Newnes, 1905), pp. 63–4.

[21] 'Socialism in the House of Commons', *Edinburgh Review*, CCIV (October 1906), p. 271.

[22] Lucy, *Diary of Two Parliaments* (Cassell, 1885), p. 103.

[23] Cited in Clegg, Fox, and Thompson, *British Trade Unions*, Vol. I, p. 279. George Howell spent some fifteen pages trying to refute Chamberlain in his *Labour Legislation, Labour Movements and Labour Leaders*. 2 vols. 2nd ed. T. F. Unwin, 1905, II, pp. 459–73. Cf. T. Burt, *Autobiography*, pp. 264–65.

[24] Lucy, *A Diary of the Salisbury Parliament, 1886–1892* (Cassell, 1896), pp. 126–27.

[25] R. Postgate, 'Class in Britain and Abroad', in R. Mabey (ed.), *Class* (Anthony Blond, 1967), p. 161.

[26] M. Cowling, *The Impact of Labour, 1920–1924* (Cambridge, The University Press, 1971), pp. 176, 289.

[27] Williams, *Derbyshire Miners*, pp. 505–10, 807–32; Garside, *Durham Miners*, pp. 322–23; Clegg, *General Union in a Changing Society*, p. 59.

[28] K. O. Morgan, *Wales in British Politics, 1868–1922* (Cardiff: University of Wales Press, 1963), pp. 198–220; Arnot, *South Wales Miners*, pp. 267–68; F. Brockway, *Inside the Left* (Allen and Unwin, 1942), pp. 36–7; Labour Representation Committee, *Conference Report* (1903), p. 15; J. Bowle, *Viscount Samuel, A Biography* (Gollancz, 1957), pp. 48–9; and Williams, *op. cit.*, p. 485. For a general discussion of this period, see R. McKibbin, *The Evolution of the Labour Party, 1910–1924* (Oxford University Press, 1974), pp. 48–71 & 112–23.

[29] Quoted in E. S. Heffer, *The Class Struggle in Parliament* (Gollancz, 1973), p. 25.

[30] Williams, *op. cit.*, pp. 491–92.

[31] In general, see Pelling, *Social Geography*, pp. xiii, 56–9, 111, 114–15, *et passim*. On working class deference, see E. A. Nordlinger, *The Working Class Tories* (MacGibbon and Kee, 1967); R. T. McKenzie and A. Silver, *Angels in Marble* (Hutchinson, 1968); and D. Butler and D. Stokes, *Political Change in Britain* (Macmillan, 1969), pp. 104–15. For particular reference to the impact of Irish Catholic immigration, see Pelling, *Geography*, pp. 284–85.

[32] Pelling, *Origins*, pp. 205–6; *Geography*, pp. 202, 236, and 253; Williams, *op. cit.*, pp. 497–8.

[33] For a thorough discussion of British theories of representation, see Birch, *Representative and Responsible Government*, and Beer, *British Politics*. Bauman, *Between Class and Elite*, pp. 204–9, calls specific attention to the role conflict of the early trade union MPs.

[34] H. Broadhurst, *H. Broadhurst, M.P.: The Story of His Life: From a Stone Mason's Bench to the Treasury Bench*, 2nd ed. (Hutchinson, 1901), p. 105. For other examples of a constituency orientation, see J. Arch, *The Story of His Life, Told by Himself*, edited by the Countess of Warwick. 2nd ed. (Hutchinson and Co. 1898), p. 357; E. Welbourne, *Miners' Unions*, p. 202; 2nd ed. W. P. Maddox, *Foreign Relations in British Labour Politics*, xerox ed. (Ann Arbor, Michigan: University Microfilm, 1964), pp. 210–14.

[35] Broadhurst, *op. cit.*, p. 77.

[36] *Parl. Deb.* 3rd series. 1880. Vol. 256, cols. 932–33 (31 August 1880).

[37] *Parl. Deb.* Series. 1882. Vol. 267, cols. 434–35 (8 March 1882).

[38] *Ibid.* 4th Series. 1902. Vol. 109, cols. 895–96 (17 June 1902).

[39] *Ibid.* 3rd Series. 1885. Vol. 298, cols. 1198–1205 (4 June 1885). Broadhurst was a member of the TUC Parliamentary Committee from 1874 until 1889 and again in 1893–94.

[40] For example, see *Parl. Deb.* 4th Series. 1898. Vol. 56, cols. 330–34 (18 April 1898); *Ibid.*, vol. 58, cols. 1027–35 (8 June 1898).

[41] W. J. Davis, *The British Trades Union Congress: History and Recollections*, 2 vols. (Co-operative Printing Society, 1910–1916), Vol. II, pp. 59–61.

[42] W. Thorne, *My Life's Battles* (George Newnes, 1925), pp. 208–9. Cf. G. Haw, *From Workhouse to Westminster* (Cassell and Co., 1907), pp. 202–7, 219–26, 230–40.

[43] Davis, Vol. I, pp. 45, 59.

[44] Labour Representation Committee, *Conference Report* (1902), p. 21.

[45] *Parl. Deb.* 3rd Series. 1879. Vol. 245, cols. 232–33 (24 April 1879).

[46] *Ibid.* 4th Series. 1898. Vol. 54, col. 1146 (9 March 1898).

[47] Arch, *His Life*, pp. 354–55. Cf. the more confused sound of Arch's maiden speech in the House of Commons, in Horn, *Joseph Arch*, pp. 240–43.

[48] Williams, *Derbyshire Miners*, pp. 496–97, quoting *The Sheffield Independent* (26 January 1907).

[49] E. W. Evans, *Mabon (William Abraham, 1842–1922)* (Cardiff: University of Wales Press, 1959), p. 34, referring to the *South Wales Daily News* (14 November 1885). The particular interest of the miners is well known. See H. J. Hanham, *Elections and Party Management* (Longmans, Green, 1959), p. 326; Cole (ed.), *Beatrice Webb's Diaries, 1912–1924*, p. 72 (entry for 8 December 1916).

[50] *Parl. Deb.* 4th Series. 1898. Vol. 59, cols. 123–33 (22 June 1898); *Ibid.*, Vol. 60, col. 30 (24 June 1898). Cf Garside, *Durham Miners*, pp. 356–59.

[51] *Parl. Deb.* 3rd Series. 1881. Vol. 262, col. 1006 (15 July 1881); *Ibid.* 4th Series. 1898. Vol. 55, col. 1234 (29 March 1898); *Ibid.*, Vol. 56, cols. 40–1 (4 April 1898).

[52] Welbourne, *Miners' Unions*, pp. 201–2.

[53] J. Hodge, *Workman's Cottage to Windsor Castle* (Sampson Low and Co. 1931), pp. 157–59. Inter-union conflict led to the defeat of Charles Duncan in 1918. See R. Hyman, *The Workers' Union* (Oxford: Clarendon Press, 1971), p. 85.

[54] Quoted in Pelling, *Origins*, p. 194.

[55] J. Wilson, *Memories of a Labour Leader* (T. Fisher Unwin, 1910), p. 284.

[56] Burt, *Autobiography*, pp. 236–38, 265–66.

[57] Clegg, Fox, and Thompson, *op. cit.*, p. 285.

[58] Hyman, *op. cit.*, pp. 154–55. Cf. the poor impression made by George Howell: in F. M. Leventhal, *Respectable Radical* (Weidenfeld and Nicolson, 1971), pp. 207–8.

[59] Davis, *Trades Union Congress*, II, p. 27. But cf. Welbourne, *op. cit.*, p. 255.

[60] For discussion and evaluation of Mabon's parliamentary career, see Evans, *Mabon*, pp. 36 ff; Morgan, *Wales in British Politics*, p. 81; Arnot, *South Wales Miners*, p. 26; and B. Turner, *About Myself* (Humphrey Toulmin, 1930), p. 286.

[61] Lucy, *Home Rule Parliament*, p. 386. Cf. Lucy, *The Balfourian Parliament, 1900–1905* (Hodder and Stoughton, 1906), p. 111.

[62] H. R. H. Weaver (ed.), *Dictionary of National Biography, 1922–1930* (Oxford University Press, 1937), p. 143. Cf. Watson, *Life of Burt*, p. 244.

[63] Lucy, *Home Rule Parliament*, p. 386.

[64] V. L. Allen, 'The Ethics of Trade Union Leaders', *British Journal of Sociology*, VII (1956), p. 320.

[65] Watson, *op. cit.*, p. 114; Burt, *Autobiography*, p. 261.

[66] Arnot, *South Wales Miners*, pp. 106–11. The tax was not removed until 1906.

[67] *Parl. Deb.* 5th Series. 1911. Vol. 21, col. 226 (7 Feb. 1911). Cf. N. Edwards, *The History of the South Wales Miners' Federation* (Lawrence and Wishart, 1938), p. 63; Bagwell, *Railwaymen*, pp. 293, 304, 337–8.

[68] Arnot, *The Miners' Federation*, I, p. 127.

[69] *Ibid.*, pp. 130–31.

[70] Arnot, *South Wales Miners*, pp. 128–29, 133–34; Morgan, *Wales in British Politics*, p. 203. Mabon's position was influenced by his struggle for control of the South Wales miners in opposition to MFGB proponents such as William Brace.

[71] Their opposition to a legislated eight hour day becomes more understandable when we note that they had already secured a seven hour day, thirty-seven hour week through collective bargaining. See S. and B. Webb, *Industrial Democracy*, new ed. (Longmans, Green, 1911), p. 255. The hours worked by various groups of miners during this period are shown in B. McCormick and J. E. Williams, 'The Miners and the Eight-Hour Day, 1863–1910', *Economic History Review*, XII (1959), pp. 237–38. Cf. Garside, *Durham Miners*, p. 25.

[72] Watson, *Burt*, p. 233. Cf. Fenwick's reason given in Arnot, *The Miners' Federation*, I, p. 181.

[73] Arnot, *ibid.*, I, p. 294; Burt, *Autobiography*, p. 208; Pelling, *Social Geography*, p. 208; Labour Representation Committee, *Annual Conference* (1902), p. 15. Perhaps the only dissenting voice was that of Broadhurst himself. See Broadhurst, p. 240.

[74] S. and B. Webb, *A History of Trade Unionism*, new ed. (Longmans, Green, 1920), pp. 567–68.

[75] Arnot, *The Miners' Federation*, I, pp. 133–34, 270–71; Williams, *Derbyshire Miners*, pp. 493, 498.

[76] Webb, *Trade Unionism*, p. 600.

[77] G. M. Tuchwell, *The Life of Sir Charles W. Dilke*, 2 vols. (J. Murray, 1917), II, pp. 342–67; R. Jenkins, *Sir Charles Dilke* (Collins, 1958), pp. 394–95; Turner, *About Myself*, p. 287.

[78] G. D. H. Cole and R. Postgate, *The Common People, 1746–1946*, 2nd ed. (Methuen, 1961), p. 459.

[79] J. A. Spender, *The Life of the Rt. Hon. Sir Henry*

Campbell-Bannerman. 2 vols. (Hodder and Stoughton, 1923), II, pp. 277–79.

[80] Clegg, Fox, and Thompson, *Trade Unions,* p. 414.

[81] For a discussion of *Osborne's* effect on Labour Party finances, see W. B. Gwyn, *Democracy and the Cost of Politics in Britain* (The Athlone Press, 1962), pp. 178–205.

[82] Bagwell, *Railwaymen,* p. 257.

[83] See A. L. Lowell, *The Influence of Party Upon Legislation in England and America* (Washington: American Historical Association Annual Report, 1902); and H. Berrington, 'Partisanship and Dissidence in the Nineteenth-century House of Commons', *Parliamentary Affairs,* XXL, No. 4 (Autumn 1968), pp. 338–74.

[84] Broadhurst, *Life,* p. 249.

[85] Clegg, Fox, and Thompson, p. 267. Cf. the disinterest of the Labour MPs immediately following the 1906 General Election. K. D. Brown, *Labour and Unemployment, 1900–1914* (Newton Abbot U.K.: David and Charles, 1971), pp. 73 ff.

[86] See G. D. H. Cole, *British Working Class Politics,* p. 214; Cole and Postgate, p. 470; Cole, *A History of the Labour Party from 1914* (Routledge and Kegan Paul, 1948), p. 2; P. Snowden, *An Autobiography.* 2 vols. (Ivor Nicholson and Watson, 1934), I, p. 216.

[87] Beer, *British Politics,* pp. 126–27.

[88] Clegg, Fox, and Thompson, pp. 271, 488; Pelling, *Origins,* pp. 205–6; Gregory, pp. 19–20.

[89] Beer, p. 112.

[90] Lucy, *Home Rule Parliament,* p. 280. Cf. Pelling, *Origins,* pp. 108–9; H. J. Hanham, 'Opposition Techniques in British Politics, 1867–1914', *Government and Opposition,* II (November 1966), p. 41.

[92] Cole, *British Working Class Politics,* p. 204.

[93] See especially Webb, *Industrial Democracy,* pp. 65–71, for a discussion of the qualifications of a 'professional representative'. Cf. Webb, *Trade Unionism,* pp. 701–2; Guttsman, *British Political Elite,* p. 230.

[94] E. Halévy, *History of the English People in the Nineteenth Century,* 6 vols. (New York: Barnes and Noble, 1961), VI, p. 93; H. Pelling, *A Short History of the Labour Party* (Macmillan 1962), p. 20.

Chapter II

[1] H. Pelling, *A History of British Trade Unionism,* pp. 261–63.

[2] H. Pelling, *Popular Politics and Society in Late Victorian Britain* (New York: St. Martin's Press, 1968), p. 106.

[3] For example, see A. R. Griffin, *The Miners of Nottinghamshire, 1914–1944* (Allen and Unwin, 1962), p. 239; J. Hodge, *Workman's Cottage,* pp. 151–52; Sir A. Pugh, *Men of Steel* (The Iron and Steel Confedera-

tion, 1951), pp. 135–39; J. Arch, *Life*, p. 391; J. H. Wilson, *My Stormy Voyage Through Life* (Co-operative Printing Society, 1925), p. 266; N. McKillop, *The Lighted Flame* (Nelson, 1950), p. 187; P. Snowden, *Autobiography*, I, pp. 161–62; J. R. Clynes, *Memoirs*. 2 vols. (Hutchinson 1937), I, p. 112; B. Turner, *About Myself*, p. 242; Sir J. Sexton, *Agitator: The Life of the Dockers' M.P.* (Faber and Faber, 1936), p. 269; G. N. Barnes, *From Workshop to War Cabinet* (Herbert Jenkins, 1929), p. 86; Clegg, *General Union in a Changing Society*, pp. 57–58; W. R. Garside, *Durham Miners*, p. 75.

⁴ See A. V. S. Lockhead, 'The Uses of Advisory Bodies by the Industrial Relations Department of the Ministry of Labour', in R. V. Vernon and N. Mansergh (eds.), *Advisory Bodies: A Study of Their Uses in Relation to Central Government, 1919–1939* (Allen and Unwin, 1940), pp. 285–291, 303.

⁵ For example, see A. Fox, *A History of the National Union of Boot and Shoe Operatives* (Oxford: Blackwell, 1958), p. 462; R. P. Arnot, *The Miners' Federation*, I, p. 219; N. Edwards, *South Wales Miners*, pp. 152–53; J. Griffiths, *Pages From Memory* (Dent, 1969), pp. 44–45; P. Bagwell, *Railwaymen* p. 535; S. Higenbottam, Comp. *Our Society's History* (Manchester: Amalgamated Society of Woodworkers, 1939), p. 283.

⁶ Giles Radice and Lisanne Radice, *Will Thorne: Constructive Militant* (George Allen and Unwin, 1974), pp. 101 ff; H. A. Clegg, *General Union* (Oxford: Blackwell, 1954), p. 99; Clegg, *General Union in a Changing Society*, pp. 135–36, 202–3; E. Taylor, "An Interview with Wesley Perrins", *Bulletin of the Society for the Study of Labour History*, no. 21 (Autumn 1970), p. 23.

⁷ Union of Postoffice Workers, Research Department, "Advantages of Direct Parliamentary Representation". (Typewritten manuscript) (2 July 1943).

⁸ Guttsman, *British Political Elite*, pp. 236–37.

⁹ The Labour Party conference *Reports* following each General Election include an appendix indicating the sponsoring body for all Labour candidates. Only in the 1920s is there some confusion.

¹⁰ E. Shinwell, *Conflict Without Malice* (Odhams Press, 1953), pp. 82 *et passim;* F. Brockway, *Socialism Over Sixty Years* (Allen and Unwin, 1946), pp. 21, 29n, 399n.

¹¹ R. E. Dowse, *Left in the Center* (Longmans, 1966), p. 177n; R. K. Middlemas, *The Clydesiders* (Hutchinson, 1965) p. 264. See also the letter by I. M. Coleman, chairman of the Scottish Divisional Council of the ILP, in the *New Statesman* (31 December 1965), p. 1029.

¹² A. Bullock, *The Life and Times of Ernest Bevin*, Vol. I: *Trade Union Leader, 1881–1940* (Heinemann, 1960), p. 204. Sometimes, as with Ben Tillett, it took more than simple encouragement.

¹³ W. I. Jennings, *Parliament*, 1st ed. (Cambridge: University Press, 1939), p. 49. Cf. Strauss, *Bevin and Company* (New York: G. P. Putnam's Sons, 1941), pp. 82–3.

¹⁴ B. Taylor, *Uphill All the Way*, p. 84. Harold Neal's experience is discussed in J. E. Williams, *Derbyshire Miners*, pp. 366–68, 873. Neal still

received some financial help from the miners at the 1966 election, but he announced his retirement in 1968 when he was seventy. He did not contest the 1970 election. See *The Times*, (30 August 1968), p. 2.

[15] R. B. McCallum and A. Readman, *The British General Election of 1945* (Oxford University Press, 1947), p. 74.

[16] Clynes, *Memoirs*, I, p. 99. (Cf. his Vol. II, p. 214.) And cf. T. J. Connelly, *The Woodworkers, 1860–1960* (Amalgamated Society of Woodworkers, 1960), p. 82; Williams, *Derbyshire Miners*, p. 488; and the comments of J. Johnston on Jack Jones, M.P. in the 1920s, in Johnston, *A Hundred Commoners* (Herbert Joseph, 1931), p. 32.

[17] Fox, *Boot and Shoe Operatives*, p. 427.

[18] M. I. Cole (ed.), *Beatrice Webb's Diaries, 1912–1924*, pp. 142–43 (entry for 14 January 1919).

[19] A. Bullock, *Trade Union Leader*, p. 416, quoting *The TGWU Record* (November 1927), pp. 104–5.

[20] Bullock, *The Life and Times of Ernest Bevin*, Vol. II: *Minister of Labour, 1940–1945* (Heinemann, 1967), p. 234.

[21] J. H. Thomas, *My Story* (Hutchinson, 1937), pp. 196–97.

[22] F. Blackburn, *George Tomlinson* (Heinemann, 1954), pp. 14–15; G. Edwards, *From Crow-Scaring to Westminster* (Labour Publishing Co., 1922), p. 223.

[23] A. E. Musson, *The Typographical Association* (New York: Oxford University Press, 1954), p. 465.

[24] N. McKillip, *The Lighted Flame*, p. 164.

[25] D. Kirkwood, *My Life of Revolt* (Harrap, 1935), p. 217. Cf. Shinwell, *I've Lived Through It All* (Gollancz, 1973), p. 24. The bulk of the trade unionists resented these attacks, and this contributed to their longstanding dislike of Herbert Morrison. See B. Donoughue and G. W. Jones, *Herbert Morrison: Portrait of a Politician* (Weidenfeld and Nicolson, 1973), pp. 246–47.

[26] Quoted in M. Foot, *Aneurin Bevan: A Biography:* Vol. I (*1897–1945*) (Macgibbon and Kee, 1962), pp. 415–16. Cf. R. Smillie, *My Life for Labour* (Mill and Boon, 1924), pp. 175–76.

[27] R. T. McKenzie, *British Political Parties*, 2nd ed. (New York: Praeger, 1963), p. 417.

[28] H. Dalton, *Memoirs*. 3 vols. (Muller, 1953–1962), I, p. 195.

[29] R. W. Lyman, 'James Ramsay MacDonald and the Leadership of the Labour Party, 1918–1922', *Journal of British Studies*, Vol. II, No. 1 (1962–1963), p. 160.

[30] McKenzie, p. 336 and sources cited there.

[31] Dowse, *Left in the Center*, p. 47.

[32] M. Bondfield, *A Life's Work* (Hutchinson, n.d. [1948]), p. 247.

[33] Lyman, "James Ramsay MacDonald . . ." *op. cit.*, pp. 135–36.

[34] McKenzie, pp. 351–53 and sources cited there.

[35] Lyman, 'MacDonald', p. 156. Cf. J. Scanlon, *The Decline and Fall of the Labour Party* (Peter Davies, 1932), p. 34.

[36] See D. Kirkwood, *Life*, p. 221; P. Snowden, *Autobiography*, II, pp. 606–8; G. Blaxland, *J. H. Thomas: A Life for Unity* (Muller, 1964), p. 166;

M. I. Cole (ed.), *Beatrice Webb's Diaries, 1912–24,* p. 261 (entry for 15 January 1924). A list of sponsored MPs in the 1924 government is found in V. L. Allen, *Trade Unions and the Government,* pp. 237–38.

[37] F. Williams, *Fifty Years March* (Odhams Press, 1950), pp. 304, 321–22; H. Pelling, 'Governing Without Power', *Political Quarterly,* XXXII, No. 1 (January-March 1961), p. 48. Cf. the similar views of Snowden, and see T. Wilson (ed.), *The Political Diaries of C. P. Scott, 1911–1928* (Collins, 1970), pp. 420, 452.

[38] Shinwell, *Conflict,* p. 91.

[39] Kirkwood, p. 221. Cf. R. W. Lyman, *The First Labour Government, 1924* (Chapman and Hall, 1957), p. 104.

[40] Lyman, *The First Labour Government,* p. 230.

[41] H. Morrison, *Herbert Morrison: An Autobiography* (Odhams Press, 1960), p. 103.

[42] S. Webb. 'The First Labour Government', *The Political Quarterly,* XXXII, No. 1 (January-March 1961), p. 16.

[43] Cole (ed.), *Beatrice Webb's Diaries, 1924–1932* (Longmans, Green, 1956), p. 13 (entry for 15 March 1924).

[44] *Ibid.,* p. 1 (entry for 8 January 1924); T. Jones, *Whitehall Diary,* Vol. I: *1916–1925,* ed. Keith Middlemas (Oxford University Press, 1969), p. 267.

[45] J. Lawson, *A Man's Life,* p. 268.

[46] Shinwell, *Conflict,* pp. 93–4.

[47] R. H. Desmarais, 'Strikebreaking and the Labour Government of 1924', *Journal of Contemporary History,* VIII, (1973), pp. 165–75: Lyman, *The First Labour Government,* p. 222.

[48] J. Symons, *The General Strike* (The Cresset Press, 1957), p. 19; M. I. Cole (ed), *Beatrice Webb's Diaries, 1924–32,* p. 114 (entry for 1 September 1926).

[49] Bullock, *Trade Union Leader,* p. 349. Cf. F. Williams, *Ernest Bevin* (Hutchinson, 1952), pp. 132–33; J. Paton, *Left Turn* (Martin Secker and Warburg, 1936), p. 247.

[50] W. Citrine, *Men and Work: An Autobiography* (Hutchinson, 1964), pp. 149–204; T. Jones, *Whitehall Diary,* Vol. II: *1926–1930,* pp. 13–15, 25 ff.

[51] Jones, *Whitehall Diary,* II, pp. 15, 18.

[52] J. Symons, *The General Strike,* pp. 41–2. Cf. Williams, *Ernest Bevin,* pp. 132–133.

[53] *Beatrice Webb's Diaries, 1924–32,* p. 139 (entry for 23 April 1927).

[54] Arnot, *The Miners' Federation,* II, p. 465; Garside, *Durham Miners,* p. 231.

[55] Clynes, *Memoirs,* II, p. 93.

[56] Snowden, *Autobiography,* II, pp. 762, 767. A list of trade unionists in the second Labour government is found in Allen, *Trade Unions,* p. 259.

[57] Morrison, *Autobiography,* p. 101; D. Carlton, *MacDonald versus Henderson* (Macmillan, 1970), pp. 80–1.

[58] R. Skidelsky, *Politicians and the Slump* (Macmillan, 1967), p. 114.

[59] *Ibid.,* pp. 128–30. The text of the Group's letter is on p. 129. Cf. Foot, *Bevan,* I, p. 111.

[60] Snowden, II, p. 846.

[61] Skidelsky, *op. cit.*, p. 269. Cf. W. Citrine, *Men and Work*, p. 281; Jones, Whitehall Diary, II, p. 236.

[62] G. McAllister, *James Maxton: The Portrait of a Rebel* (John Murray, 1935), p. 216. The Bill went through twelve drafts before being published. See Skidelsky, pp. 112–13, 131–33.

[63] R. Bassett, *Nineteen Thirty-one, Political Crisis* (Macmillan, 1958), p. 139. Thomas had earlier been critical of 'rigid Trade Union methods' which hampered the fight against unemployment. See Jones, *Whitehall Diary*, II, p. 241.

[64] Allen, *Trade Unions*, p. 301.

[65] W. Golant, 'The Emergence of C. R. Attlee as Leader of the Parliamentary Labour Party in 1935', *The Historical Journal*, XIII (1970), pp. 330–31; R. Jenkins, *Mr. Attlee* (Heinemann, 1948), p. 167; H. Dalton, *Memoirs*, II, pp. 80–81; Donoughue and Jones, *Morrison*, p. 242.

[66] Bullock, *Trade Union Leader*, p. 593. Cf. Williams, *Bevin*, p. 203.

[67] Dalton, II, p. 136.

[68] Allen, *Trade Unions*, p. 12.

[69] Bullock, *Minister of Labour*, p. 5.

[70] *Ibid.*, p. 39. Cf. *Ibid.*, pp. 37, 99–102, 107–8, and 182–84.

[71] H. Morrison, *Government and Parliament*, 3rd ed. (Oxford University Press, 1964), p. 120.

[72] Bullock, *Minister of Labour*, pp. 118, 244–45.

[73] Allen, *Trade Unions*, pp. 36–37. Cf. J. F. Clarke, 'An Interview With Sir William Lawther', *Bulletin of the Society for the Study of Labour History*, No. 19 (Autumn 1969), p. 15; Johnston, *A Hundred Commoners*, p. 97; Snowden, I, p. 507; Lyman, *First Labour Government*, pp. 3–4.

Chapter III

[1] D. Butler and J. Freeman (eds.), *British Political Facts, 1900–1967*, 2nd ed. (Macmillan, 1968), p. 198. Trade union efforts to expand educational opportunity are discussed in R. Barker, *Education and Politics, 1900–1951: A Study of The Labour Party* (Oxford: Clarendon Press, 1972), pp. 120–35. The increasing acceptance of this expansion and the resulting political problems are discussed in W. G. Runciman, *Relative Deprivation and Social Justice* (Penguin Books, 1972), pp. 118–20.

[2] B. Magee, *The New Radicalism* (New York: St. Martin's Press, 1963), p. 185.

[3] H. Hopkins, *The New Look* (Secker and Warburg, 1963), pp. 166–67. Cf. R. Hoggart, *The Uses of Literacy* (Penguin Books, 1958), *passim*. E. Taylor, 'An Interview with Wesley Perrins', *Bull. Soc. Study of Labour History*, No. 21 (Autumn 1970), p. 24.

[4] See J. Hughes, 'Patterns of Trade Union Growth', in M. Brown and K. Coates (eds.), *Trade Union Register: 3* (Spokesman Books, 1973), pp. 47–52; K. Hindell, 'Trade Union Membership', *Planning*, XXVIII, No. 463 (2 July 1962), p. 156; and J. Hughes, *Changes in the Trade Unions* (Fabian Society, 1964), p. 6.

[5] See G. S. Bain, *Trade Union Growth and Recognition* (H.M.S.O. [Research Paper No. 6 for the Royal Commission on Trade Unions and Employers' Associations (The Donovan Commission)], 1967), pp. 111–14; Bain, *The Growth of White Collar Unionism* (Oxford: Clarendon Press, 1970), Table 3A–1 (facing p. 200).

[6] For example, see J. Bocock, 'The Politics of White-Collar Unionization', *Political Quarterly*, XLIV (1973), pp. 294–303; J. H. Goldthorpe, *et. al.*, *The Affluent Worker: Political Attitudes and Behaviour* (Cambridge: University Press, 1968), pp. 25–28; and M. Harrison, *Trade Unions and the Labour Party*, p. 25.

[7] These percentages are based on the number of affiliated members reported in Trades Union Congress *Reports* and the Labour Party Annual Conference *Reports* for 1966 thru 1973. For further discussion of this under- and overrepresentation, see A. Watkins, 'Buying the Vote', *New Statesman* (18 September 1970), p. 323. For a general discussion of the 'political levy' see Harrison, *Trade Unions*, pp. 21–65.

[8] R. Fletcher, 'Where Did It All Go Wrong?' *Encounter* (November 1969), p. 12. That Fletcher is sponsored by Jones' union, the TGWU, should not conceal the basic political and class feeling that he is expressing.

[9] J. Torode, 'White Collar Blue Collar', *Socialist Commentary* (August 1970), p. 21. Torode suggests that Feather was joking, but was he? On union resentment of the Labour government, see J. P. Mackintosh, 'The Problems of the Labour Party', *Political Quarterly*, XLIII (1972), p. 5; and E. Heffer, *Class Struggle in Parliament, passim.*

[10] For a general discussion of the AEF in this regard, see J. D. Edelstein, 'Democracy in A National Union: The British AEU', *Industrial Relations*, IV, No. 3 (May 1965), pp. 105–25. For reference to the impact of such procedures on the union's confrontation with the Industrial Relations Court, see *The Economist* (11 May 1974), pp. 89–90.

[11] For a general treatment of British union organisation, see V. L. Allen, *Power in Trade Unions* (Longmans, Green, 1954). On the TGWU, see Allen's *Trade Union Leadership* (Longmans, Green, 1957); and J. Goldstein, *The Government of British Trade Unions* (Allen and Unwin, 1952);

[12] E. Taylor, *The House of Commons at Work*, 5th rev. ed. (Penguin Books, 1963), p. 134. Cf. S. E. Finer, *Anonymous Empire*, 2nd ed. (Pall Mall Press, 1966).

[13] H. Morrison, *Government and Parliament*, pp. 35–6, 50.

[14] Beer, *British Politics*; Allen, *Trade Unions and the Government*, pp. 33–43, 304.

[15] Amalgamated Engineering Union, *Report and Proceedings of the National Committee* (1959), pp. 36–7.

[16] *The Times* (30 November 1964), p. 6. An overall evaluation of union representatives on advisory bodies is given in Allen, *Trade Unions*, pp. 34–41; PEP, *Advisory . . .* p. 43.

[17] *The Times* (1 September 1967), p. 1. But contrast *The Times* of 18 August 1969, p. 2.

[18] *Parl. Deb.* 5th Series 1945–46. Vol. 426, col. 43 (24 July 1946).

[19] P. G. Richards, *Patronage in British Government* (Allen and Unwin,

1963), pp. 99–100; W. G. Runciman, *Relative Deprivation*, pp. 124–27; A. Fels, *The British Prices and Incomes Board* (Cambridge: University Press, 1972), pp. 255–57.

[20] Gaitskell's speech was reprinted in a number of union journals. For example, see *The Locomotive Journal*, LXXII (October 1959), p. 314.

[21] C. Attlee, *The Labour Party in Perspective and Twelve Years Later* (Gollancz, 1949), p. 61.

[22] G. Radice, 'What About the Workers?' *Socialist Commentary* (February 1971), p. 6.

[23] For example, see the National Union of General and Municipal Workers, *Congress* (1967), p. 240. Cf. the views of the AEF as expressed in I. Richter, *Political Purpose in Trade Unions* (Allen and Unwin, 1973), pp. 63, 89–90.

[24] D. Wood, 'Trade Unions Rediscover Parliament', *The Times* (11 November 1970), p. 4. In an era that takes consultation for granted, Wood's article is very revealing on its limitations.

[25] P. G. Richards, *Honourable Members* 2nd ed. (Faber, 1964), p. 185; D. Houghton, 'Trade Union M.P.s in the British House of Commons', in *Members' Interests Report*, Appendix III, p. 125. But contrast the reactions to 'In Place of Strife' in 1968 and 1969 and to the Conservative Industrial Relations Bill in 1970 and 1971: see Heffer, *Class Struggle, passim*.

[26] H. A. Clegg, *General Union in a Changing Society*, pp. 202–3.

[27] *The Times* (4 Feb. 1971), p. 2.

[28] For example, see *Parl. Deb.* 1951–1952. Vol. 494, col. 1155 (27 Nov. 1951); Foot, *Bevan*, I, p. 413; *Daily Telegraph* (23 March 1964); P. Paterson, 'The Unions and Labour: Has the Time Come for a Reappraisal of the Alliance?' *New Statesman* (2 Sept 1966), p. 314; and Richter, *op. cit.*, pp. 60–1.

[29] This was especially true after the electoral defeats in 1959 and 1970. See Parliamentary Labour Party, Trade Union Group, *Annual Report, 1958–1959* (mimeographed), p. 2. See also: *Parl. Deb.* 1959–60. Vol. 612, col. 119 (27 October 1959); *The Times* (22 October 1959), p. 14; R. Prentice, 'What Kind of Labour Party?' *Socialist Commentary* (April 1973), p. 5; and G. Radice, 'Trade Unions and the Labour Party', *Socialist Commentary* (November 1970), p. 8.

[30] G. D. H. Cole, *History of the Labour Party from 1914*, p. 220. On the 1927 act, see M. C. Schefftz, 'The Trade Disputes and Trade Unions Act of 1927: the Aftermath of the General Strike', *Review of Politics*, XXIX (1967), pp. 387–406.

[31] J. E. Williams, *Derbyshire Miners*, pp. 836–39; A. Bullock, *Trade Union Leader*, pp. 533–34.

[32] Labour Party Annual Conference, *Report* (1968), Appendix 11, p. 377n. See M. Harrison, pp. 80–5 for discussion of the amounts paid by various unions between 1945 and 1958.

[33] For an example of such confusion involving Robert Mellish, see *The Observer* (7 December 1969), p. 3; *ibid.* (14 Dec. 1969), p. 5.

[34] Labour Party, *Interim Report of the Sub-Committee on Party Organisation* (1955) (The Wilson Committee), p. 16, para. 68, and pp

26–7, paras. 124–29. No final report was issued. Cf. R. T. McKenzie's argument in *The Observer* (25 Sept. 1966), and the discussion at the 1968 Labour Party conference: Annual Conference *Report* (1968), p. 224. But Harrison has argued that there is no relation between sponsorship and the state of a CLP's organization and finances. (*Trade Unions*, p. 84).

[35] A. Moffat, *My Life With the Miners* (Lawrence and Wishart, 1965), pp. 73, 222–23; T. F. Carbery, *Consumers in Politics* (Manchester: The University Press, 1969), pp. 129–34.

[36] But see A. Ranney, *Pathways to Parliament* (Madison and Milwaukee: University of Wisconsin Press, 1965), pp. 129–247; M. Rush, *The Selection of Parliamentary Candidates* (Nelson, 1969), pp. 149, 165–83.

[37] See Harrison, *op. cit.*, pp. 279–83. and Rush, pp. 291–94, for further details of these procedures.

[38] L. Gabbitas, 'Grooming for Parliament', *New Dawn*, XVII (1963), p. 319; author's interview with USDAW official, 11 August 1967; letter to author from H. G. Pridmore, chief administrative officer, USDAW, 11 June 1969; and *The Times* (9 Oct. 1969), p. 10.

[39] National Union of Mineworkers' Annual Conference *Report* (1965), pp. x, 119–24; *ibid.* (1967), pp. xi, 302–3; and A. Moffat, *Life*, pp. 226–27.

[40] Personal interview with NUVB MP, July 28, 1964; National Union of Vehicle Builders' *Rules Conference* (1962), Amendments.

[41] For similar procedures used before World War II, see Sir A. Pugh, *Men of Steel*, p. 567; R. L. Leonard, 'Morrison's Political Bequest', *New Society*, XI (4 Jan. 1968), pp. 5–6.

[42] Letter from G. F. Smith, general secretary, Amalgamated Society of Woodworkers, 22 Dec. 1967.

[43] Personal interviews with AEF assistant general secretaries, 5 August 1964 and 10 August 1967; A. Howard, 'Parliament and the Unions', *New Statesman* (29 March 1963), p. 446; I. Richter, *Political Purpose*, p. 55.

[44] A. Ranney, *Pathways to Parliament*, p. 154.

[45] Union of Postoffice Workers' Annual Conference, *Report* (1962), p. 6; Union of Postoffice Workers, *The Post*, LXIX, No. 2 (25 Jan. 1964), p. 29.

[46] Ranney, *op. cit.*, pp. 223–24.

[47] Union of Shop, Distributive and Allied Workers, *Reports and Proceedings* (1960), p. 111.

[48] National Union of General and Municipal Workers, *Congress* (1963), pp. 372–75.

[49] Author's interview with AEF assistant general secretary, 5 August 1964.

[50] For example, see Transport and General Workers' Union, *Minutes* (1959), p. 45 (Minute No. 103).

[51] 'The Union's Political Representation', *NUGMW Journal*, XXII (1959), pp. 98–9. Letter to author from Lord Cooper, then general secretary of the NUGMW, 31 July 1967. Both Gaitskell and Wilson received a nominal sum from the NUGMW when they served as leaders of the PLP. Personal interview with NUGMW official, 27 August 1964.

[52] M. Stewart, *Frank Cousins* (Hutchinson, 1968), p. 38; *The Observer* (2 Oct. 1968) and *The Daily Telegraph* (26 Feb. 1964).

[53] A number of AEF MPs interviewed during the summer of 1964 were especially bitter about the activities of both the TGWU and the NUGMW in this regard.

[54] *The Times* (12 March 1968), p. 3; (1 May 1975), p. 16; Richter, *op. cit.*, pp. 49–69.

[55] See C. Hitchens, 'The Miners and Labour,' *The New Statesman* (9 July 1974), p. 10; L. Abse, *Private Member* (Macdonald, 1973), pp. 37–38; and M. Edelman, 'Inside Westminster – Where Does Power Lie?' *New Humanist* (June 1972), pp. 49–50.

[56] This was A. P. Herbert's comment on the Labour MPs in 1945. See his *Independent Member* (Methuen, 1950), p. 371. The change in Labour representation in the 1960s has been widely commented on. For example, see: D. Butler and A. King, *The British General Election of 1966* (Macmillan, 1966), pp. 204–11; P. G. J. Pulzer, *Political Representation and Elections* (New York: Praeger, 1967), pp. 71–2; D. Butler and M. Pinto-Duschinsky, *The British General Election of 1970* (Macmillan, 1971), p. 302; G. Brown, *In My Way* (Gollancz, 1971), p. 90; A. Watkins, 'What About the Workers?' *New Statesman* (28 Aug. 1970), p. 227; R. W. Johnson, 'British Political Elite . . . ', pp. 60–1; H. Hutchinson, 'It Looks like No More Bevins and No More Bevans', *The Sun* (22 April 1966); R. Butt, 'Front Bench Rivals', *The Sunday Times* (14 June 1970), p. 20; and *The Economist* (2 March 1974), p. 67.

[57] A. Howard, 'Trade Unions and Labour', *Manchester Guardian* (8 July 1959); G. Cyriax, 'Labour and the Unions', *Political Quarterly*, XXXI, (1960), p. 331; and, especially, B. Magee, *New Radicalism*, pp. 157–58.

[58] Cross-Bencher, 'The Death of a Hero', *Sunday Express* (7 June 1959).

[59] H. A. Clegg, A. J. Killick, and R. Adams, *Trade Union Officers* (Oxford: Blackwells, 1961), p. 47. The figure is only approximate. Trade-union members of the party tend to be older than non-union party members. See B. Hindess, *The Decline of Working Class Politics* (Macgibbon and Kee, 1971), p. 93, Table 5.1.

[60] *The Times* (6 Feb. 1950), p. 7. But contrast M. Harrison, *Trade Unions*, p. 281.

[61] C. Pannell, 'Twenty A.E.U. M.P.'s Next Time', *Amalgamated Engineering Union Journal*, XXIV, No. 4 (April 1957), p. 107. Cf. Griffiths, *Pages From Memory*, p. 54.

[62] For example, see. F. Allaum, 'Wanted – More Trade Union M.P.s' *New Dawn*, XX, No. 11 (21 May 1966), pp. 323–24. Cf. H. Wilson's Forward to Bernard Taylor's memoirs. Taylor, *Uphill*, p. xi.

[63] " 'Professional' Labour M.P.s – A Warning", *The Times* (7 June 1966), p. 8. Cf. *The London Evening News* (19 June 1970), p. 10.

[64] Ron Hayward, Labour Party National Agent as quoted in A. King and A. Sloman, *Westminster and Beyond* (Macmillan, 1973), p. 51. Cf. *The Times* (11 November 1970), p. 3.

[65] R. Hughes, "Personally Speaking", *Tribune* (29 August 1969). Hughes reaffirmed his point in a letter to *Tribune* two weeks later in which he complained about cuts in the original article. See *Tribune* (12 September 1969).

[66] Stewart, *Frank Cousins*, p. 4.

[67] Brown, *In My Way*, pp. 88–90.

[68] Matthew Coady, 'A Leader for the Left', *New Statesman* (8 July 1966), p. 38. Cf. R. Crossman, "The Crossman Diaries," *The Sunday Times* (9 February 1975), p. 13.

[69] Gallup Poll, *Trade Unions and the Public in 1964* (1964), Section 2, Table 7. Two years later the proportion supporting trade-union sponsorship of MPs had dropped to 29 per cent. *Gallup Political Index*, Report No. 77 (September 1966), Table 6, Question 2.

[70] Trades Union Congress, *Trade Unionism: The Evidence of the Trades Union Congress to the Royal Commission on Trade Unions and Employers' Associations*, 2nd ed. (TUC, 1967), p. 57, para. 152.

[71] Letter to author from John Milhench, secretary of the United Textile Factory Workers' Association, 14 August 1964. Similar views were expressed by almost all union officials and sponsored MPs interviewed in 1964 and 1967. Cf. W. R. Garside, *Durham Miners*, p. 29.

[72] Harrison, *Trade Unions*, p. 280. Their fears must have been assuaged in 1970 when they adopted Ronald W. Brown as a sponsored MP.

[73] *Parl. Deb.* 1960–61. Vol. 636, col 1960 (17 March 1960), National Union of General and Municipal Workers, *Congress* (1959), p. 363; J. McCann, 'Beneath Big Ben', *Amalgamated Engineering Union Journal*, XXVII, No. 3 (March 1960), p. 85; and an article by E. J. Milne (sponsored by USDAW) defending the sponsored MPs, reprinted in *Members' Interests Report*, Appendix VIII, pp. 129–30.

[74] Tradition was cited by only a few of the union officials and MPs interviewed in 1964 and 1967, but it seemed to underlie the position of many who justified sponsorship on the grounds of utility.

[75] Interview with USDAW official, 9 August 1964 and with TSSA official, 8 August 1967. Cf. A. E. Griffiths, 'From the General Secretary's Desk: A. A. D. – Political Fund', *The Locomotive Journal*, LXXIX, No. 8 (August 1960), p. 186; and Garside, *op. cit.*, p. 65.

[76] Interview with Woodworkers' official, 12 August 1964.

[77] Stewart, *British Pressure Groups*, p. 177 (emphasis added). Cf. J. Blondel, *Voters*, p. 215; Richter, *op. cit.*, pp. 54, 66, 109.

[78] *The Woodworkers' Journal* (July 1967), p. 139.

[79] For example, see the Transport and General Workers' Union, *Minutes* (1957), p. 51 (Minute No. 121); Transport Salaried Staffs' Association, *Minutes* (1962), pp. 48–9 (Resolution 76); the Union of Shop, Distributive and Allied Workers, *Reports and Proceedings* (1966), p. 25; *ibid.* (1967), pp. 21–2.

[80] Harrison, p. 297; J. McCann, 'Beneath Big Ben', *loc. cit.*

[81] Webb, *Industrial Democracy*, pp. 65–71.

Chapter IV

[1] Trade Union Group, Parliamentary Labour Party, *Report* (1957–58), pp. 1–2 (mimeographed; hereafter referred to as Union Group *Report*). I am indebted to the Rt. Hon. Charles Pannell, sometime hon. secretary of the

Group, for access to some of the Group's annual reports.

[2] Union Group *Report* (1961–62), pp. 3–4. For further discussion of the Group's activity, see I. Richter, *Political Purpose in Trade Unions*, ch. VII, VIII; J. Ellis and R. W. Johnson, *Members from Unions*, pp. 15–25.

[3] Union Group *Report* (1962–63), p. 1.

[4] R. Marsh, 'The P.L.P. and the Trade Unions', revised copy (Fabian Society, 1963) (mimeographed). I am indebted to the Rt. Hon. Richard Marsh for permission to use his studies.

[5] Personal interview with Group officer during the summer of 1964.

[6] Interview with sponsored MP, summer of 1964.

[7] *The Times* (5 Feb. 1954), p. 3. Cf. A. Watkins, 'Labour: Paper Tigers', *New Statesman* (10 January 1969), p. 34. The paper tigers in question were the members of the Trade Union Group.

[8] Personal interview with PLP whip in the summer of 1964; and Union Group *Report* (1957–58), pp. 1–2.

[9] Union Group *Report* (1959–60); p. 3; *ibid.* (1961–62), p. 1; D. Houghton, 'Trade-Union MPs in the British House of Commons', in *Members' Interests Report*, p. 123.

[10] *The Daily Telegraph* (2 Nov. 1960); *The Times* (8 Nov. 1961), p. 5.

[11] *Yorkshire Evening Post* (3 Nov. 1960).

[12] *The Times* (16 Dec. 1971), p. 4.

[13] J. L. Lynskey, 'The Role of British Backbenchers in the Modification of Government Policy', *Western Political Quarterly*, XXII (1970), p. 336; F. Boyd, 'How Labour Was Saved in 1951', *The Guardian* (1 July 1964), p. 10.

[14] National Union of Railwaymen, *Annual General Meeting* (1960), Vol. II (6th day), p. 58.

[15] *The Times* (8 Nov. 1960), p. 12. Cf. *The Daily Telegraph* (15 Dec. 1960), p. 1; *The Times* (15 Dec. 1960), p. 10.

[16] 'Labour's New Men of Power: The Golden Boy', *New Statesman* (22 May 1964), p. 805.

[17] Union Group *Report* (1962–63), p. 1. Cf. the Group's action in the 1961 contest for the deputy party leadership: *ibid.* (1961–62), p. 1.

[18] *Ibid.* (1959–60), p. 2; *ibid.* (1960–61), pp. 3–4.

[19] *Ibid.* (1960–61), pp. 2–3. Cf. J. McCann, 'Beneath Big Ben', *Amalgamated Engineering Union Journal*, XXVIII, No. 8 (August 1961), p. 246.

[20] Union Group *Report* (1960–61), p. 3.

[21] *The Times* (3 Oct. 1961), p. 18.

[22] E. Heffer, *Class Struggle*, p. 99. Heffer, whose book includes two chapters on the struggle over 'In Place of Strife', is sponsored by the ASW and was a participant in the events he describes. Also see P. Jenkins, *The Battle of Downing Street* (Charles Knight, 1970) for a journalistic account of the conflict; and H. Wilson, *The Labour Government, 1964–1970* (Weidenfeld and Nicolson and Michael Joseph, 1971), pp. 591 ff., for the Prime Minister's view.

[23] The results of the poll are reported in *The Times* (8 Jan. 1969), p. 1. Heffer reports that he could find no member of the Group who had been

contacted by the poll. *Op. cit.*, pp. 105–7, 118.

[24] *Parl. Deb.* 1968–69. Vol. 779, cols. 163–66, division 106 (3 March 1969).

[25] Jenkins, *Battle of Downing Street*, p. 82. Callaghan's position benefited from this action when elections were held for the PLP Parliamentary Committee in July 1970: see *The Times* (6 July 1970), p. 8. Richard Marsh's and Roy Mason's positions are reported in Auberon Waugh, 'Far From the Ol' Folks at Home', *The Spectator* (10 Jan. 1969), p. 35; A. Watkins, 'No Plan at the Top', *New Statesman* (24 Jan. 1969), p. 102, and 'The Cabinet and the Bill', *New Statesman* (13 June 1969), p. 822.

[26] Jenkins, *op. cit.*, p. 136. And four TGWU MPs, including two who had not actively opposed 'In Place of Strife', were denied sponsorship just before the 1970 election.

[27] *Ibid.*, pp. 153–54. Contrast the account in Wilson, *Labour Government*, pp. 656–57.

[28] Heffer, *op. cit.*, p. 107.

[29] R. Crossman, "The Crossman Diaries", *The Sunday Times* (9 February 1975), p. 13.

[30] Heffer, *op. cit.* pp. 178, 186; *The Times* (6 Nov. 1970), p. 6.

[31] Heffer, pp. 178–79; *The Times* (11 Nov. 1970), p. 4, and 24 Nov. 1970, p. 2; J. Torode, 'White Collar Blue Collar', *Socialist Commentary* (August 1970), p. 21.

[32] W. Rodgers, 'Personal Column', *Socialist Commentary* (April 1971), p. 13. For the makeup of the working party and some of the details of the parliamentary struggle, see Labour Party Annual Conference, *Report* (1971), pp. 72, 88–9; and Heffer, *op. cit.*, pp. 169–205, 218–62.

[33] See M. Shanks, 'The English Sickness', *Encounter* (Jan. 1972), pp. 84–8; *The Economist* (27 April 1974), pp. 78–9; and B. Hepple, 'Adieu to the NIRC', *New Society* (8 Aug. 1974), pp. 354–55.

[34] *The Economist* (11 May 1974), pp. 89–93.

[35] For example, see Foot's letter to *The Times* on 13 August 1974, p. 13.

[36] Personal interview with sponsored MP in the summer of 1964; J. P. W. Mallalieu, 'The Trade Union MP', *New Statesman* (28 Nov. 1959), p. 734.

[37] *News Chronicle* (11 Dec. 1959). Cf. *The Economist* (19 Dec. 1959), p. 1144, on elections to the PLP's transport group.

[38] S. E. Finer, *et. al.*, *Backbench Opinion in the House of Commons* (Pergamon Press, 1961), pp. 57–8.

[39] This is the conclusion of an unpublished seminar paper prepared by Miss C. Rupert, State University of New York, Fredonia, January 1971. P. G. Richards, *Parliament and Conscience* (Allen and Unwin, 1970), pp. 179–96. Richards does not include sponsored status in his analysis.

[40] PEP, *Advisory Committees...* p. 71; F. Blackburn, *George Tomlinson*, p. 1.

[41] P. Strauss, *Bevin and Company*, p. 80.

[42] M. Stewart, *Frank Cousins*, pp. 26–7; cf. P. G. Walker, 'On Being a Cabinet Minister', *Encounter* (April 1956), pp. 18–19.

[43] R. M. Punnett, *Front-Bench Opposition* (Heinemann, 1973), pp. 124–25; Ian Aitken, 'The Structure of the Labour Party', in G. Kaufman

(ed.), *The Left* (Anthony Blond, 1966), p. 18; *The Times* (21 Jan. 1963), p. 13.

[44] M. Coady, 'Two Men on a Tightrope', *New Statesman* (10 Dec. 1965), p. 910.

[45] *The Times* (23 Jan. 1972), p. 2; *ibid.* (24 Jan. 1972), p. 2.

[46] R. J. Jackson, *Rebels and Whips* (New York: St. Martin's Press, 1968), pp. 82–3, 135, 160, 185–86, 192–93; Finer *et al.*, pp. 27 *et passim*.

[47] J. Griffiths, *Pages From Memory*, p. 126. Cf. G. Rogers, 'When Visions Disappear', *TSS Journal*, LXIV (1967), p. 183.

[48] J. P. Mackintosh, 'Socialism or Social Democracy? The Choice for the Labour Party', *Political Quarterly*, XLIII (1972), pp. 480–81; *The Economist* (26 April 1975), pp. 17–8.

[49] Based on figures reported in *The Political Companion*, No. 9 (October–December, 1971), pp. 76 85.

[50] C. Attlee, *As It Happened* (Heinemann, 1954), p. 156; L. Hunter, *The Road to Brighton Pier* (Arthur Barker, 1959), p. 151; Dalton, *Memoirs*, III, p. 240.

[51] See Allen, *Trade Unions and the Government*, pp. 291–93, for a list of sponsored MPs in the 1945 Labour government.

[52] Dalton, III, p. 159. Contrast H. Morrison, *Autobiography*, p. 249.

[53] Dalton, III, p. 361.

[54] F. Williams, *A Prime Minister Remembers* (Heinemann, 1961), pp. 220–21.

[55] The sponsored MPs on the committee thus reflected the divisions within the Trade Union Group itself: see Punnett, *Front-Bench Opposition*, pp. 124–25.

[56] M. Foot. *Bevan*, II: *1945–1960*, pp. 102–218; J. B. Christoph, 'The Advent of the National Health Service', in Christoph and B. E. Brown (eds.), *Cases in Comparative Politics*, 2nd ed. (Boston; Little, Brown, 1969), pp. 35–74.

[57] Foot, *Bevan*, I, p. 97.

[58] *The Times* (16 March 1959), p. 6. Cf. *The Economist* (18 June 1960), p. 1188.

[59] See R. M. Punnett, 'The Labour Shadow Cabinet, 1955–1964', *Parliamentary Affairs*, XVIII (Winter, 1964–65), p. 64.

[60] *The Times* (4 May 1968), p. 7.

[61] National Union of Mineworkers, *Annual Conference Report* (1957), pp. 141–42.

[62] *Daily Mirror* (5 July 1957).

[63] *The Times* (17 July 1957), p. 10; *ibid.* (25 July 1957), p. 6.

[64] H. B. Boyne, 'That Ticket to Westminster', *Daily Telegraph* (18 July 1957).

[65] R. K. Alderman, 'Parliamentary Party Discipline in Opposition: The Parliamentary Labour Party, 1951–1964', *Parliamentary Affairs*, XXI, No. 2 (Spring 1968), p. 131; B. Magee, 'Candidates: How They Pick Them: Labour: The Missing Talents', *New Statesman* (5 Feb. 1965), p. 189. In light of Magee's remarks here and in *The New Radicalism*, one must wonder about his reception in the House after the February 1974 election

[66] Williams, *A Prime Minister Remembers,* p. 81. Cf. M. Beloff, 'Reflections on the British General Election of 1966', *Government and Opposition,* I (August 1966), pp. 530–31; A. H. Birch, *Representative and Responsible Government,* p. 232; Rose, *Politics in England,* p. 93.

[67] Griffiths, *Pages From Memory,* p. 196; D. Houghton, 'The Labour Back-bencher', *Political Quarterly,* XL (1969), p. 461.

[68] *The Times* (3 July 1968), p. 2; *The Listener* (11 July 1968), pp. 39 ff. When Gunter resigned the Labour Party whip in 1972, he reaffirmed this class orientation when he wrote to the PLP's chief whip; I would be ' . . . less than human if I did not shrink from being kicked out by the middle-class intellectuals who now control the party'. *The Times* (17 Feb. 1972), pp. 1, 2. Contrast Wilson, *op. cit.,* p. 541, who seemed totally unaware of this aspect of Gunter's resignation in 1968.

[69] J. M. Boyd, 'Ray Gunter's Errors', *Amalgamated Engineering Union Journal,* XXXI, No. 5 (May 1964), p. 158.

[70] See the list of candidates for the Parliamentary Committee in *The Political Companion,* No. 17 (Winter 1973), pp. 63–4.

[71] Labour Party Annual Conference, *Report* (1973), pp. 63–4.

[72] See Punnett, *op. cit.,* pp. 139–42, on the problems of persuading some MPs to accept appointment as Opposition spokesmen.

[73] For discussions on the evolving nature of the Labour Party leadership, see Guttsman, *British Political Elite,* pp. 225–77; J. Bonnor, 'The Four Labour Cabinets', *Sociological Review,* VI (1958), pp. 37–47; Johnson, 'British Political Elite', *loc. cit.,* pp. 44–5, 48–51; and V. J. Hanby, 'A Changing Labour Elite: The National Executive Committee of the Labour Party, 1900–1972', in I. Crewe (ed.) *British Political Sociology Yearbook,* Vol. I: *Elites in Western Democracy* (Croom Helm, 1974), pp. 126–58.

[74] Peter Kellner, "Anatomy of the Vote", *New Statesman* (2 April 1976), p. 462.

[75] Morrison, *Autobiography,* pp. 249–50; Dalton, III, p. 415.

[76] Based on the list of whips given in F. M. G. Willson, 'Some Career Patterns in British Politics: Whips in the House of Commons, 1906–1966', *Parliamentary Affairs,* XXIV, No. 1 (Winter 1970–71), pp. 41–2.

[77] *Ibid.,* p. 37; and F. M. G. Willson, 'The Routes of Entry of New Members of the British Cabinet', *Political Studies,* VII (1959), p. 231.

Chapter V

[1] Portions of the following material have appeared in W. D. Muller, 'Trade Union M.P.s and Parliamentary Specialization', *Political Studies,* XX, No. 3 (1972), pp. 317–24.

[2] See *Members' Interests Report, op. cit.,* and the resulting debate in the House of Commons: *Parl. Deb.* 1968–69. Vol. 779, col. 1148 (11 March 1969), and cols. 1562–64 (13 March 1969).

[3] For a listing of the number of Questions directed at all departments in 1962–63, see W. D. Muller, *The Parliamentary Activity of Trade Union*

MPs, 1959–64, (Unpublished doctoral dissertation, University of Florida, Gainseville, Fla., 1966), appendix VIII, p. 312.

[4] J. F. S. Ross, *Parliamentary Representation,* 2nd enlarged ed. (Eyre and Spottiswood, 1948), p. 138; P. G. Richards, *Parliament and Foreign Affairs* (Allen and Unwin, 1967), p. 87; H. Pelling, *A Short History of the Labour Party* (Macmillan, 1962), p. 29; Snowden, *Autobiography,* II, pp. 530–31; Maddox, *Foreign Relations,* pp. 38–46, 196–234; Harrod, *Trade Union Foreign Policy,* p. 103; and Finer, *et al, Backbench Opinion,* pp. 15–75.

[5] *Parl. Deb.* 1960–61. Vol. 632, cols. 219–354 (13 Dec. 1960).

[6] *Ibid.* 1962–63. Vol. 670, cols. 975ff, 1915ff. (30 Jan. 1963). Hynd had been a chancellor of the Duchy of Lancaster in the 1945–50 Labour government, with special responsibility for occupied Germany. The only other trade unionist to be active in defence debates was Fred Mulley, shadow minister of air from 1960 until 1964.

[7] *Parl. Deb.* 1962–63. Vol. 668, cols. 97–120 (30 Nov. 1962); *ibid.,* cols. 227–30 (6 Dec. 1962); *ibid.,* Vol. 669, cols. 15–19 (10 Dec. 1962); and *ibid.,* cols. 142–48 (17 Dec. 1962).

[8] *Ibid.* 1962–63. Vol. 669, cols. 570–71 (13 Dec. 1962).

[9] *Ibid.* 1961–62. Vol. 648, col. 450 (2 Nov. 1961).

[10] *Ibid.* 1962–63. Vol. 666, col. 261 (31 Oct. 1962).

[11] A. King and A. Sloman, *Westminster and Beyond,* p. 138.

[12] Some of the debates which served as the basis of this discussion are: *Parl. Deb.* 1960–61. Vol. 636, cols. 1913 ff (11 March 1961); *ibid.* 1961–62. Vol. 652, cols. 720 ff (29 Jan. 1962); *ibid.* 1962–63. Vol. 671, cols. 1503 ff (14 Feb. 1963); *ibid.* 1963–64. Vol. 684, cols. 1001 ff (20 Nov. 1963); *ibid.* Vol. 687, cols. 961 ff (21 Jan. 1964). Others are cited in the following notes.

[13] *Ibid.* 1959–60. Vol. 620, col. 1367 (30 March 1960).

[14] *Ibid.* Vol. 615, cols. 907 ff (11 Nov. 1959). It is significant that of the 40 union-sponsored Members who took part in the division on the second reading of Marsh's bill, there were only seven miners. An offices bill, of course, would not apply to the coal mines.

[15] *Ibid.* 1962–63. Vol. 667, cols. 588 ff (15 Nov. 1962).

[16] *Ibid.* 1961–62. Vol. 652, cols. 720 ff (29 Jan. 1962).

[17] *Ibid.* col. 788.

[18] This discussion is based on the official records of the Select Committees. See Great Britain, House of Commons, *Returns of Select Committees,* 1959–64. (mimeographed). Also, see D. Coombes, *The Member of Parliament and the Administration* (Allen and Unwin, 1966), pp. 88–89, 123.

[19] This discussion is based on personal interviews with a number of the MPs sponsored by the NUM in the summer of 1964.

[20] The members who supplied this information asked to remain anonymous to preserve the domestic tranquillity of the miners' group. Cf. M. Coady, 'Fall-out from the Pits', *New Statesman* (30 June 1967), p. 897.

[21] The following discussion is based on: *Parl. Deb.* 1945–46. Vol. 418, cols. 701 ff. (29 Jan. 1946); Vol. 422, cols. 1501 ff. (13 May 1946); Vol. 423, cols. 44 ff (20 May 1946); Vol. 425, cols. 399 ff (10 July 1946); Vol. 426,

cols. 45 ff. (24 July 1946); *Ibid.* 1946–47. Vol. 433, cols. 62 ff. (10 Feb. 1947); Vol. 440, cols. 603 ff (17 July 1947); *Ibid.* 1947–48. Vol. 450, cols. 1969 ff. (11 May 1948); Vol. 452. col. 1576 (24 June 1948); *Ibid.* 1948–49. Vol. 467, cols. 2335 ff. (26 July 1949); Vol. 469, cols. 1415 ff. (10 Nov. 1949).

[22] See E. Shinwell, *Conflict without Malice*, pp. 172–75. Shinwell was the minister in charge of the nationalisation measure.

[23] Some of the debates directly affecting the mining industry are: *Parl. Deb.* 1960–61. Vol. 635, cols. 36 ff. (20 Feb. 1961); Vol. 646, col. 758 ff. (24 Oct. 1961); *Ibid.* 1961–62. Vol. 650, cols. 449 ff. (29 Nov. 1961), as well as those in the following notes.

[24] This analysis is based on the following debates during the 1971–72 session: *Parl. Deb.* 1971–72. Vol. 826, cols. 1096 ff. (22 Nov. 1971); *Ibid.* Vol. 829, cols. 228 ff. (18 Jan. 1972); *Ibid.* Vol. 830, cols. 800 ff. (3 Feb. 1972); *Ibid.* Vol. 830, cols. 1143 ff. (8 Feb. 1972); and *Ibid.* Vol. 833, cols. 1145 ff. (20 March 1972). The two brief responses to the Wilberforce Report are not included.

[25] *Parl. Deb.* 1959–60. Vol. 614, cols. 44 ff (23 Nov. 1959); *Ibid.* Vol. 616, cols. 176 ff. (27 Jan. 1960); *Ibid.* Vol. 617, cols. 1155 ff. (16 Feb. 1960).

[26] *Ibid.* (1962–63). Vol. 667, cols. 1020 ff. (20 Nov. 1962).

[27] *Ibid.* 1959–60. Vol. 616, cols. 267–68, division 27 (27 Jan. 1960).

[28] For a discussion of these and other examples of the mining MPs' activity, see Stewart, *British Pressure Groups*, p. 77; A. Horner, *Incorrigible Rebel* (MacGibbon and Kee, 1960), pp. 205–6; Taylor, *Uphill*, pp. 131–32; 146–48; Moffat, *My Life with the Miners*, p. 79.

[29] *Parl. Deb.* 1959–60. Vol. 614, cols. 78 (23 Nov. 1959).

[30] *Ibid.* 1961–62. Vol. 650, col. 671 (4 Dec. 1961).

[31] *Ibid.* 1971–72. Vol. 833, col. 1188 (20 March 1972).

[32] *Ibid.* Vol. 829, col. 277 (18 Jan. 1972).

[33] *Ibid.* col. 324.

[34] *Ibid.* 1959–60. Vol. 614, cols. 92 ff. (23 Nov. 1959).

[35] *Ibid.* Vol. 616, cols. 223 ff. (27 Nov. 1959).

[36] *Ibid.* 1971–72. Vol. 829, col. 325–26 (18 Jan. 1972).

[37] National Union of Mineworkers, *Information Bulletin*, XVI (1961), p. 3.

[38] *Ibid., Annual Conference Report* (1964), p. 157.

[39] *Parl. Deb.* 1971–72. Vol. 826, cols. 1096 ff. (22 Nov. 1971). Three miners, Dennis Skinner, George Grant, and Roy Mason, took part in this debate.

[40] M. Coady, 'Fall-out from the Pits', *loc. cit.* Cf. H. Thomas, 'Pit Closures', (letter) *New Statesman* (7 July 1967), pp. 16–17. See also A. Eadie's reference to 'snide' remarks about the mining MPs during the 1972 strike: *Parl. Deb.* 1971–72. Vol. 833, col. 1161 (20 March 1972). The remarks had appeared in *The Daily Telegraph*.

[41] W. Paynter, *My Generation*, pp. 139–43. The use of sponsored MPs as scapegoats or as a safety valve was also suggested by an NUM official in an interview with the author on 14 Aug. 1967. Cf. I. Richter, *Political Purpose,*

p. 65; and an interview with an official of the ASW, 5 Aug. 1967.
[42] *The Times* (13 Jan. 1972), p. 2; *Ibid.* (3 Feb. 1972), p. 2. Fifteen miners' MPs were reported picketing the Battersea power station in the second incident and two of them had their picture in *The Times*. After a picket was killed, another MP, Dennis Skinner, referred to an accident that occurred to him while picketing. See *Parl. Deb.* 1971–72. Vol. 830, col. 806 (3 Feb. 1972).
[43] *The Times* (10 Nov. 1967), p. 1; *ibid.* (13 Nov. 1967), p. 1.
[44] *Ibid.* (22 Aug. 1966), p. 17; *Ibid.* (6 Sept. 1968), p. 23; *Ibid.* (24 Dec. 1968), p. 15. Mason's inability to do more contributed to a growing disenchantment with the Labour Party among the miners. See C. Hitchens, 'The Miners and Labour', New Statesman (5 July 1974), p. 10.
[45] For an analysis of production and contraction of the coal industry between 1947 and 1971, see *Parl. Deb.* 1971–72, Vol. 830, cols. *15–16* (31 Jan. 1972). Replies to Written Questions. The question which elicited this information was asked by Joseph Harper, an NUM-sponsored MP.
[46] *Parl. Deb.* 1971–72. Vol. 829, col. 331 (18 Jan. 1972). The meeting was announced on 20 Jan. *The Times* (20 Jan. 1972), p. 1.
[47] 'Candidus', 'Panic Talk', *Socialist Commentary* (Dec. 1967), p. 14.
[48] *Parl. Deb.* 1971–72. Vols. 829, 830, and 831.
[49] *Ibid.* Vol. 830, col. 677 (3 Feb. 1972).
[50] The same type of specialisation was reported for the late nineteenth century by Hanham, *Elections and Party Management*, p. 326; and for the third decade of the twentieth century by Johnston, *A Hundred Commoners*, p. 227.
[51] Letter to the author from R. Main, secretary, Northumberland Area, National Union of Mineworkers, 17 Aug. 1964.
[52] Personal interview with NUR official, 16 Aug. 1967.
[53] P. Bagwell, *Railwaymen*, pp. 600–2.
[54] Major transport debates directly involving the railroads during the 1959–64 Parliament include: *Parl. Deb.* 1959–60, Vol. 627, cols. 2358 ff. (26 Oct. 1960); *Ibid.* 1960–61. Vol. 633, cols. 615 ff. (30 January 1961); *Ibid.* Vol. 637, cols. 930–1058, 1153–1275 (20 and 21 Nov. 1961); *Ibid.* 1963–64. Vol. 698, cols. 425 ff. (8 July 1964).
[55] Author's interviews with two railway MPs, 20 and 28 July 1964.
[56] National Union of Railwaymen, *Annual General Meeting* (1960), Vol. II (6th day), p. 61; H. Howarth, 'Dealing With Transport and Rates', *TSS Journal*, LXII (1965), pp. 568–69.
[57] For example, see *Parl. Deb.* 1960–61. Vol. 637, col. 289 (21 March 1961); *Ibid.* 1963–64. Vol. 698, cols. 501 ff. (8 July 1964).
[58] National Union of Railwaymen, *Annual General Meeting* (1962), Vol. I, pp. 471–72; *Ibid., General Secretaries' Report* (1966), p. 3; and Transport Salaried Staffs' Association, *Report* (1962), pp. 33–4, para. 278.
[59] For one declaration see *Parl. Deb.* 1960–61. Vol. 633, col. 702 (30 Jan. 1961).
[60] *Parl. Deb.* 1963–64. Vol. 698, cols. 502–9 (8 July 1964).
[61] *Parl. Deb.* 1974–75, Vol. 884, col. 1132 (20 Jan. 1975) (daily edition).
[62] *Ibid.*, cols. 1157–62. Three days after the vote, it was announced that

Walter Johnson was resigning his position as an assistant whip. Johnson had a history of disagreement with the Government's policy and was also a national officer of TSSA. On Jan. 13, a week before the vote, he had written to Robert Mellish, the Chief Whip, asking to be relieved. See *The Evening Standard*, (23 Jan. 1975), p. 7; *The Times* (24 Jan. 1975), p. 2.

[63] National Union of Railwaymen, *Annual General Meeting* (1960), *Proceedings*, Vol. II (sixth day), p. 63.

[64] *Parl. Deb.* 1963–64. Vol. 698, cols. 436–37 (8 July 1964).

[65] The activity of the railwaymen in the House of Commons is recognised by their unions. For example, see Transport Salaried Staffs' Association *Report* (1961), p. 34. para. 276; *Ibid.* (1962), pp. 33–4, paras. 273, 278; *Ibid.* (1963), p. 36, para. 302.

[66] *T & G W Record*, XLI (January 1961), p. 38; *Ibid.*, XLVI (August 1966), p. 43; Cf. a letter to *The Daily Telegraph* (9 June 1966) by R. Fletcher.

[67] A. Creech-Jones, 'Parliament, 1959–64 – Work of the Union's Group', *T & G W Record*, XLIV (September 1964), pp. 24–6.

[68] *Parl. Deb.* 1959–60. Vol. 617, col. 599 (10 Feb. 1960).

[69] *Ibid.*, cols. 599–615; and 'A Prayer in the House', *The Land Worker*, XLI (March 1960), p. 4.

[70] Interview with NUAW research officer, 20 Aug. 1964.

[71] 'The Tied Cottage', *The Land Worker*, XLI (October 1960), p. 7. Cf. *The Economist* (18 February 1961), p. 648; *The Times* (4 Aug. 1966), p. 9.

[72] *Parl. Deb.* 1960–61. Vol. 634, col. 288 (7 Feb. 1961).

[73] R. E. Winterbottom, 'Selective Employment Tax', *New Dawn*, XX, No. 15 (16 July 1966), pp. 451–52, 462. The original version of the speech is found at *Parl. Deb.* 1966–67. Vol. 730, cols. 987–93 (23 June 1966).

[74] *Parl. Deb.* 1966–67. Vol. 738, cols. 379–380 (21 Dec. 1966) (replies to Written Questions).

[75] *Public Employees Journal* (March 1967), p. 3.

[76] For example, see *DATA Journal* (April 1966), p. 6; and Stewart, *British Pressure Groups*, pp. 81, 85, for earlier examples.

[77] Dalton, *Memoirs*, III, p. 135; Sir A. Pugh, *Men of Steel*, pp. 589–93.

[78] Both Richards and Wilkie were supported by the Ship Constructors and Shipwrights Union. See G. N. Barnes, *From Workshop to War Cabinet* (Herbert Jenkins, 1929), p. 83.

[79] S. Webb, 'The First Labour Government', *The Political Quarterly*, XXXII, (1961), p. 15.

[80] For example, see the explanation of the representative's role given in A. J. Junz, *The Student Guide to Parliament* (Hansard Society, 1960), p. 5.

[81] How the indices used to measure the various types of activity were constructed, and what was the nature of the groups used for comparison with the union-sponsored MPs, are discussed in appendices II and III.

[82] R. Rose, *Politics in England*, p. 93.

[83] Finer, *et al*, *Backbench Opinion*, pp. 14–23; Ross, *Parliamentary Representation*, p. 27; R. E. Dowse, 'The Parliamentary Labour Party in Opposition', *Parliamentary Affairs*, XIII, No. 4 (Autumn 1960), pp. 520–29; and P. G. Richards, *Parliament and Conscience*, pp. 32, 189–91.

[84] Cf. P. W. Buck, *Amateurs and Professionals in British Politics, 1918–59* (Chicago: University of Chicago Press, 1963), p. 66.

[85] See *The Times* (25 Feb. 1970), p. 1.

[86] A. Bevan, *In Place of Fear* (New York: Simon and Schuster, 1952), p. 6. Bevan entered the House at the age of twenty-nine, unusually early for sponsored MPs.

[87] Author's interview with PLP whip, summer 1964.

[88] For example: H. W. Lucy, *A Diary of the Unionist Parliament, 1895–1900* (Bristol, England: J. W. Arrowsmith, 1901), p. 47; J. L. Garvin, *The Life of Joseph Chamberlain*, 3 vols. (Macmillan, 1932), I, pp. 229–30; K. Feiling, *The Life of Neville Chamberlain* (Macmillan, 1946, p. 77; H. Nicolson, *Diaries and Letters, 1930–39*, ed. N. Nicolson (Fontana Books, 1969), p. 86; H. Laski, *Parliamentary Government in England* (Allen and Unwin, 1938), p. 162; A. Bullock, *Minister of Labour*, p. 107; J. Griffiths, *Pages from Memory*, p. 126; D. Kirkwood, *Life*, pp. 247–48; W. L. Guttsman, *Political Elite*, p. 201.

[89] G. Brown, *In My Way*, p. 89.

Chapter VI

[1] R. Marsh, 'The P.L.P. and the Trade Unions', Revised copy (Fabian Society, 1963), pp. 3–4 (mimeographed).

[2] Personal interview with assistant general secretary, AEF, 5 Aug. 1964. Cf. Marsh, *op. cit.*, p. 2.

[3] *The Daily Worker* (2 April, 1965).

[4] Unions doing this when they have sponsored MPs include: the AEF, NUTGW, NUM, BISAKTA, the Musicians, and the NUR. For a discussion of the AEF meetings, see Richter, *Political Purpose in Trade Unions*, pp. 62 ff. On the NUM, see W. Paynter, *My Generation*, p. 96.

[5] Author's interviews with NUR officials in 1964 and 1967; National Union of Railwaymen, *Annual General Meeting* (1961), Vol. I (4th day), p. 61.

[6] Unions doing this include: the UPW, USDAW, NUPE, CAWU, and the NUM. For the passage of specific documents, see Moffat, *My Life with the Miners*, pp. 154–55; Transport Salaried Staffs Association, Annual Delegate conference (1963), *Minutes*, p. 97 (Resolution 107); and Amalgamated Engineering Union, *Report of Proceedings of the National Committee* (1959), p. 199.

[7] For example, in the 1959–64 Parliament: *1.* TSSA (Ray Gunter, president and Tom G. Bradley, treasurer); *2.* NUAW (Edwin Gooch, president and Albert V. Hilton, vice president); *3.* UPA (Ellis Smith, president); *4.* USDAW (Walter Padley, president); *5.* UTFWA (Ernest Thornton, president of the Weavers' union and member of UTFWA's executive committee). Most of these offices are primarily honorary.

[8] Attempts to verify Kerr's status with the union were unsuccessful. Alone of the nearly twenty unions contacted for this study, ASTMS refused to cooperate in any way.

234 The 'Kept Men'?

[9] Personal interview with ASW official, 12 Aug. 1964.

[10] See R. Mason, 'I Speak for 100 Gagged Men', *The People* (22 Nov. 1959), p. 12; P. G. Richards, *Honourable Members,* p. 185; D. Houghton, 'Trade Union M.P.s in the British House of Commons', in *Members' Interests Report,* Appendix III, p. 125.

[11] Unions doing this include the TGWU, UPW, USDAW, and the NUR. In the NUR the reports are written by the union staff, not by the MPs.

[12] TSSA, UPW, NUPE, and NUGMW.

[13] NUM, AEF, NUGMW, NUVB, NGA, CAWU, and DATA.

[14] NUR and ASW.

[15] National Union of Mineworkers, *Conference Report* (1964), p. 157.

[16] This is true of the TGWU.

[17] For example, see National Union of General and Municipal Workers, *Congress* (1965), p. 332.

[18] Social Survey, *Gallup Poll on the Trade Unions* (1959), p. 10 (Table 10). For a general discussion of the union journals, see D. F. Selvin, 'Communication in Trade Unions: A Study of Union Journals', *British Journal of Industrial Relations,* I (1963), pp. 75–93.

[19] *Gallup Poll on the Trade Unions* (1959), *loc. cit.*

[20] G. Cyriax and R. Oakeshott, *The Bargainers: A Survey of Modern British Trade Unionism* (New York: Praeger, 1961), p. 71. For the most recent treatment of the role of the shop steward, see W. E. J. McCarthy, *The Role of Shop Stewards in British Industrial Relations.* Research Paper No. 1 for the Royal Commission on Trade Unions and Employers' Associations. (H.M.S.O., 1967).

[21] B. Hennessy, 'Trade Unions and the British Labor Party', *The American Political Science Review,* XLIX (1955), pp. 1063–64; E. Wigham, *What's Wrong with the Unions?* (Baltimore: Penguin Books, 1961), pp. 57–70.

[22] Interview with TUC officer, summer 1967.

[23] Webb, *A History of Trade Unionism,* p. 570; W. Citrine, *Men and Work,* p. 345.

[24] R. Marsh, 'The Trade Union Movement and the Parliamentary Labour Party', (The Fabian Society, n.d. [1962?], pp. 1–2) (mimeographed). This is the original version of the Marsh paper previously cited.

[25] Interviews with AEF assistant general secretary (5 Aug. 1964) and with an NUM-sponsored MP (25 June 1964).

[26] Harrison, p. 297. Cf. Houghton, 'Trade Union M.P.s . . .', *loc. cit.,* pp. 124–5; and T. F. Carbery, *Consumers in Politics,* pp. 91–3.

[27] J. McCann, 'Beneath Big Ben', *Amalgamated Engineering Union Journal,* XXVII, No. 3 (March 1960), p. 85. Cf. Richter, *Political Purpose,* p. 101.

[28] For example, see *Members' Interests Report, op. cit.;* A. Roth, *Business Background of Members of Parliament,* p. xi; K. I. Vijay, 'The Declaration of Interests', *loc. cit.,* pp. 478–86.

[29] *Daily Sketch* (11 Feb. 1965); *Evening Standard* (2 Feb. 1965); and personal interview with AEF assistant general secretary, 10 Aug. 1967.

[30] *Members' Interests Report,* p. xxxiii, para. 114. It should be

emphasised that this does not refer to payments under the Hastings Agreement, but only to whatever supplementary payments may exist among the sponsored MPs. There is frequent confusion between the two, and the sponsored MPs are quite concerned to make the distinction. See *The Observer*, 7 Dec. 1969, p. 3; 14 Dec. 1969, p. 5; and 23 April 1972, p. 25.

[31] Harrison, pp. 293–94. In another situation involving S. O. Davies and the miners' union during the defence dispute of 1960–61, the union did not cease its financial aid to Davies despite both his loss of the Whip and his opposition to NUM policy. Davies had a history of conflict with the union but his strong local support enabled him to win election as an Independent in 1970 over the opposition of the Labour Party and the national NUM. Author's interview with NUM official, 28 July 1964; *The Daily Telegraph* (28 June 1953).

[32] For references to Milne's situation, see A. King, 'The MPs' New Freedom', *New Society* (14 March 1974), p. 640; C. Hitchens, 'Labour and the North East,' *New Statesman* (17 May 1974), p. 684. Milne was denied the opportunity to speak to the 1974 USDAW conference and in early 1975 he announced that he would sue the union for a job. See Union of Shop, Distributive and Allied Workers, *Report of Proceedings at the Annual Conference* (1974), pp. 23–24; *Sunday Telegraph* (2 Feb. 1975); and *The Financial Times* (3 Feb. 1975).

[33] N. Beloff, 'Why the Unions Need Wilson', *The Observer* (21 July 1968), p. 7. Cf. F. McLeavy, 'Trade Union M.P.', *T & G W Record*, XL (Jan., 1960), p. 38.

[34] *Parl. Deb.* 1974–75, Vol. 889, cols 1689–90 (11 April 1975) (daily edition). Mr. Lyon was replying to specific charges that the sponsored MPs were subject to communist pressure because of communist representation on union executive boards. Not surprisingly since the debate took place on a Friday, it was little noticed by sponsored MPs.

[35] Portions of the following material have previously appeared in W. D. Muller, 'Union–MP Conflict: An Overview', *Parliamentary Affairs*, XXVI, No. 3 (Summer 1973), pp. 336–55.

[36] Ranney, *Pathways to Parliament*, p. 21; Richards, *Honourable Members*, p. 22; King and Sloman, *Westminster and Beyond*, pp. 49–50; and A. Watkins, 'Trouble at the Grass Roots', *Spectator* (23 Feb. 1966), p. 220.

[37] Richter, pp. 60 *et. passim.*; N. Barou, *British Trade Unions* (Gollancz, 1949), p. 137.

[38] Bagwell, *Railwaymen*, p. 232.

[39] Clegg, Fox, and Thompson, *History of Trade Unions*, p. 421n.

[40] Bagwell, p. 237.

[41] *Ibid.*, pp. 239–40.

[42] Thomas reported that Bell tried to keep the seat for a Liberal and opposed Thomas' own candidature. Thomas, *My Story*, pp. 24–26.

[43] Evans, *Mabon*, pp. 38, 74–78; Stead, *op. cit.*, p. 339.

[44] Burt, *Autobiography*, p. 290; Gregory, *Miners*, pp. 33–37.

[45] Pelling, *Social Geography*, pp. 339–45.

[46] Griffin, *Miners of Nottinghamshire*, p. 22. Cf. Williams, *Derbyshire*

Miners, pp. 498–505, 807–824. For a discussion of some of the factors in the miners' union that allowed Hancock and, at a more recent date, Aneurin Bevan and S. O. Davies to withstand pressure from union headquarters, see Paynter, *My Generation,* pp. 109–11; and J. D. Edelstein, 'Countervailing Powers and the Political Process in the British Mineworkers' Union', *International Journal of Comparative Sociology,* IX (1968), pp. 255–88.

[47] *The Times* (23 Feb. 1927), p. 12. For a complete discussion of Spencer's problems with the Nottingham miners, see Griffin, *op. cit.,* pp. 150–236.

[48] Thomas, *op. cit.,* pp. 196–98.

[49] Bagwell, *op. cit.,* pp. 531–52; Blaxland, *J. H. Thomas,* p. 254. Thomas was also denied his union pension.

[50] Cole, *A History of the Labour Party from 1914,* p. 88. But Lyman (*The First Labour Government,* p. 9) views the resignation as the result of constituency pressure.

[51] *Parl. Deb.* 1930–31, Vol. 256, cols. 5–8 (8 Sept. 1931).

[52] J. McGovern, *Without Fear or Favour* (Blond, 1960), p. 170; Middlemas, *Clydesiders,* pp. 269, 275.

[53] Interview with NUM-sponsored MP, 23 July 1964.

[54] See *The Times* (1 July 1963), p. 7; G. A. Greenwood, 'Men, Women and Matters', *New Dawn,* XVII (1963), pp. 503–4; Roth, *Business Background,* pp. xii–xiv.

[55] Brown, *In My Way,* pp. 86–88; Butler and Pinto-Duschinsky, *British Election of 1970,* p. 298.

[56] National Union of Railwaymen, *Proceedings and Reports* (1962), Part I: *Executive Committee Minutes* (September 1962), p. 69, Item 69; *Ibid.* (December 1962), pp. 32–39, Item 2914; *Railway Review* (10 Jan. 1964), p. 7.

[57] Rush, *Parliamentary Candidates,* pp. 140–41.

[58] *The Times* (3 April 1970), p. 8.

[59] Interview with AEF assistant general secretary, 10 Aug. 1967; Amalgamated Engineering Union, *National Committee Report* (1966), p. 297 (Sir William Carron's presidential address).

[60] Bevan, *In Place of Fear,* p. 15.

[61] McGovern, *op. cit.,* p. 117. But contrast the account given by Foot, *Bevan,* I, pp. 131–33.

[62] Horner, *Incorrigible Rebel,* p. 64; Foot, *Bevan,* I, pp. 270–99; Paynter, *My Generation,* p. 116.

[63] Foot, *Bevan,* I, p. 355. But contrast the account given by Morrison (*Autobiography,* p. 224) which does not refer to the TUC spokesman. Cf. Donoughue and Jones, *Morrison,* pp. 299–300.

[64] Foot, *Bevan,* I, p. 462. The two Ebby Edwards are the same person. Bullock, *Minister of Labour,* p. 303, makes no reference to the threat of union action. In March 1955 Bevan again threatened to invoke the claim of privilege, this time against party action. See Foot, *Bevan,* II, p. 475.

[65] For a' thorough analysis of Britain's successful effort to join the Common Market and the domestic political struggle it caused, see Uwe Kitzinger, *Diplomacy and Persuasion: How Britain Joined the Common*

Market (Thames and Hudson, 1973). The following discussion is largely based on Kitzinger's study.

[66] Kitzinger, Appendix I, p. 401.

[67] The relvant portions of the press article citing the TGWU speech by Alex Kitson are reprinted in *Parl. Deb.* 1970–71, Vol. 821, cols. 516–17 (14 July 1971).

[68] *The Times* (17 July 1971), p. 2. Kitzinger (Appendix I, p. 403) reports general pressure on sponsored MPs from unions opposing entry. And one MP acknowledged such pressure in A. King, *British Members of Parliament: A Self Portrait* (Macmillan with Granada Television, 1974), p. 7. In the spring of 1975 it was too soon to tell what the impact of the struggle to stay in the EEC would have in this regard.

[69] *The Times* (19 April 1972), p. 2. In any case, both Albu and Pannell retired in 1974.

[70] *Ibid.* (26 June 1975), pp. 1, 2.

[71] *Ibid.* (28 June 1975), pp. 1, 14.

[72] Great Britain, Parliamentary Papers (1974–75). Accounts and Papers 634 (Report from the Committee of Privileges).

[73] *The Times* (30 June 1975), p. 3; (2 July 1975), p. 4; (21 July 1975), p. 2.

[74] *Ibid.* (11 August 1975), p. 1.

[75] *Glasgow Herald* (27 March 1972). Nonetheless, Doig was readopted as a candidate by his Dundee West CLP and reelected in 1974.

[76] *Daily Telegraph* (19 March 1973); *Labour Weekly* (23 March 1973).

[77] *The Times* (1 July 1975), p. 2; (4 July 1975), p. 4. The press was full of articles about Prentice in the weeks leading up to the meeting of his Newham, N. E. CLP on July 23rd and immediately following the meeting.

[78] *Ibid.* (8 July 1975), p. 15; (10 July 1975), p. 15.

[79] *Glasgow Herald* (27 Jan. 1975); and J. Torode, 'London Letter', *The Guardian* (28 Jan. 1975), p. 13. Kitson was the same TGWU official who had made the 1971 speech about supporters of the EEC.

[80] R. J. Jackson, *Rebels and Whips*, p. 222.

[81] This was the usual response of more than 30 sponsored MPs interviewed in the summer of 1964. Cf. Brown, *In My Way*, p. 87.

[82] Harrison, *Trade Unions*, p. 293, n. 1.

[83] *The Times* (17 December 1975), p. 2; *Ibid.* (18 December 1975), pp. 2, 4.

[84] Great Britain, Parliamentary Papers (1943–44), Accounts and Papers 84 (*Report from the Committee of Privileges*), para. 4.

[85] *Ibid.* (1946–47), Accounts and Papers 118 (*Report from the Committee of Privileges*), para. 12. For a personal account of Brown's frequently stormy relations with his civil servants' union, see W. J. Brown, *So Far . . .* (Allen and Unwin, 1942), *passim*.

[86] *Parl. Deb.* 1966–67. Vol. 731, cols. 976–80 (11 July 1966).

[87] *Ibid.* 1970–71. Vol. 821, col. 1072 (19 July 1971). The entire discussion on the matter begins with col. 1059.

[88] *The Times* (6 Aug. 1971), p. 3.

[89] A. King, 'The MPs' New Freedom', *New Society* (14 March 1974), pp. 639–40.

Chapter VII

[1] Portions of this chapter were published in *Parliamentary Affairs*, XXIII, No. 3 (Summer 1970), pp. 258–76.

[2] Social Survey, *Gallup Poll on the Trade Unions* (1959), Table II; The Gallup Poll, *Trades Unions and the Public in 1964*, (1964), Table 10.

[3] Lord Windlesham, *Communication and Political Power* (Jonathan Cape, 1966), p. 122, n. 1; Labour Party Annual Conference, *Report* (1961), p. 182.

[4] *Ibid.* (1960), p. 14.

[5] Quoted in Stewart, *Frank Cousins*, p. 94.

[6] The Congress of the NUGMW voted for the unilateralist resolution while some 75 delegates were absent at the beach or on the way home. *The Economist* (13 June 1959), pp. 998–99. The decision was speedily reversed at a recalled conference a few weeks later. *The Economist* (29 Aug. 1959), p. 615.

[7] Labour Party Annual Conference, *Report* (1960), p. 176.

[8] *Ibid.*, p. 201.

[9] See L. Epstein, 'Who Makes Party Policy: British Labour, 1960–61', *Midwest Journal of Political Science*, VI (1962), pp. 165–82.

[10] *The Guardian* (2 Sept. 1960).

[11] A. Fox. 'The Unions and Defence', *Socialist Commentary*, (February 1961), p. 5. Cf. Windlesham, pp. 112–13.

[12] Fox, 'The Unions and Defence,' p. 7; Windlesham, *Communication*, p. 120; W. Wyatt, 'The Man Who Split the Labour Party', *The Sunday Times* (30 Oct. 1960).

[13] Wyatt, *op. cit.* Wyatt saw Communists as the chief reason for the outcome in the NUR and in several other unions including the AEF.

[14] L. Thompson, 'Twenty Union Chiefs for Gaitskell', *The Observer* (30 Oct. 1960). The reverse of this was to be seen in the National Union of Vehicle Builders, which voted to join the multilateralists over the objections of their leaders. *The Daily Telegraph* (9 June 1961).

[15] Windlesham, *op. cit.*, pp. 119–40.

[16] The actual vote was 166 for Gaitskell and 81 for Wilson. *The Times* (4 Nov. 1960), p. 12.

[17] *The Times* (11 Nov. 1960), p. 12; and 18 Nov. 1960, p. 14; *The Daily Telegraph* (12 Nov. 1960).

[18] Parliamentary Labour Party, Trade Union Group, *Report* (1959–60), p. 3 (mimeographed).

[19] *Parl. Deb.* 1960–61. Vol. 632, cols. 350–54, division 22 (13 Dec. 1960).

[20] L. Epstein, 'New M.P.s and the Politics of the P.L.P.', *Political Studies*, X (1962), p. 122. An alternative source for data on the position of individual Members of Parliament in the controversy is found in the publication of the pro-Gaitskell Campaign for Democratic Socialism. E.g. see 'M.P.'s Supporting the Campaign', *Campaign*, No. 3 (March 1961). But the listings of the

CDS are incomplete and not always reliable.

[21] *The Economist* (17 Dec. 1960), p. 1214. It is relevant to note that the number of Labour Members who did not vote in division 22 of 13 Dec. 1960 is not much larger than Harold Wilson's poll of 81 votes in the leadership fight in November 1960.

[22] For a detailed listing of the sponsored MPs who did not take part in Division 22, see W. D. Muller, 'Trade Union Sponsored Members of Parliament in the Defence Dispute of 1960–1961', *Parliamentary Affairs*, XXIII, No. 3 (Summer, 1970), p. 264, Table I, and sources cited there.

[23] K. Hindell and P. Williams, 'Scarborough and Blackpool: An Analysis of Some Votes at the Labour Party Conferences of 1960 and 1961', *The Political Quarterly*, XXXIII, No. 3 (July–Sept. 1962), p. 309.

[24] For the detailed analysis on which this conclusion concerning the miners is based, see Muller, *op. cit.*, pp. 266–7, Tables IV and V.

[25] For an outline of the types of union–MP interaction, see W. D. Muller, 'Union–MP Conflict: An Overview', *Parliamentary Affairs*, XXVI, No. 3 (Summer, 1973), p. 346, Table I.

[26] National Union of Mineworkers, *Annual Conference Report* (1961), pp. 304–5.

[27] Union of Shop, Distributive and Allied Workers, *Report of Conference Proceedings* (1962), p. 17.

[28] *Ibid.* Padley's views are shared by other leaders of his union (personal interview with Union of Shop, Distributive and Allied Workers' official, 10 Aug. 1964). Cf. M. Harrison. *Trade Unions*, pp. 293–94.

[29] Union of Postoffice Workers, Annual Conference, *Report* (1961), p. 46.

[30] Amalgamated Engineering Union, *Report of Proceedings of the National Committee* (1961), p. 232. The conference also had a resolution praising its sponsored Members of Parliament, but it was not considered. *Ibid.*, p. 239.

[31] National Union of General and Municipal Workers, *Report of Congress*,(1961), pp. 324–29. Resolution 110.

[32] Transport Salaried Staffs Association, Annual Delegate Conference (1961), *Minutes*, p. 45. Resolution 162.

[33] Letter from Mr. H. Wynn, secretary, Derbyshire Area, National Union of Mineworkers, 17 Aug. 1964, quoting the text of the council's resolution. Cf. the actions of the Scottish miners, A. Moffat, *Life*, pp. 204–5.

[34] *The Times* (29 Dec. 1960), p. 3; Cf. *The Sunday Express* (1 Jan. 1961). Neal was dropped as an NUM-sponsored candidate in 1966 because he had passed the Derbyshire miners new retirement age for MPs. Nevertheless he was re-elected to Parliament in 1966.

[35] National Union of Railwaymen, Annual General Meeting (1961) (hereafter cited as Railwaymen), *Agenda*, p. 20. Resolution 21.

[36] *Ibid.* It was withdrawn in favour of a resolution on the general issue of defence policy with no reference to the PLP or to the union's parliamentary panel. *Ibid.*, pp. 166–77. Resolution 179.

[37] *Ibid.*, pp. 19–20. Resolution 18.

[38] Railwaymen, *Proceedings*, Vol. I (first day), pp. 23–25. At the time the union was paying the Members £100 per year in addition to helping with

election expenses and constituency upkeep under terms of the Hastings Agreement.

[39] Railwaymen, *Proceedings*, Vol. I (first day), pp. 30–31. It was not possible to discover the details of the other instances of union–Member conflict to which Greene refers.

[40] Railwaymen, *Agenda*, p. 20.

[41] Interview with National Union of Railwaymen official, 19 Aug. 1964. I am indebted to the National Union of Railwaymen's secretarial department for access to the report of the union's conferences and the minutes of the Union's executive committee.

It may be relevant to note here that several members of the Railwaymen's staff expressed the casual view that the sponsored members of Parliament 'are expected to follow our policy;' moreover the NUR refused to support Stan Mills' efforts to get on List B.

[42] Railwaymen, *Proceedings*, Vol. I (fourth day), pp. 60–67.

[43] *Ibid.*, pp. 68–70. In 1962 Popplewell took a similar independent stand when confronted by union pressure to oppose the entry of Britain into the Common Market. National Union of Railwaymen, Annual General Meeting (1962), *Proceedings*, Vol. I, p. 469.

[44] T. Corfield, 'Fashioning a World of Tomorrow: Report on the Labour Party Conference, 1960', *T & G W Record*, XL (November 1960), p. 37.

[45] Transport and General Workers' Union, *Annual Report* (1960), p. 188.

[46] Personal interview with a TGWU-sponsored MP, summer 1964.

[47] On this, see the perceptive article by J. Cole, 'Mr. Cousins Holds Transport Union to Unilateralism', *The Guardian* (14 July 1961).

[48] Transport and General Workers' Union Conference (1961), *Minutes*, p. 30. Minute No. 54. Cousins' role is recognised in Brown's memoirs, *In My Way*, pp. 87–8.

[49] I. Coulter, 'Toe Cousins Line, Move on M.P.s', *Sunday Times* 7 May 1961; *Sunday Telegraph* (7 May 1961).

[50] *The Times* (5 Oct. 1960), p. 12.

[51] E.g. see A. Albu, 'Beneath Big Ben,' *Amalgamated Engineering Union Journal*, XXVII, No. 7 (July 1960), p. 207; W. W. Small, 'Beneath Big Ben', *op. cit.*, XXVIII, No. 3 (March 1961), p. 80.

[52] Stewart, *Cousins*, p. 33. An MP usually accompanies the TGWU party conference delegation, thus giving Mellish an opportunity which Brown would not have.

[53] J. Cole, 'Mr. Brown's Challenge to Mr. Cousins', *Guardian* (10 July 1961), p. 16; *The Times* (10 and 12 July 1961); and *The Economist* (15 July 1961), p. 236.

[54] Stewart, *Cousins*, p. 105. Brown's efforts did not even commend themselves to those other TGWU MPs who agreed with his goals.

[55] Windlesham, *Communication*, p. 113.

[56] *Ibid.*, p. 138.

[57] G. Deer in *The Newark Herald* (England) (1 Aug. 1959). Cf. Deer, 'Alive and Kicking', *T & G W Record*, XL (Sept. 1960), p. 42.

[58] This was the usual reaction of most of the more than 30 sponsored MPs interviewed in the summer of 1964.

[59] Letter from Mr. R. Main, secretary, Northumberland Area, National Union of Mineworkers, 17 Aug. 1964. Cf. the comments of another official of the miners' union: '. . . all Mining Members of Parliament, including the ones representing South Wales are responsible not to the individual areas but to the National Executive Committee of the miners' union on matters of broad policy'. Letter to the author from Mr. D. Francis, secretary, South Wales Area, National Union of Mineworkers, 18 Aug. 1964.

Chapter VIII

[1] For a general analysis of the problems of the British economy in the later 1960s, see R. Bailey, *Managing the British Economy* (Hutchinson, 1968); W. Davis, *Three Years Hard Labour* (Andre Deutsch, 1968); R. E. Caves *et al.*, *Britain's Economic Prospects* (Washington: Brookings Institution, 1968). The Bailey and Davis books pay more attention to the economic performance of the Wilson government, while Caves is more general and theoretical.

[2] A. Watkins, 'The Revolt Against Mr. Brown's Bill', *Spectator* (11 Feb. 1966), p. 160.

[3] PEP, *Growth in the British Economy* (Allen and Unwin, 1960), p. 192.

[4] The text of Cousins' letter of resignation and Wilson's reply is found in *The Times* (4 July 1966), p. 1. See also Stewart, *Frank Cousins*, pp. 140–44: Wilson, *Labour Government*, p. 222.

[5] In fact, the power to compel witnesses was never invoked by the PIB. See A. Fels, *Prices and Incomes Board*, p. 38.

[6] Great Britain, House of Commons, *Order Paper* (1966–67). p. 2302 (14 July 1966).

[7] Other leading revolts are recorded in: *Parl. Deb.* 1966–67. Vol. 733, cols. 605–10, division 156 (3 Aug. 1966); *Ibid.* Vol. 734, cols. 965–70, division 178 (25 Oct. 1966); House of Commons, *Order Paper* (1966–67), p. 5179 (Nov. 1966); *Ibid.*, p. 5234 (1 Dec. 1966); *Parl. Deb.* 1966–67. Vol. 748, cols. 439–44, division 363 (13 June 1967); *Ibid.* 1967–68. Vol. 765, cols. 419–24, division 154 (21 May, 1968); *Ibid.* 1969–70. Vol. 793, cols. 1477–82, division 40 (17 Dec. 1969).

[8] *The Sunday Times* (4 Sept. 1966), p. 1.

[9] *The Times* (5 Sept. 1966), p. 7; 17 July 1968, p. 1.

[10] *The Economist*: 4 Feb. 1967, p. 397; 11 Feb. 1967, p. 494; 25 Feb. 1967, p. 706; and 4 March 1967, p. 798.

[11] *The Times* (9 May 1968), p. 2.

[12] Personal interview with DATA official, 18 Aug. 1967.

[13] Referred to in D. Houghton, 'Trade Union M.P.s in the British House of Commons', in *Members' Interests Report*, p. 120.

[14] 'Miners' M.P. Explains', *Scotsman* (Edinburgh) (4 Sept. 1966); 'Miners' M.P.s Under Fire', *The Financial Times* (30 Aug. 1966); 'Unions Advised to Think Twice', *The Guardian* (30 Aug. 1966).

[15] 'Mineworkers Slam M.P.s Over Wage Freeze Support', *The Morning Star* (21 Nov. 1966). The MPs were reported to have had a rough time since many of the miners were very much opposed to the policy. It should be pointed out that the Scottish miners have a longstanding reputation for radicalism within the NUM.

[16] E.g. see *The Times* (1 Sept. 1967), p. 3.

[17] For a discussion of the tendency of union members to contract out, see J. Torode, 'White Collar Blue Collar', *Socialist Commentary* (June 1968), pp. 26–7. A year earlier, *The Times* (3 Aug. 1967, p. 3) was reporting that there was only a marginal decrease.

[18] J. Bonfield, 'On Political Affiliation', *The Graphical Journal*, IV (1967), p. 178.

[19] *The Times* (3 Aug. 1967), p. 3.

[20] Labour Party Annual Conference, *Report* (1970), p. 56.

[21] National Union of Public Employees, *Conference Report* (1967), p. 116.

[22] E. S. D. Bishop, 'A Fairer Distribution of Wealth and Income', *Data Journal* (October 1966), pp. 21–2.

[23] L. Formby, 'A Fairer Distribution of Wealth and Income?' *Data Journal* (November 1966), p. 14. The second and far less specific, letter was by A. E. Rabone, 'Distribution of Wealth', *Data Journal* (December 1966), p. 26.

[24] E. S. D. Bishop, 'A Reply to Mr. Formby', *Data Journal* (January 1967), p. 21.

[25] L. Formby, 'Incomes Policy', *Data Journal* (March 1967), pp. 28–9.

[26] T. Bishop, 'Parliament: Rights and Responsibilities,' *Data Journal* (April 1967), p. 22.

[27] P. Williams, 'Conflict of Loyalties', *The New Dawn*, XX, No. 22 (22 Oct. 1966), p. 704.

[28] H. Smallwood, 'The Democratic Way', *The New Dawn*, XX, No. 23 (5 Nov. 1966), p. 736.

[29] S. Dunn, 'The Wage Freeze', *The New Dawn*, XX, No. 24 (19 Nov. 1966), p. 768.

[30] Union of Shop, Distributive and Allied Workers, *Report and Proceedings* (1967), pp. 22–4.

[31] *Ibid.*, pp. 52–68.

[32] M. Brandt, 'Our Leaders Must Lead', *The Graphical Journal*, III (1966), p. 248.

[33] Amalgamated Engineering Union, National Committee *Report* (1966), pp. 196, 199; *Ibid.* (1967), pp. 206, 285. Transport Salaried Staffs Association, *Minutes of Annual Delegate Conference* (1966), p. 56.

[34] *The Times* (3 March 1966), p. 12, and 9 March 1966, p. 10. Brown had a history of conflict with the busmen.

[35] N. Beloff, 'Can Wilson Keep Labour Together?' *The Observer* (10 July 1966).

[36] *The Guardian* (13 July 1966). The headline in *The Financial Times* (13 July 1966) read, 'Poor Support for Cousins in Opposing Incomes Bill'. In sharp contrast *The Daily Mail* headline read, 'Cousins Wins Support as Union M.P.s Meet' (13 July 1966).

[37] *Parl. Deb.* 1966–67. Vol. 731, cols. 976–80 (11 July 1966).

[38] 'TGWU Advises Cousins to Quit Parliament', *Financial Times* (23 Sept. 1966).

[39] P. Paterson, 'Cousins Faces Row on His "Rebel" M.P.s', *Sunday Telegraph* (9 July 1967).

[40] The text of the resolution is found in *The T & G W Record* (September 1967), p. 21. On 2 Oct. 1966 *The Observer* reported that the union was making no demands on the MPs for their support in the dispute.

[41] Quoted in G. Whiteley, 'TGWU To Keep Closer Watch on Sponsored M.P.s', *The Guardian* (14 July 1967).

[42] *The Times* (14 July 1967), p. 1. The following quotes are taken from the same article.

[43] *Parl. Deb.* 1966–67. Vol. 750, cols. 1535–41 (17 July 1967) and col. 1724 (18 July 1967).

[44] See *The Sunday Times* (16 July 1967).

[45] Interview with Labour Party official, 22 Aug. 1967; Brown, *In My Way*, pp. 87–8.

[46] *The Times* (5 June 1970), p. 8. J. Ellis is wrong when he claims that only one of the MPs, George Brown, lost his sponsorship. See Ellis and Johnson, *Members From Unions*, p. 27. J. M. H. Lee regained his sponsored status and a seat in the House of Commons in February, 1974.

[47] *Daily Telegraph* (26 Feb. 1964).

[48] Interview with NUPE official, summer 1967.

[49] *The Times* (30 Sept. 1965), p. 12.

[50] *Ibid.* (29 April 1967), p. 2. A condensed version of Fred Lee's speech was published in the *AEU Journal* (June 1967), pp. 231–32.

[51] *Sunday Telegraph* (9 May 1965). In contrast, Cousins was invited to speak to the same conference.

[52] 'George Brown Talks About Prices, Productivity and Incomes', *T & G W Record*, XLV (May 1965), pp. 16–18.

[53] See the *T & G W Record*, XLVI (September 1966).

[54] T. Park, 'Parliamentary News', *T & G W Record*, XLVI (October 1966), pp. 22–3.

Conclusion

[1] W. G. Runciman, *Relative Deprivation and Social Justice*, pp. 143–44.

[2] R. W. Johnson, 'The British Political Elite', *op. cit.*, p. 69.

[3] See A. H. Birch, *Representative and Responsible Government*, pp. 14–17.

Appendix II

[1] Parliamentary Questions have been the subject of three extended studies: P. Howarth, *Questions in the House* (Bodley Head, 1956) deals with the historical development of the Question Hour through the end of the nineteenth century. D. N. Chester and N. Bowring, *Questions in Parliament* (Oxford: Clarendon Press, 1962), examine the the contemporary Question Hour in a comprehensive fashion. R. W. McCulloch's *Parliamentary Control: Question Hour in The English House of Commons* (Ann Arbor: University Microfilms, n.d. [Publication Number 11, 127]) is a useful comparative study of Britain, the French Third Republic, and Weimar Germany.

[2] Chester and Bowring, p. 196.

[3] *Ibid.*, p. 219.

[4] This technique is used by Chester and Bowring, pp. 192–99, and by R. W. McCulloch, 'Question Time in the British House of Commons', *American Political Science Review*, XXVII (1933) pp. 971–75.

[5] The standing committees of the House of Commons have received little attention, but see the chapter on legislative committees in K. C. Wheare, *Government by Committee* (Oxford: Clarendon Press, 1955), pp. 119–62. See also R. Kimber and J. J. Richardson, 'Specialisation and Parliamentary Standing Committees', *Political Studies*, XVI (1968), pp. 97–101.

[6] Cf. B. Crick, *The Reform of Parliament* (Weidenfeld and Nicholson, 1964), pp. 82–5.

[7] This technique has been borrowed from P. G. Richards, *Honourable Members*, pp. 79–82. Since we have already measured activity in the Question Hour, Richards' technique has been modified to the extent of our using only that portion of the index entry headed 'Debate' and measuring it in centimeters rather than fractional columns. This basic technique has received criticism from Eric Nordlinger for failing to take into account the quality of an MP's speeches. See Nordlinger, 'Leading From Behind', *New Society* (21 May 1964), p. 26.

Select Bibliography

Select Bibliography

(Interviews, correspondence, and trade union documents and journals are not included)

BRITISH GOVERNMENT PUBLICATIONS AND DOCUMENTS (published by HMSO):

House of Commons.

Debates.

Order Paper.

Returns of Select Committees, 1959–70 (printed and mimeographed annually).

Returns of Standing Committees, 1959–64.

Parliamentary Papers, 1943–44. Accounts and Papers No. 84. *Report From the Committee of Privileges* (Robinson Case Report).

Parliamentary Papers, 1946–47. Accounts and Papers No. 118. *Report From the Committee of Privileges* (Brown Case Report).

Parliamentary Papers 1969–70. Accounts and Papers No. 57. *Report From the Select Committee on Members' Interests (Declarations).*

Royal Commission on Trade Unions and Employers' Association. 1965–68. *Report.* (CMND. 3263).

Research Papers No. 1: *The Role of Shop Stewards in British Industrial Relations* (by W. E. J. McCarthy).

Research Papers No. 3: *Industrial Sociology and Industrial Relations* (by Alan Fox).

Research Papers No. 5, Part 1: *Trade Union Structure and Government* (by John Hughes).

Research Paper No. 5, Part 2: *Membership Participation and Trade Union Government* (by John Hughes).

247

248 *The 'Kept Men'?*

Research Papers No. 6: *Trade Union Growth and Recognition* (by George Sayers Bain).
Research Papers No. 10: *Shop Stewards and Workshop Relations* (by W. E. J. McCarthy and S. R. Parker).
Minutes of Evidence, 35 (26 April 1966). Witness: Inns of Court Conservative and Unionists Society.
Minutes of Evidence, 55 (1 November 1966). Witness: Fabian Society.

Labour Party Publications:

Constitution and Standing Orders, 1960.
Election Who's Who, 1959, 1964, 1966, 1970, 1974.
Interim Report of the Sub-Committee on Party Organization (Wilson Report), 1955.
Labour Organizer, XXXII (January 1954); XLIII (July 1964).
Labour Party Conference. *Reports* (almost every year since 1906).
Labour Representation Committee. *Reports,* 1901–05.
Parliamentary Labour Party. Trade Union Group. *Reports,* 1957–58; 1959–64 (mimeographed annually).
Report of the Conference on Labour Representation, 1900.

Books (the place of publication is London unless otherwise stated):

Abse, Leo. *Private Member,* Macdonald, 1973.
Alcock, G. W. *Fifty Years of Railway Trade Unionism.* Co-operative Printing Society, 1922.
Alexander, Andrew, and Watkins, Alan. *The Making of the Prime Minister, 1970.* Macdonald, 1970.
Allen, V. L. *Power in Trade Unions.* Longmans, Green, 1954
Trade Union Leadership. Longmans, Green, 1957.
Trade Unions and the Government. Longmans, Green, 1960.
Amery, J. *The Life of Joseph Chamberlain,* Vol. IV. Macmillan, 1952. (see Garvin, J. L.)
Amery, L. S. *My Political Life.* 3 vols. Hutchinson, 1953.
Arch, Joseph. *The Story of His Life, Told by Himself.* Edited by the Countess of Warwick. 2nd ed. Hutchinson and Co., 1898.
Arnot, R. Page. *A History of the Miners' Federation of Great Britain.* 3 vols. Allen and Unwin, 1949–61.
South Wales Miners (Glowyr de Cymru): A History of the South Wales Miners' Federation (1890–1914). George Allen and Unwin, 1967.
Arthur, Sir George. *George V.* New York: Jonathan Cape and Harrison Smith, 1930.
The Earl of Oxford and Asquith (H. H. Asquith). *Fifty Years of British Parliament.* 2 vols. Boston: Little, Brown, 1926.
Memories and Reflections, 1852–1927. 2 vols. Boston: Little, Brown, 1928.
Attlee, Clement. *As It Happened.* Heinemann, 1954.

The Labour Party in Perspective – and Twelve Years Later. Gollancz. 1949.

Bagwell, Philip S. *The Railwaymen*. George Allen and Unwin, 1963.

Bailey, Richard. *Managing the British Economy*. Hutchinson, 1968.

Barker, Rodney. *Education and Politics, 1900–1951: A Study of the Labour Party*. Oxford: Clarendon Press, 1972.

Barnes, George N. *From Workshop to War Cabinet*. Herbert Jenkins, 1929.

Barou, N. *British Trade Unions*. Gollancz, 1949.

Bassett, Reginald. *Nineteen Thirty-one, Political Crisis*. Macmillan, 1958.

Bauman, Zygmunt. *Between Class and Elite*. Trans. by Sheila Patterson. Manchester: Manchester University Press, 1972.

Bealey, F., and Pelling, H. *Labour and Politics, 1900–1906*. Macmillan, 1958.

Beer, Samuel H. *British Politics in the Collectivist Age*. New York: Alfred A. Knopf, 1965.

Bevan, Aneurin. *In Place of Fear*. New York: Simon and Schuster, 1952.

Lord Beveridge (W. H.). *Power and Influence*. Hodder and Stoughton, 1953.

Birch, A. H. *Representative and Responsible Government*. George Allen and Unwin, 1964.

Blackburn, Fred. *George Tomlinson*. Heinemann, 1954.

Blake, Robert. *Disraeli*. New York: St. Martin's Press, 1967.
The Unknown Prime Minister. Eyre and Spottiswoode, 1955.

Blank, Stephen. *Industry and Government in Britain: The Federation of British Industries in Politics, 1945–1965*. Saxon House/D. C. Heath, 1973.

Blaxland, Gregory. *J. H. Thomas: A Life for Unity*. Muller, 1964.

Blondel, Jean. *Voters, Parties and Leaders*. Revised ed. Penguin Books, 1969.

Blythe, Ronald. *The Age of Illusion*. Penguin Books, 1964.

Bondfield, Margaret. *A Life's Work*. Hutchinson, n.d. (1948?).

Bowle, J. *Viscount Samuel: A Biography*. Gollancz, 1957.

Braddock, Jack and Bessie. *The Braddocks*. Macdonald, 1963.

Brand, Carl F. *British Labour's Rise to Power*. Stanford: Stanford University Press, 1941.

Briggs, A., and Saville, J. (eds.). *Essays in Labour History*. Macmillan, 1960.

Broadhurst, H. *H. Broadhurst, M.P.: The Story of His Life: From a Stone Mason's Bench to the Treasury Bench*. 2nd ed. Hutchinson, 1901.

Brockway, Fenner. *Inside the Left*. George Allen and Unwin, 1942.
Socialism Over Sixty Years. George Allen and Unwin, 1946.

Brome, Vincent. *Aneurin Bevan*. Longmans, Green, 1953.

Brown, George (Lord George Brown). *In My Way*. Gollancz, 1971.

Brown, Kenneth D. *Labour and Unemployment, 1900–1914*. David and Charles, 1971.

Brown, W. J. *So Far . . .* George Allen and Unwin, 1943.

Buck, Philip W. *Amateurs and Professionals in British Politics, 1918–1959*. Chicago: University of Chicago Press, 1963.

Bullock, Alan. *The Life and Times of Ernest Bevin*, Vol. I: *Trade Union Leader, 1881–1940*. Heinemann, 1960. Vol. II: *Minister of Labour, 1940–1945*. Heinemann, 1967.

Bulmer-Thomas, Ivor. *The Growth of the British Party System*. 2 vols. New York: Humanities Press, 1965.

Burt, Thomas. *An Autobiography* (with supplementary chapters by Aaron Watson). T. Fisher Unwin, 1924.

Butler, David. *The British General Election of 1951*. Macmillan, 1952. *The British General Election of 1955*. Macmillan, 1955.

Butler, David, and Freeman, Jennie (eds.). *British Political Facts, 1900–1967*. 2nd ed. Macmillan, 1968.

Butler, David, and King, Anthony. *The British General Election of 1964*. Macmillan, 1965.
The British General Election of 1966. Macmillan, 1966.
Macmillan, 1966.

Butler, David, and Pinto-Duschinsky, Michael. *The British General Election of 1970*. Macmillan, 1971.

Butler, David, and Rose, Richard. *The British General Election of 1959*. Macmillan, 1960.

Butler, David, and Stokes, Donald. *Political Change in Britain*. Macmillan, 1969.

Carbery, Thomas F. *Consumers in Politics*. Manchester: the University Press, 1969.

Carlton, David. *MacDonald versus Henderson*. Macmillan, 1970.

'Cassandra'. *George Brown: A Profile and Pictorial Biography*. Oxford: Pergamon Press, 1964.

Caves, Richard, *et al*. *Britain's Economic Prospects*. Washington: Brookings Institution, 1968.

Chamberlain, Sir Austin. *Politics from Inside*. Cassell, 1936.

Chapman, Richard A. *Decision Making*. Routledge and Kegan Paul, 1968.

Chester, D. N. and Bowring, Nona. *Questions in Parliament*. Oxford: Clarendon Press, 1962.

Viscount Chilston (Eric Alexander). *Chief Whip*. Routledge and Kegan Paul, 1961.

Citrine, W. *Men and Work: An Autobiography*. Hutchinson, 1964.

Clegg, H. A. *General Union*. Oxford: Blackwell, 1954.
General Union in a Changing Society. Oxford: Blackwell, 1964.

Clegg, H. A., Fox, Alan, and Thompson, A. F. *A History of British Trade Unions Since 1889*, Vol. I: 1889–1910. Oxford: Clarendon Press, 1964.

Cline, Catherine Ann. *Recruits to Labour: The British Labour Party, 1914–1931*. Syracuse: Syracuse University Press, 1963.

Clynes, J. R. *Memoirs*. 2 vols. Hutchinson, 1937.

Cole, G. D. H. *British Working Class Politics, 1832–1914*. Routledge, 1941.
A History of the Labour Party From 1914. Routledge and Kegan Paul, 1948.

Cole, G. D. H. and Postgate, Raymond. *The Common People, 1746–1946*. 2nd ed. Methuen, 1961.

Cole, Margaret I. (ed.). *Beatrice Webb's Diaries, 1912–1924*. Longmans,

Green, 1952.
Beatrice Webb's Diaries, 1924–1932. Longmans, Green, 1956.
Connelly, T. J. *The Woodworkers, 1860–1960.* Amalgamated Society of Woodworkers, 1960.
Cooke, Colin. *The Life of Richard Stafford Cripps.* Hodder and Stoughton, 1957.
Coombes, David. *The Member of Parliament and the Administration.* George Allen and Unwin, 1966.
Cowling, Maurice. *The Impact of Labour, 1920–1924.* Cambridge: the University Press, 1971.
Craig, F. W. (ed.). *British Parliamentary Election Statistics, 1918–1968.* Glasgow: Political Reference Publications, 1968.
Craik, William. *Sydney Hill and the National Union of Public Employees.* George Allen and Unwin, 1968.
Crick, Bernard. *The Reform of Parliament.* Weidenfeld and Nicolson, 1964.
Cross, Colin. *Philip Snowden.* Barrie and Rockliff, 1966.
Cyriax, George, and Oakeshott, R. *The Bargainers: A Survey of Modern British Trade Unionism.* New York: Praeger, 1961.
Dalton, Hugh. *Memoirs.* 3 vols. Muller, 1953–62.
Dangerfield, G. *The Strange Death of Liberal England.* New York: Capricorn Books, 1961.
Davis, William. *Three Years Hard Labour.* Andre Deutsch, 1968.
Davis, W. J. *The British Trades Union Congress.* 2 vols. Co-operative Printing Society (for the Trades Union Congress, Parliamentary Committee), 1910–13.
Donoughue, Bernard and Jones, G. W. *Herbert Morrison: Portrait of a Politician.* Weidenfeld and Nicolson, 1973.
Dowse, R. E. *Left in the Center.* Longmans, 1966.
Easton, David. *A Systems Analysis of Political Life.* New York: John Wiley, 1965.
Eckstein, Harry. *Pressure Group Politics: The Case of the British Medical Association.* George Allen and Unwin, 1960.
Edelman, Murray. *The Symbolic Uses of Politics.* Urbana: University of Illinois Press, 1964.
Edwards, George. *From Crow Scaring to Westminster.* Labour Publishing Co., 1922.
Edwards, Ness. *The History of the South Wales Miners' Federation.* Lawrence and Wishart, 1938.
Ellis, John, and Johnson, R. W. *Members From Unions.* Fabian Society, 1974.
Epstein, Leon D. *Britain – Uneasy Ally.* Chicago: University of Chicago Press, 1954.
Evans, E. W. *Mabon (William Abraham, 1842–1922).* Cardiff: University of Wales Press, 1959.
The Miners of South Wales. Cardiff: University of Wales Press, 1961.
Evans, Howard. *Sir Randal Cremer.* Boston: Ginn and Co. (for the International School of Peace), 1910.
Feiling, Keith. *Life of Neville Chamberlain.* Macmillan, 1946.

Fels, Allan. *The British Prices and Incomes Board.* Cambridge: the University Press, 1972.

Ferris, Paul. *The New Militants: Crisis in the Trade Unions.* Penguin Books, 1972.

Finer, S. E., Berrington, H. B., and Bartholomew, D. J. *Backbench Opinion in the House of Commons, 1955–1959.* New York: Pergamon Press, 1961.

Flanders, Allan. *British Trade Unionism.* Bureau of Current Affairs, 1948.

Foot, Michael. *Aneurin Bevan,* Vol. I: *1897–1945.* Macgibbon and Kee, 1965.

   Aneurin Bevan, Vol. II: *1945–1960.* Davis-Poynter, 1973.

Fox, A., *A History of the National Union of Boot and Shoe Operatives, 1874–1957.* Oxford: Blackwell, 1958.

Frankenburg, R. *Communities in Britain.* Penguin Books, 1966.

Gardiner, A. G. *Life of Sir William Harcourt.* 2 vols. Constable, 1923.

Garside, W. R. *The Durham Miners, 1919–1960.* Allen and Unwin, 1971.

Garvin, J. L. *The Life of Joseph Chamberlain,* Vols. I–III. Macmillan, 1932. (See Amery, J.)

Glass, S. T. *The Responsible Society.* Longmans, 1966.

Goldstein, Joseph. *The Government of British Trade Unions.* Allen and Unwin, 1952.

Goldthorpe, John H., Lockwood, David, Bechhofer, Frank, and Platt, Jennifer. *The Affluent Worker: Industrial Attitudes and Behaviour.* Cambridge: the University Press, 1968.

   The Affluent Worker: Political Attitudes and Behaviour. Cambridge: the University Press, 1968.

   The Affluent Worker in the Class Structure. Cambridge: the University Press, 1969.

Gosling, Harry. *Up and Down Stream.* Methuen, 1927.

Graves, Robert, and Hodge, Alan. *The Long Week-end; A Social History of Great Britain, 1918–1939.* 2nd ed. New York: W. W. Norton and Company, 1963.

Gregory, Roy. *The Miners and British Politics, 1906–1914.* Oxford University Press, 1968.

Griffin, Alan R. *The Miners of Nottinghamshire, 1914–1944.* George Allen and Unwin, 1962.

Griffiths, James. *Pages from Memory.* Dent, 1969.

Groves, Reg. *Sharpen the Sickle!* The Porcupine Press, 1949.

Gulley, Elsie Elizabeth. *Joseph Chamberlain and English Social Politics.* New York: Columbia University Press, 1926.

Guttsman, W. L. *The British Political Elite.* Macgibbon and Kee, 1963.

Gwyn, William B. *Democracy and the Cost of Politics in Britain.* The Athlone Press, 1962.

Lord Haldane (R. B.). *Autobiography.* Hodder and Stoughton, 1929.

Halevy, Elje. *History of the English People in the Nineteenth Century.* 6 vols. New York: Barnes and Noble, 1961.

Hamilton, Mary Agnes. *Arthur Henderson: A Biography.* Heinemann, 1938.

Hanham, H. J. *Elections and Party Management*. Longmans, Green, 1959.
Hare, A. Paul. *Handbook of Small Group Research*. New York: The Free Press, 1962.
Harrison, Martin. *Trade Unions and the Labour Party Since 1945*. Detroit: Wayne State University Press, 1960.
Harrod, J. *Trade Union Foreign Policy*. Garden City, N.Y.: Anchor Doubleday, 1972.
Hastings, Sir Patrick. *Autobiography*. Heinemann, 1948.
Haw, George. *From Workhouse to Westminster*. Cassell. 1907.
Heffer, Eric S. *The Class Struggle in Parliament*. Gollancz, 1973.
Herbert, A. P. *Independent Member*. Methuen, 1950.
Higenbottam, S. (comp.). *Our Society's History*. Manchester: Amalgamated Society of Woodworkers, 1939.
Hilton, W. S. *Foes to Tyranny: A History of the Amalgamated Union of Building Trade Workers*. AUBTW, 1963.
Hindess, Barry. *The Decline of Working Class Politics*. Macgibbon and Kee, 1971.
Hobsbawn, E. J. *Labour Men: Studies in the History of Labour*. Garden City, N.Y.: Anchor Books, 1967.
Hodge, John. *Workman's Cottage to Windsor Castle*. Sampson Low, 1931.
Hoffman, J. D. *The Conservative Party in Opposition, 1945–1951*. Macgibbon and Kee, 1964.
Hogan, James. *Election and Representation*. Cork: Cork University Press, 1945.
Hoggart, Richard. *The Uses of Literacy*. Penguin Books, 1958.
Hopkins Harry. *The New Look*. Secker and Warburg, 1963.
Horn, Pamela. *Joseph Arch (1826–1919): The Farm Workers' Leader*. Kineton, England: The Roundwood Press, 1971.
Horner, Arthur. *Incorrigible Rebel*. Macgibbon and Kee, 1960.
Howarth, P. *Questions in the House*. The Bodley Head, 1956.
Howard, Anthony, and West, Richard. *The Making of the Prime Minister*. Jonathan Cape, 1965.
Howell, George. *The Conflict of Capital and Labour*. 2nd ed. Macmillan, 1890.
　　Labour Legislation, Labour Movements and Labour Leaders. 2 vols. 2nd ed. T. F. Unwin, 1905.
Hughes, Emrys. *Keir Hardie*. George Allen and Unwin, 1956.
Hughes, Fred. *By Hand and Brain*. Lawrence and Wishart (for the Clerical and Administrative Workers' Union), 1953.
Hughes, John. *Change in the Trade Unions*. Fabian Society, 1964.
Humphrey, A. W. *A History of Labour Representation*. Constable, 1913.
Hunter, Leslie. *The Road to Brighton Pier*. Arthur Barker, 1959.
Hyman, Richard. *The Workers' Union*. Oxford: Clarendon Press, 1971.
Jackson, Robert J. *Rebels and Whips*. New York: St. Martin's Press, 1968.
Janosik, Edward G. *Constituency Labour Parties in Britain*. Pall Mall Press, 1968.
Jenkins, Peter. *The Battle of Downing Street*. Charles Knight, 1970.
Jenkins, Roy. *Mr. Attlee*. Heinemann, 1948.

Sir Charles Dilke. Collins, 1958.

Jennings, W. Ivor. *Parliament.* Cambridge: the University Press, 1939.

Johnson, Nevil. *Parliament and Administration: The Estimates Committee, 1945–1965.* George Allen and Unwin, 1966.

Johnston, James. *A Hundred Commoners.* Herbert Joseph, 1931.

Jones, Thomas. *Whitehall Diary,* 2 vols. Edited by Keith Middlemas. Oxford University Press, 1969.

Junz, Alfred J. *The Student Guide to Parliament.* Hansard Society, 1960.

Kaplan, Abraham. *The Conduct of Inquiry.* San Francisco: Chandler Publishing Co., 1964.

Kaufman, Gerald (ed.). *The Left.* Anthony Blond, 1966.

Kent, William. *John Burns: Labour's Lost Leader.* Williams and Norgate, 1950.

Kerr, Russell, *et. al. Beyond the Freeze.* 1966.

King, Anthony. *British Members of Parliament: A Self-Portrait,* Macmillan with Granada Television, 1974.

King, Anthony, and Sloman, Anne. *Westminster and Beyond.* Macmillan, 1973.

Kirkwood, David. *My Life of Revolt.* Harrap, 1935.

Kitzinger, Uwe. *Diplomacy and Persuasion.* Thames and Hudson, 1973.

Krug, Mark M. *Aneurin Bevan: Cautious Rebel.* New York: Thomas Yoseloff, 1961.

Laski, Harold J. *Parliamentary Government in England.* George Allen and Unwin, 1938.

Lawson, Jack. *A Man's Life.* Hodder and Stoughton, 1932.

Leonard, Dick and Herman, Valentine (eds.). *The Backbencher and Parliament.* Macmillan, 1972.

Leonard, R. L. *Guide to the General Election.* Pan Books, 1964.

Leventhal, F. M. *Respectable Radical: George Howell and Victorian Working Class Politics.* Weidenfeld and Nicolson, 1971.

Lowe, David. *From Pit to Parliament.* The Labour Publishing Company, 1923.

Lowell, A. Lawrence. *The Influence of Party Upon Legislation in England and America.* Washington: American Historical Association Annual Report, 1902.

Lucy, Henry W. *The Balfourian Parliament, 1900–1905.* Hodder and Stoughton, 1906.

A Diary of the Home Rule Parliament, 1892–1895. Cassell, 1896.

A Diary of the Salisbury Parliament, 1886–1892. Cassell, 1892.

Diary of Two Parliaments. Cassell, 1885.

A Diary of the Unionist Parliament, 1895–1900. Bristol: J. W. Arrowsmith, 1901.

Later Peeps at Parliament. G. Newnes, 1905.

Memories of Eight Parliaments. Heinemann, 1908.

Peeps at Parliament. G. Newnes, 1903.

Lyman, R. W. *The First Labour Government, 1924.* Chapman and Hall, 1957.

Mabey, Richard (ed.). *Class.* Anthony Blond, 1967.

Maddox, William P. *Foreign Relations in British Labour Politics*. Xerox edition. Ann Arbor: University Microfilms, 1964. First published by Harvard University Press, 1934.

Magee, Bryan. *The New Radicalism*. New York: St. Martin's Press, 1963.

Mann, Tom. *Memoirs*. Labour Publishing Company, 1923.

Manzer, Ronald A. *Teachers and Politics*. Manchester: Manchester University Press, 1970.

Marsh, David C. *The Changing Social Structure of England and Wales*. Routledge and Kegan Paul, 1965.

Martin, Kingsley. *Harold Laski*. Gollancz, 1953.

Matthews, Donald S. *The Social Background of Political Decision Makers*. New York: Random House, 1955.

Maurice, Sir Frederick. *The Life of Viscount Haldane of Cloan*. 2 vols. Faber and Faber, 1937.

McAllister, Gilbert. *James Maxton: The Portrait of A Rebel*. John Murray, 1935.

McBriar, A. M. *Fabian Socialism and English Politics, 1884–1918*. Cambridge: the University Press, 1966.

McCallum, R. B. and Readman, A. *The British General Election of 1945*. Oxford University Press, 1947.

MacDonald, Donald Farquhar. *The State and the Trade Unions*. Macmillan, 1960.

McGovern, J. *Without Fear of Favour*. Blandford, 1960.

McHenry, D. E. *The Labour Party in Transition, 1931–38*. George Routledge and Sons, 1938.

McKenzie, R. T. *British Political Parties*. 2nd ed. New York: Praeger, 1963.

McKenzie, R. T., and Silver, Allan. *Angels in Marble: Working Class Conservatives in Urban England*. Heinemann, 1968.

McKibbin, Ross. *The Evolution of the Labour Party, 1910–1924*. Oxford University Press, 1974.

McKillop, Norman. *The Lighted Flame*. Thomas Nelson, 1950.

Mackintosh, John P. *The British Cabinet*. Toronto: University of Toronto Press, 1962.

McNair, J. *James Maxton: The Beloved Rebel*. Allen and Unwin, 1956.

Macridis, Roy C. (ed.). *Political Parties: Contemporary Trends and Ideas*. New York: Harper Torchbooks, 1967.

Meehan, Eugene J. *The British Left Wing and Foreign Policy*. New Brunswick: Rutgers University Press, 1960.

Meyers, Frederic. *European Coal Mining Unions*. Los Angeles: Institute of Industrial Relations of the University of California, 1961.

Middlemas, Robert Keith. *The Clydesiders*. Hutchinson, 1965.

Milliband, Ralph. *Parliamentary Socialism*. Merlin Press, 1964.

Moffat, Abe. *My Life with the Miners*. Lawrence and Wishart, 1965.

Moneypenny, W. F. and Buckle G. E. *The Life of Benjamin Disraeli*. New ed. in 2 vols. John Murray, 1929.

Moran, James. *NATSOPA: Seventy Five Years*. Heinemann (on behalf of NATSOPA), 1964.

Morgan, Kenneth O. *Wales in British Politics, 1868–1922*. Cardiff: University of Wales Press, 1963.

Morrison, H. *Government and Parliament.* 3rd ed. Oxford University Press, 1964.

    Herbert Morrison: An Autobiography. Odhams Press, 1960.

Mulley, F. *The Politics of Western Defense.* New York: Praeger, 1962.

Murphy, J. T. *Labour's Big Three.* Bodley Head, 1948.

Musson, A. E. *The Typographical Association.* New York: Oxford University Press, 1954.

Nicholas, H. G. *The British General Election of 1950.* Macmillan, 1951.

Nicolson, Harold. *Diaries and Letters, 1930–39.* Edited by Nigel Nicolson. Fontana Books, 1969.

Nicolson, Sir Harold. *King George V.* Constable, 1952.

Nordlinger, Eric A. *The Working Class Tories.* Macgibbon and Kee, 1967.

Ostrogorski, M. *Democracy and the Organization of Political Parties,* Vol. 1: *England.* Edited by S. M. Lipset. New York: Anchor Doubleday Books, 1964.

Parkin, Frank. *Middle Class Radicalism: The Social Bases of the British Campaign for Nuclear Disarmament.* Manchester: Manchester University Press, 1968.

Parris, Henry. *Government and the Railways in Nineteenth Century Britain.* Routledge and Kegan Paul, 1965.

Paton, John. *Left Turn!* Martin Secker and Warburg, 1936.

Paynter, Will. *My Generation.* Allen and Unwin, 1972.

PEP. *Advisory Committees in British Government.* George Allen and Unwin, 1960.

Pelling, Henry. *A History of British Trade Unionism.* Penguin Books, 1963.

    Origins of the Labour Party, 1880–1900. 2nd. ed. Oxford: Clarendon Press, 1965.

    Popular Politics and Society in Late Victorian Britain. New York: St. Martin's Press, 1968.

    A Short History of the Labour Party. Macmillan, 1962.

    Social Geography of British Elections, 1885–1910. Macmillan, 1967.

Pollard, Sidney. *A History of Labour in Sheffield.* Liverpool: Liverpool University Press, 1959.

Potter, Allen. *Organized Groups in British National Politics.* Faber and Faber, 1961.

Pritt, D. N. *The Labour Government, 1945–1951.* Lawrence and Wishart, 1963.

Pugh, Sir Arthur. *Men of Steel.* The Iron and Steel Trades Confederation, 1951.

Pulzer, Peter G. J. *Political Representation and Elections: Parties and Voting in Great Britain.* New York: Praeger, 1967.

Punnett, R. M. *Front-Bench Opposition.* Heinemann, 1973.

Radice, Giles, and Radice, Lisanne. *Will Thorne: Constructive Militant.* George Allen and Unwin, 1974.

Ranney, Austin. *Pathways to Parliament.* Madison and Milwaukee: University of Wisconsin Press, 1965.

Reid, J. H. Stewart. *The Origins of the Labour Party.* Minneapolis: University of Minnesota Press, 1955.

Richards, Peter G. *The Backbenchers*. Faber, 1972.
Honourable Members: A study of the British Backbencher. 2nd ed. Faber and Faber. 1964.
Parliament and Conscience. George Allen and Unwin, 1970.
Parliament and Foreign Affairs. George Allen and Unwin, 1967.
Patronage in British Government. George Allen and Unwin, 1963.

Richter, Irving. *Political Purpose in Trade Unions*. Allen and Unwin, 1973.

Roberts, B. C. *The Trades Union Congress, 1868–1921*. Cambridge, Mass.: Harvard University Press, 1958.

Rodgers, W. T. (ed.). *Hugh Gaitskell, 1906–1963*. Thames and Hudson, 1964.

Rose, Richard. *Politics in England*. Boston: Little, Brown, 1964.

Ross, J. F. S. *Parliamentary Representation*. 2nd, enlarged ed. Eyre and Spottiswood, 1948.

Roth, Andrew. *The Business Background of Members of Parliament*. Parliamentary Profiles, n.d. (1963?).

Runciman, W. G. *Relative Deprivation and Social Justice*. Penguin Books, 1972.

Rush, Michael. *The Selection of Parliamentary Candidates*. Nelson, 1969.

Russell, A. K. *Liberal Landslide: The General Election of 1906*. Newton Abbot, U.K, David and Charles, 1973.

Lord Samuel (H.L.S.). *Memoirs*. Cresset, 1945.

Scanlon, John. *The Decline and Fall of the Labour Party*. Peter Davies, 1932.

Scott, C. P. *The Political Diaries of C. P. Scott, 1911–1928*. Edited by Trevor Wilson. Collins, 1970.

Self, Peter, and Storing, H. *The State and the Farmer*. George Allen and Unwin, 1962.

Sexton, Sir James. *Agitator: The Life of the Dockers' M.P.* Faber and Faber, 1936.

Shanks, M. *The Stagnant Society*. Penguin Books, 1961.

Shinwell, Emanuel. *Conflict Without Malice*. Odhams Press, 1955.
I've Lived Through it All. Gollancz, 1973.

Shrimsley, Anthony. *The First Hundred Days of Harold Wilson*. New York: Praeger, 1965.

Viscount Simon (John Allsebrock). *Retrospect*. Hutchinson, 1952.

Skidelsky, Robert. *Politicians and the Slump*. Macmillan, 1967.

Smellie, K. B. *Great Britain Since 1688: A Modern History*. Ann Arbor: University of Michigan Press, 1962.

Smillie, Robert. *My Life for Labour*. Mill and Boon, 1924.

Smith, Dudley. *Harold Wilson: A Critical Biography*. Robert Hale, 1964.

Smith, Leslie. *Harold Wilson: The Authentic Portrait*. New York: Charles Scribner's, 1964.

Snowden, Philip. *An Autobiography*. 2 vols. Ivor Nicholson and Watson, 1934.

Sommer, D. *Haldane of Cloan*. Allen and Unwin, 1960.

Spender, J. A. *The Life of the Rt. Hon. Sir Henry Campbell-Bannerman*, 2 vols. Hodder and Stoughton, 1923.

and Asquith, Cyril. *Life of Herbert Henry, Lord Oxford and Asquith.* 2 vols. Hutchinson and Co., 1932.

Spoor, Alec. *White-Collar Union: 60 years of NALGO.* Heinemann, 1967.

Stansky, Peter. *Ambitions and Strategies.* Oxford: Clarendon Press, 1964.

Stewart, J. D. *British Pressure Groups: Their Role in Relation to the House of Commons.* Oxford: Clarendon Press, 1958.

Stewart, Margaret. *Frank Cousins: A Study.* Hutchinson, 1968.

Strauss, Patricia. *Bevin and Company.* New York: G. P. Putnam's Sons, 1941.

Symons, Julian. *The General Strike.* The Cresset Press, 1957.

Taylor, A. J. P. *English History, 1914–1945.* Oxford University Press, 1965.

Taylor, Bernard (Lord Taylor of Mansfield). *Uphill All the Way: A Miner's Struggle.* Sedgwick and Jackson, 1972.

Taylor, Eric. *The House of Commons at Work.* 5th rev. ed. Penguin Books, 1963.

Thomas, John A. *The House of Commons, 1832–1901.* Cardiff: University of Wales Press, 1937.

Thomas, J. H. *My Story.* Hutchinson, 1937.

Thorne, Will. *My Life's Battle.* George Newnes, 1925.

Tillett, Ben. *Memories and Reflections.* J. Long, 1931.

Tuckwell, G. M. *The Life of Sir Charles W. Dilke.* 2 vols. J. Murray, 1917.

Tracey, H. (ed.). *The Book of the Labour Party.* 3 vols. Caxton Publishing Co., 1925.

Turner, Ben. *About Myself, 1863–1930.* Humphrey Toulmin, 1930.

Turner, D. R. *The Shadow Cabinet in British Politics.* Routledge and Kegan Paul, 1969.

Vernon, R. V., and Mansergh, N. (eds.). *Advisory Bodies: A Study of Their Uses in Relation to Central Government, 1919–1937.* Allen and Unwin, 1940.

Wahlke, J. C., Eulau, Heinz, Buchanan, W., and Ferguson, Leroy C. *The Legislative System.* New York: John Wiley and Sons, 1962.

Watkins, Ernest. *The Cautious Revolution.* New York: Farrar, Strauss and Co., 1950.

Watson, Aaron. *A Great Labour Leader, Being the Life of the Right Hon. Thomas Burt, M.P.* Brown, Langham, 1908.

Weaver, H. R. H. (ed.). *Dictionary of National Biography, 1922–1930.* Oxford University Press, 1937.

Webb, Sidney. *The Story of the Durham Miners, 1662–1921.* Fabian Society and Labour Publishing Co., 1921.

Webb, Sidney and Beatrice. *The History of Trade Unionism.* New ed. Longmans, Green, 1920.

Industrial Democracy. New ed. Longmans, Green, 1911.

Wedgwood, Josiah. *Memories of a Fighting Life.* Hutchinson, 1940.

A Testament to Democracy. Hutchinson, 1942.

Welbourne, E. *The Miners' Unions of Northumberland and Durham.* Cambridge: the University Press, 1923.

Wheare, K. C. *Government by Committee*. Oxford: Clarendon Press, 1955.
Wheeler-Bennett, John W. *John Anderson, Viscount Waverley*. Macmillan, 1962.
King George VI. Macmillan, 1958.
Whyte, F. *The Life of W. T. Stead*. 2 vols. Boston: Houghton Mifflin, 1925.
Wigham, Eric. *What's Wrong with the Unions?* Baltimore, Md.: Penguin Books, 1961.
Wilkinson, Ellen. *Peeps at Politicians*. Philip Allan, 1930.
Williams, Francis. *Ernest Bevin*. Hutchinson, 1952.
Fifty Years March. Odhams Press, 1950.
Magnificent Journey. Odhams Press, 1954.
A Prime Minister Remembers. Heinemann, 1961.
Williams, J. E. *The Derbyshire Miners*. George Allen and Unwin, 1962.
Wilson, Harold. *The Labour Government, 1964–1970*. Weidenfeld and Nicolson and Michael Joseph, 1971.
Wilson, J. Havelock. *My Stormy Voyage Through Life*. Cooperative Printing Society, 1925.
Wilson, John. *Memories of a Labour Leader*. T. Fisher Unwin, 1910.
Lord Windlesham. *Communication and Political Power*. Jonathan Cape, 1966.
Earl Winterton. *Orders of the Day*. Cassell, 1953.
Lord Woolton. *Memoirs*. Cassell, 1959.
Wootton, Graham, *Workers, Unions and the State*. New York: Schocken, 1967.
Young, G. M. *Stanley Baldwin*. Rupert Hart-Davis, 1952.

Newspapers and Periodicals (General):

Separate entries for items in the following publications are not included in the next section.
The Economist
The Listener
New Society
The New Statesman
The Spectator
The Times (London)
The newspaper clipping files of the Labour Party Library (The overwhelming bulk of newspaper citations are taken from these files. I am indebted to Mrs. Irene Wagner for permission to use them.)

Other Articles:

Alderman, R. C. 'Discipline in the Parliamentary Labour Party, 1945–1951', *Parliamentary Affairs*, XVIII (Summer 1965), pp. 293–306.
'Parliamentary Party Discipline in Opposition: The Parliamentary Labour Party, 1951–1964', *Parliamentary Affairs*, XXI (Spring 1968), pp. 124–36.

Allen, V. L. 'The Ethics of Trade Union Leaders', *British Journal of Sociology*, VII (1956), pp. 314–36.

'The Re-organisation of the Trades Union Congress, 1918–1927', *British Journal of Sociology*, XI (1960), pp. 23–43.

Baldwin, G. B. 'Structural Reform in the British Miners' Union', *Quarterly Journal of Economics*, LXVII (1953), pp. 576–97.

Barker, Anthony. 'Parliament and Patience', *Political Studies*, XV (1967), pp. 74–81.

Beloff, Max. 'Reflections on the British General Election of 1966', *Government and Opposition*, I (August 1966), pp. 529–34.

Bendix, R. and Lipset, S. M. 'Political Sociology', *Current Sociology*, VI, No. 2 (1957), pp. 79–169.

Berrington, Hugh. 'Partisanship and Dissidence in the Nineteenth Century House of Commons', *Parliamentary Affairs*, XXI (Autumn 1968), pp. 338–74.

Bocock, Jean. 'The Politics of White-Collar Unionisation', *Political Quarterly*, XLIV (1973), pp. 294–303.

Bonnor, J. 'The Four Labour Cabinets', *Sociological Review*, VI (1958), pp. 37–47.

Brand, C. F. 'The Conversion of the British Trade Unions to Political Action', *American Historical Review*, XXX (January 1925), pp. 251–70.

Brenner, Michael J. 'Functional Representation and Interest Group Theory: Some Notes on British Practice', *Comparative Politics*, II (1969–70), pp. 111–34.

Bromhead, Peter. 'The British Constitution in 1966', *Parliamentary Affairs*, XX (Spring 1967), pp. 106–19.

'The British Constitution in 1967', *Parliamentary Affairs*, XXI (Spring 1968), pp. 107–23.

Burns, J. M. 'The Parliamentary Labour Party in Great Britain', *American Political Science Review*, XLIV (1950), pp. 855–71.

'Candidus'. 'Dog Days', *Socialist Commentary* (August 1967), pp. 10–11.

'Panic Talk', *Socialist Commentary* (December 1967), pp. 13–14.

Carter, Tony. 'The Government and Positive Industrial Relations', *Socialist Commentary* (June 1974), pp. 6–7.

'Catalpa'. 'In and Out of Parliament', *Socialist Commentary* (August 1967), pp. 23–24.

Christoph, James B. 'The Advent of the National Health Service', *in* James B. Christoph and Bernard E. Brown (eds.), *Cases in Comparative Politics*, 2nd ed. Boston: Little, Brown, 1969, pp. 35–74.

Clarke, J. F. 'An Interview with Sir William Lawther', *Bulletin of the Society for the Study of Labour History*, No. 19 (Autumn 1969), pp. 14–21.

Cole, Margaret. 'British Trade Unions and the Labour Government', *Industrial and Labor Relations Review*, I (July, 1948), pp. 573–79.

Crick, B. 'The Future of the Labour Government', *Political Quarterly*, XXXVIII (1967), pp. 375–88.

Crossman, Richard. 'The Crossman Diaries', *The Sunday Times* (9 Feb. 1975), pp. 12–15.

Cyriax, G. 'Labour and the Unions', *Political Quarterly*, XXXI (1960), pp.

324–32.

Dahl, Robert A. 'Workers' Control of Industry and the British Labour Party', *American Political Science Review*, XLI (1947), pp. 875–900.

Desmarais, Ralph H. 'Strikebreaking and the Labour Government of 1924', *Journal of Contemporary History*, VIII (1973), pp. 165–75.

Dowse, R. E. 'The Entry of the Liberals into the Labour Party, 1914–1920', *Yorkshire Bulletin of Economic and Social Research*, XIII (November 1961), pp. 78–87.

'The Left Wing Opposition During the First Two Labour Governments', *Parliamentary Affairs*, XIV (1960–61), pp. 80–93, 229–43.

'The Parliamentary Labour Party in Opposition', *Parliamentary Affairs*, XIII (1959–60), pp. 520–29.

Duffy, A. E. P. 'Differing Policies and Personal Rivalries in the Origins of the I. L. P.', *Victorian Studies*, VI (September 1962), pp. 43–65.

'The Eight Hours Day Movement in Britain, 1886–1893', *The Manchester School*, XXXVI (1968), pp. 203–22, 345–63.

'New Unionism in Britain, 1889–1890: A Reappraisal', *Economic History Review*, XIV (1961), pp. 313–15.

Edelman, Maurice, 'Inside Westminster – Where Does Power Lie?' *New Humanist* (June 1972), pp. 49–50.

Edelstein, J. David. 'Countervailing Powers and the Political Process in the British Mineworkers' Union', *International Journal of Comparative Sociology*, IX (1968), pp. 255–88.

'Democracy in a National Union: The British AEU', *Industrial Relations*, IV, No. 3 (May 1965), pp. 105–25.

Edelstein, J. David, and Ruppel, H. J. 'Convention Frequency and Oligarchic Degeneration in British and American Unions', *Administrative Sciences Quarterly*, XV (1970), pp. 47–56.

Epstein, L. D. 'New M.P.s and the Politics of the PLP', *Political Studies*, X (1962), pp. 121–29.

'The Nuclear Deterrent and the British Election of 1964', *The Journal of British Studies*, V, (1965–66), pp. 139–63.

'Who Makes Party Policy: British Labour, 1960–61', *Midwest Journal of Political Science*, VI (1962), pp. 165–82.

Fairlie, Henry. 'The Lives of Politicians', *Encounter* (August 1967), pp. 18–37.

Fletcher, Raymond, 'Where Did It All Go Wrong?' *Encounter* (November 1969), pp. 8–16.

'Where Do We Go From Here?' *Encounter* (December 1970), pp. 3–8.

Fox, Alan, 'The Unions and Defence', *Socialist Commentary* (February 1961), pp. 4–9.

Golant, W. 'The Emergence of C. R. Attlee as Leader of the Parliamentary Labour Party in 1935', *The Historical Journal*, XIII (1970), pp. 318–32.

Goodman, Jay S. 'A Note on Legislative Research: Labour Representation in Rhode Island', *American Political Science Review*, LXI (1967), pp. 468–73.

Grunfeld, C. 'Political Independence in British Trade Unions', *British Journal of Industrial Relations*, I (1963), pp. 23–42.

Hacker, Andrew. 'Original Sin vs. Utopia in British Socialism', *Review of Politics*, XVIII (1956), pp. 184–206.

Hammill, F. 'Labour Representation', *Fortnightly Review*, LXI (1894), pp. 546–56.

Hanby, Victor J. 'A Changing Labour Elite: The National Executive Committee of the Labour Party, 1900–72', *in* Ivor Crewe (ed.) *British Political Sociology Yearbook*, Vol. I: *Elites in Western Democracy*. Croom Helm, 1974, pp. 126–58.

Hanham, H. J. 'Opposition Techniques in British Politics, 1867–1914', *Government and Opposition*, II (November 1966), pp. 35–48.

Henderson, Arthur, and MacDonald, J. Ramsay. 'Trade Unions and Parliamentary Representation', *Contemporary Review*, XLV (February 1909), pp. 173–79.

Hennessy, B. 'Trade Unions and the British Labour Party', *American Political Science Review*, XLIX (1955), pp. 1050–67.

Hindell, Keith. 'Trade Union Membership', *Planning*, XXVIII, No. 463 (2 July 1963), pp. 153–200.

Hindell, Keith, and Williams, P. 'Scarborough and Blackpool: An Analysis of Some Votes at the Labour Party Conferences of 1960 and 1961', *Political Quarterly*, XXXIII (July–September 1962), pp. 306–20.

Horwill, H. W. 'The Payment of Labour Representatives in the British House of Commons', *Political Science Quarterly*, XXV (June 1910), pp. 312–27.

Houghton, Douglas. 'The Labour Back-bencher', *Political Quarterly*, XL (1969), pp. 454–63.

Howe, Irving. 'Hardy as a "Modern" Novelist', *The New Republic* (26 June 1965), pp. 19–22.

Hughes, John. 'Patterns of Trade Union Growth', *in* Michael Barratt Brown and Ken Coates (eds.). *Trade Union Register: 3*. Spokesman Books, 1973, pp. 47–60.

Jefferson, C. W., Sams, K. I., and Swann, D. 'The Control of Incomes and Prices in the United Kingdom, 1964–1967: Policy and Experience', *Canadian Journal of Economics*, I (1968), pp. 269–94.

Johnson, R. W. 'The British Political Elite, 1955–1972', *European Journal of Sociology*, XIV (1973), pp. 35–77.

Jones, Aubrey. 'The National Board for Prices and Incomes', *Political Quarterly*, XXXIX (1969), pp. 122–33.

Kimber, Richard, and Richardson, J. J. 'Specialization and Parliamentary Standing Committees', *Political Studies*, XVI (1968), pp. 97–101.

Laws, Brian. 'The Durham Miners' Gala', *Socialist Commentary* (August 1973), pp. 14–15.

Lyman, Richard W. 'James Ramsay MacDonald and the Leadership of the Labour Party, 1918–22', *Journal of British Studies*, II (1962–63), pp. 132–60.

Lynskey, James J. 'The Role of British Backbenchers in the Modification of Government Policy', *Western Political Quarterly*, XXII (1970), pp. 333–47.

McCormick, B. and Williams, J. E. 'The Miners and the Eight-Hour Day,

1863–1910', *Economic History Review*, XII (1959), pp. 222–38.

McCulloch, R. W. 'Question Time in the British House of Commons', *American Political Science Review*, XXVII (1933), pp. 971–75.

Mackintosh, John P. 'Anybody Still for Democracy?' *Encounter* (November 1972), pp. 19–27.

'A Bed of Thistles', *Socialist Commentary* (December 1967), pp. 11–12.

'The Problems of the Labour Party', *Political Quarterly*, XLIII (1972), pp. 2–18.

'Socialism or Social Democracy? The Choice for the Labour Party', *Political Quarterly*, XLIII (1972), pp. 470–84.

McKenzie, R. T., and Silver, A. 'Conservatism, Industrialism and the Working Class Tory in England', *Transactions of the Fifth World Congress of Sociology* (2–8 Sept. 1962), Vol. III, pp. 191–202. Washington: International Sociological Association, 1964.

Madgwick, P. J. 'Resignations', *Parliamentary Affairs*, XX (Winter, 1966–67), pp. 59–76.

Marwick, Arthur. 'The Labour Party and the Welfare State in Britain, 1900–1948', *American Historical Review*, LXXIII (December 1967), pp. 380–403.

Milburn, Josephine F. 'The Fabian Society and the British Labour Party', *Western Political Quarterly*, XL (1958), pp. 319–39.

'Trade Unions in Politics in the British Commonwealth', *Western Political Quarterly*, XVII (1964), pp. 273–83.

Millett, J. H. 'The Role of an Interest Group Leader in the House of Commons', *Western Political Quarterly*, IX (1956), pp. 915–26.

Mortimer, Jim. 'Trade Unions and the State', *Socialist Commentary* (July 1970), pp. 8–10.

Muller, William D. 'Trade Union M.P.s and Parliamentary Specialization', *Political Studies*, XX (1972), pp. 317–24.

'Trade Union Sponsored Members of Parliament in the Defence Dispute of 1960–1961', *Parliamentary Affairs*, XXIII, No. 3 (Summer 1970), pp. 258–76.

'Union-MP Conflict: An Overview', *Parliamentary Affairs*, XXVI, No. 3 (Summer 1973), pp. 336–55.

Mulley, F. W. 'NATO's Nuclear Problems: Control or Consultation', *Orbis*, VIII (Spring 1964), pp. 21–35.

Paynter, Will. 'Trade Unions and Government', *Political Quarterly*, XLI (1970), pp. 444–54.

PEP. 'The Structure and Organization of British Trade Unions', *Planning*, XXIX, No. 477 (2 Dec. 1963), pp. 433–84.

Pelling, Henry. 'Governing Without Power', *Political Quarterly*, XXXII (1961), pp. 45–52.

Prentice, Reg. 'What Kind of Labour Party?' *Socialist Commentary* (April 1973), pp. 4–6.

Punnett, R. M. 'The Labour Shadow Cabinet, 1955–1964', *Parliamentary Affairs*, XVIII (Winter 1964–65), pp. 61–70.

Radice, Giles. 'Trade Unions and the Labour Party', *Socialist Commentary* (November 1970), pp. 7–8, 10.

'What About the Workers?' *Socialist Commentary* (February 1971), pp. 6–7.

Rodgers, William. 'Personal Column', *Socialist Commentary* (April 1971), pp. 13–14.

Roberts, B. C. 'On the Origins and Resolution of English Working-Class Protest', *in* Hugh David Graham and Ted Robert Gurr (eds.). *The History of Violence: Historical and Comparative Perspectives.* New York: Bantam Books, 1969, pp. 245–80.

Sarbin, T. 'Role Theory', in Gardner Lindzey (ed.). *Handbook of Social Psychology,* 2 vols. Cambridge, Mass.: Addison-Wesley, 1954, I, pp. 223–58.

Schefftz, M. C. 'The Trade Disputes and Trade Unions Act of 1927: the Aftermath of the General Strike', *Review of Politics,* XXIX (1967), pp. 387–406.

Seligman, L. G. 'Elite Recruitment and Political Development', *Journal of Politics,* XXVI (1964), pp. 612–26.

'Political Parties and the Recruitment of Political Leadership', *in* Lewis J. Edinger (ed.). *Political Leadership in Industrialized Societies.* New York: John Wiley and Sons, 1967, pp. 294–315.

'Political Recruitment and Party Structure', *American Political Science Review,* LV (1961), pp. 77–86.

'Recruitment in Politics', *PROD,* I, No. 4 (1958), pp. 14–17.

Selvin, David F. 'Communications in Trade Unions: A Study of Union Journals', *British Journal of Industrial Relations,* I (1963); pp. 75–93.

Shanks, Michael. 'The English Sickness', *Encounter* (January 1972), pp. 79–93.

Sires, R. V. 'The Beginnings of British Legislation for Old Age Pensions', *Journal of Economic History,* XIV (1954), pp. 229–53.

'Socialism in the House of Commons', *Edinburgh Review,* CCIV (October 1906), pp. 271–73.

Stead, Peter. 'Working-Class Leadership in South Wales, 1900–1920,' *Welsh History Review,* VI (1973), pp. 329–54.

Steck, Henry J. 'The Re-emergence of Ideological Politics in Great Britain: The Campaign for Nuclear Disarmament', *The Western Political Quarterly,* XVIII (1965), pp. 87–103.

Stone, F. O. 'The Labour Party and the Trade Unions', *Nineteenth Century,* XCVII (March, 1925), pp. 309–25.

Taylor, Eric. 'An Interview with Wesley Perrins', *Bulletin of the Society for the Study of Labour History,* No. 21 (Autumn 1970), pp. 16–24.

Terrill, Ross. 'The Office of Deputy Leader in the British Labour Party', *in* John D. Montgomery and Albert O. Hirschman (eds.). *Public Policy,* Vol. XVII, Cambridge: Harvard University Press, 1968, pp. 439–67.

Thomas, Peter D. G. 'Check List of M.P.s Speaking in the House of Commons, 1768 to 1774', *Bulletin of the Institute of Historical Research,* XXXV, No. 92 (November 1962), pp. 220–26.

Thompson, P. 'Liberals, Radicals and Labour in London, 1880–1900', *Past and Present,* No. 27 (1964), pp. 73–101.

Torode, John, 'Do White Collar Unions Prosper?' *Socialist Commentary*

(September 1967), pp. 32–33.

'Prince Philip and George Brown', *Socialist Commentary* (December 1969), pp. 20–22.

'Unions and Politics', *Socialist Commentary* (October 1967), pp. 15–16.

'White Collar, Blue Collar', *Socialist Commentary* (June 1968), pp. 26–28 and (August 1970), pp. 21–22.

Valen, Henry. 'The Recruitment of Parliamentary Nominees in Norway', *Scandinavian Political Studies*, I (1966), pp. 121–66.

Vijay, K. I. 'The Declaration of Interests by M.P.s: An Analysis of the Current Campaign for Reform', *Political Quarterly*, XLIV (1973), pp. 478–86.

Walker, Patrick Gordon. 'On Being a Cabinet Minister', *Encounter* (April 1956), pp. 17–24.

Webb, Sidney. 'The First Labour Government', *The Political Quarterly*, XXXII (January–March 1961), pp. 6–34.

Willson, F. M. G. 'The Routes of Entry of New Members of the British Cabinet', *Political Studies*, VII (1959), pp. 222-32.

'Some Career Patterns in British Politics; Whips in the House of Commons, 1906-1966', *Parliamentary Affairs*, XXIV, No. 1 (Winter, 1970–71), pp. 33–42.

Williams, J. E. 'The Political Activities of a Trade Union, 1906–1914', *International Review of Social History*, II (1957), pp. 1–21.

Miscellaneous:

Aiken Charles. 'Representation and Functional Representation: Bases and Operations'. Paper prepared for the 7th World Congress of the International Political Science Association. Brussels, 1967. (mimeographed).

Birch, A. H. 'The Theory and Practice of Representation', Paper prepared for the International Political Science Association Round Table on Problems of Representation. Jablonna, 1966. (mimeographed).

Campaign for Democratic Socialism. *Campaign*. No. 1, January 1961. No. 22, December 1962.

Dodds' Parliamentary Companion (published annually).

Ehrlich, Stanislaw. 'On Functional Representation in the West', Paper prepared for the 7th World Congress of the International Political Science Association. Brussells, 1967. (mimeographed).

Gallup Poll. *Trade Unions and the Public in 1964* (1964).

Marsh, Richard. 'The Trade Union Movement and the Parliamentary Labour Party'. London: Fabian Society, n.d. (mimeographed).

'The P.L.P. and the Trade Unions'. Revised copy. London: The Fabian Society, 1963 (mimeographed).

McCulloch, Robert W. *Parliamentary Control: Question Hour in the English House of Commons*. Ann Arbor: University Microfilms, n.d. (Publication No. 11, 127).

Oden, William E. *A Critique of Selected Theories of Functional Representation*. Unpublished Ph.D. Dissertation, Indiana University, n.d. (1958?).

The Political Companion, No. 1, October/December 1969. No. 18, Spring 1974.

Roberts, H. R. 'The Union's Political Representation'. National Union of General and Municipal Workers, n.d. (mimeographed).

Rupert, Cynthia. 'The Voting of British Trade Union MP's on Social Reform'. Unpublished seminar paper. State University of New York, Fredonia (January 1971).

Social Survey. *Gallup Poll on the Trade Unions*. 1959.

Gallup Political Index, No. 48, January 1964. No. 88, August 1967.

Spiro, Herbert J. 'Functional Representation and the Danger of Compartmentalization'. Paper prepared for the 7th World Congress of the International Political Science Association. Brussels, 1967. (mimeographed).

The Times Guide to the House of Commons. London: The Times Publishing Company, following each General Election, 1945–74.

Wahlke, John C. 'Public Policy and Representative Government: The Role of the Represented'. Paper prepared for the 7th World Congress of the International Political Science Association. Brussels, 1967. (mimeographed).

Index

267